THE
OXFORD
BOOK
OF
DAYS

MARILYN YURDAN

First published 2013

The History Press
The Mill, Brimscombe Port
Stroud, Gloucestershire, GL5 2QG
www.thehistorypress.co.uk

British Library Cataloguing in Publication Data.
A catalogue record for this book is available from the British Library.

ISBN 978 0 7524 6550 0

Typesetting and origination by The History Press
Printed in India

JANUARY 1ST

1862: On this day the Ancient Order of Druids of Oxford, Lodge 59, met in the Town Hall for their annual festival. The festival started with the toast 'The health of the Queen' and went on to express the entire nation's grief at the demise of Prince Albert, which had left the Queen 'widowed, and her children fatherless'. The next toast was to 'The High Steward of the City of Oxford, the Earl of Abingdon', which was followed by a long and patriotic speech about the wonderful character and achievements of the British race. Then followed 'Prosperity to Lodge 59' (cheers); 'the health of the Mayor of Oxford' (cheers); the 'Prosperity of the University of Oxford' (no cheers). In a very long speech, a Mr Neate said of the Americans, 'so long as they were not our actual enemies' he felt 'bound to treat them as our brethren.' Unsurprisingly, the next speaker 'could not refrain from saying that it was the dullest Druid's [*sic*] dinner' that he had ever attended. Then the health of the chairman was drunk, followed by a toast to the 'Prosperity of the Philanthropic Fund', and no less than eleven more toasts and responses were enacted. (*Jackson's Oxford Journal*)

JANUARY 2ND

1889: On this second day of the year, at 6 p.m., the servants of Exeter College, consisting of some forty men and youths, sat down to an excellent dinner in the college hall. In the chair, presiding over the festivities, was the college manciple, Mr Phillips, and its chief cook, Mr Newman, who took the role of vice-chairman. There were several toasts, the main one being to 'The Rector and Fellows of Exeter College'. These gentlemen had provided the feast, so this toast was greeted with great enthusiasm.

After everyone had eaten and the table had been cleared, the common-room man, Mr Birrill, brought in wines and spirits and tobacco and pipes, which he placed on the table, and the evening was passed in a very sociable way. Several members of the company, notably Messrs C. Phillips, A.W. Hollis, H. Brimfield, R. Ward, A. Thomas and C. Robbins, got up and sang, and their efforts were well received by their colleagues. The hall-man, Mr Hollis, was congratulated on all the work which he had put into decorating the hall for the event. The party broke up at about 11.30 p.m., and everybody left the college very satisfied with their Christmas entertainment. (*Jackson's Oxford Journal*)

JANUARY 3RD

1889: About 100 wives and children of Exeter College servants gathered in the college hall where 'a sumptuous tea was provided, after which games and music were indulged in' on this night in 1889. Several songs were sung, which appeared to give great pleasure to the company. Then Mr Phillips [the college Manciple] introduced his toy 'German Band', which consisted of five wind instruments – one played by Mr Phillips and the others by four of his sons. 'This peculiar class of music caused much wonder and amusement.' Another son, Master E.A. Phillips, then played the violin, accompanied by his little sister on the piano, 'which was received with much acclamation'. The musical turns were followed by a magic lantern show which proved to be one of the highlights of the evening, and the 'comic scenes caused much merriment with the juveniles'. The evening finished with a 'fancy fair' which was great fun, and there was a free raffle with 'useful and ornamental articles' for prizes. The catering, which was done by Mr Birrill, was voted a great success, and the party broke up at 9.30 p.m., by which time the younger guests were very tired but very happy with their evening. (*Jackson's Oxford Journal*)

JANUARY 4TH

1893: Over two days, all of the cabmen, tramcar and bath-chair men of the city were invited to go round to Oriel College for a meal and entertainment in the college hall. This was the fifth year that the event had taken place, on alternate years. The guests were given 'an excellent meat tea, with plum puddings and mince pies' which were provided by Mr Arnatt of St Ebbe's Street. After all the food had been disposed of, a report on the state of the Cabmen's Benefit Club was read out, and judged to be 'of a satisfactory character'. When £24 10s had been given out in sick benefit, £61 4s 1d was left to be divided among the club's sixty-seven members (which worked out at 18s 4d each), leaving £20 in the kitty. On both nights the men were given an address by a local clergyman followed by some light relief. On the Wednesday this consisted of conjuring by Professor Carl de Louis, and on the Thursday a display of views by Mr Taunt, 'by means of the oxy-hydrogen light, the subject of the entertainment being "Our Native Land", and the views included a large number of places in this locality'. (*Jackson's Oxford Journal*)

JANUARY 5TH

1892: On this day Henry Taunt, the accomplished photographer, held the first of his annual Christmas parties for the year. The party for adults took place in the evening in Oxford Town Hall, while the children's event was held one afternoon. Taunt was known not only for his photographs, postcards and book illustrations, many of which survive, but also for his magic lantern shows, which were well attended. Advertising the event in advance, *Jackson's Oxford Journal* wrote:

> The trip this year is to Madeira, with an imaginary run over the Island, and to go to Madeira and back for a shilling is very cheap indeed, besides we get as well a whole series of other things for the same money, and we know from past experience how thoroughly Mr Taunt caters for the pleasure of his universally large audiences. The children are taken with Alice 'through the Looking Glass' and thus treated to a series of amusements beyond – so we can only wish Mr Taunt the success he deserves and advise our readers to secure tickets at once at 9 and 10 Broad-street.

Over a century later, Taunt's photographs continue to provide a visual history of the city. (*Jackson's Oxford Journal*)

JANUARY 6TH

1899: New Year celebrations at the Radcliffe Infirmary began with the time-honoured amateur theatricals in the large hall in the outpatients department in 1899. The entertainment included 'three humorous farces which were admirably presented and were accompanied with a good deal of laughter and applause at the end'. These plays were entitled *The Burglar and the Judge*, *Cheerful and Musical* and *My Lord in Livery*. The ladies' Orchestra, under the direction of Mr Proudfoot, also gave their services. After 'God Save the Queen' had been sung, the company went off happily to their homes.

The following Tuesday, the traditional Christmas tree was put up in outpatients. That year it was a huge one which reached from floor to ceiling. It was 'profusely decorated with a variety of multi-coloured fairy lamps and a large collection of toys, sweets, bon-bons, books, and prettily-dressed dolls', while around the base were parcels containing 'useful articles'. All the members of the hospital staff, as well as the patients, were given presents. The children sat in a circle round the tree while it was being stripped of the presents, with others watching from their bath-chairs. Numerous visitors dropped in, refreshments were served and there was music at intervals. (*Jackson's Oxford Journal*)

JANUARY 7TH

2002: This was the day when the workers and management at the BMW car factory at Cowley were celebrating receiving a very important honour. The new Mini Cooper model was being named North American Car of the Year at the Detroit International Auto Show, adding its most prestigious accolade to date to its already impressive array of awards amassed during its first full year in production. Mini's general manager, Trevor Houghton-Berry, stated that the United States was a key market for the Mini and that the award was a tremendous achievement; it was great news for anyone involved in its manufacture and sale. The first consignment of 20,000 Minis, which was shipped to the United States after its launch the previous March, had sold out almost immediately, thanks to customers who had placed advance orders. These had been the first Minis to be sold in the United States since 1967. A further 5,000 had been exported and were expected to be snapped up. To get the award, the Mini had to fight off competition from the Nissan 350Z and Infiniti G35. Other accolades had been the *Independent* and *Times* newspapers' Car of the Year, BBC2's *Top Gear* Best Small Car award, and Channel 4's *Driven* Car of the Series. (*Oxford Mail*)

January 8th

1942: On this day Stephen William Hawking was born in Oxford. His parents were from north London, but he was evacuated as a baby at the outbreak of the Second World War to the safe haven of Oxford. The Hawking family moved to St Albans when he was eight, and three years later he started at St Albans School. Stephen returned to Oxford to read Physics at University College, where his father had been educated. His father wanted him to study Medicine and Stephen's own choice was Maths, but his college did not offer it. Three years later he completed a first-class degree in Natural Sciences. He then went to Cambridge to undertake research in Cosmology because there was nobody suitable to supervise him at Oxford at that time. After finishing his PhD, he became a Research Fellow and later a Professorial Fellow at Gonville and Caius College. Hawking moved from the Institute of Astronomy in 1973, and started at the Department of Applied Mathematics and Theoretical Physics in 1979, where he was Lucasian Professor of Mathematics until 2009 (one of his predecessors was Isaac Newton in 1669). He is currently Director of Research at the Centre for Theoretical Cosmology at the Department of Applied Mathematics and Theoretical Physics in Cambridge.

JANUARY 9TH

1810: On this day Magdalen Hall (as opposed to Magdalen College), in Catte Street, was burnt to the ground. This was not looked on as a great loss by the people of Oxford as the building had been virtually falling down. However, this notice was placed in *Jackson's Oxford Journal*:

> The principal, vice-principal and resident undergraduates of Magdalen Hall most thankfully acknowledge that they are indebted, under Providence, for the lives of the inhabitants and the preservation of the buildings from entire destruction, to the exertions of many Members of the University and City who so generously exposed themselves to danger on behalf of their Society during the late awful fire. They are desirous of expressing their sense of their obligations in person to all these friends, but as in many cases they are prevented by ignorance of names from performing this pleasant duty, they beg them all to accept this public declaration of their cordial gratitude and be assured that they feel how inadequate words are to describe the deep impression that has been made upon their hearts by the kind and essential services so promptly and cheerfully rendered to them by the University and City.

(*Jackson's Oxford Journal*)

JANUARY 10TH

2001: On this day Colin Dexter, Cambridge graduate and creator of *Inspector Morse*, said how proud he was to have been made a Freeman of the City of Oxford, and toasted Morse during his speech. The previous day, councillors at Oxford's Strategy and Resources Committee meeting had voted unanimously for Mr Dexter to be given this rare honour. Councillor Alex Hollingsworth said, 'We would like to thank Colin Dexter for putting Oxford on the TV map by killing off 80 of our residents.' When he was told the good news, the crime novelist commented, 'I hope I don't end up in jail like the other two,' in reference to the only other living holders of the distinction – Nelson Mandela and Aung San Suu Kyi, the Burmese human rights campaigner. He was particularly delighted with the honour as, despite the fact that he was not an Oxford man, he had been accepted and recognised. Colin has lived in Oxford since 1966, when he took up a post at the now-defunct University of Oxford Delegacy of Local Examinations. He claimed that the Freedom of the City meant more to him than the OBE he had received from Prince Charles at Buckingham Palace the previous October. (*Oxford Mail*)

January 11th

2008: This was the day when readers of the *Oxford Mail* were asked to listen to a podcast of bagpipe music and make up their minds about whether or not it should be banned from a main Oxford street. The reason for this was that bagpipe-playing Heath Richardson had presented a petition with 1,150 names to the city councillors. Heath, aged thirty-two, had been playing in Cornmarket Street for fourteen years, but the previous month some of the traders in Cornmarket had complained about his music and had started a petition to have him moved. Dr William Waggott, a medical publisher based in the street, collected 400 names, but Heath started a counter-petition and persuaded more than 1,000 people to sign it within the first week. Heath, from Chipping Norton, went into Oxford Town Hall to present his petition to Jean Fooks, executive member for the cleaner city campaign. He said that he had been totally overwhelmed by the support which he had received from people in the city centre. Dr Waggott, whose petition called for tighter regulations regarding busking, was unavailable for comment. Ms Fooks said, 'It's only fair that we receive the busker's petition as well as the petition from the traders.' (*Oxford Mail*)

JANUARY 12TH

2000: This was the day that Professor John Bayley, who was widowed after a forty-three-year marriage to award-winning novelist Dame Iris Murdoch, spoke about his love for a family friend and their plans to be married that summer. After spending many years nursing his wife, who had suffered from Alzheimer's disease, and overcoming his grief at her death the previous February aged seventy-nine, he said that he had found someone else whom he could love and care for. The bride-to-be was a long-standing friend, and fellow widow, Norwegian-born Audi Villers. Talking to the *Oxford Mail* at his home in North Oxford, Professor Bayley said that it seemed as if he had always known her and that he honestly couldn't remember how they had become so close. They used to holiday together in Lanzarote, where Audi now spent most of her time. She suffered badly from asthma and allergies and, although the air greatly improved her condition, he believed that she would benefit from his nursing and care. He added, 'Having looked after Iris for all those years, I rather like the idea of looking after someone again. Nursing someone you love is very agreeable.' (*Oxford Mail*)

JANUARY 13TH

2003: This was the day when a twenty-five-year-old Oxford academic, who had never had a book published, became the youngest person to appear on a list of the country's most promising writers. Previous to this, Adam Thirlwell, a Fellow of prestigious All Souls College, had only had one piece of fiction published; this was a 3,000-word extract from his novel, *Politics*, which had appeared in the Oxford literary magazine, *Arete*, of which he was the joint editor. The judges at the journal *Granta* were so impressed by his work that they named him as one of Britain's twenty best novelists under the age of forty. One of them told how he had received a dog-eared manuscript, read through it, and 'that was that'. He described it as 'a lovely book, very funny, a sexual comedy about a love triangle'. The praise was expected to prove a useful advertisement for *Politics* which was due to be published that autumn, as the list of promising young writers was only compiled once every ten years. Adam, who was doing research at All Souls into the modern European novel, said that if the book turned out to be a best-seller, he wanted to write full time. (*Oxford Mail*)

JANUARY 14TH

2001: One of Oxford's greatest idiosyncrasies is the Ceremony of the Hunting of the Mallard at All Souls College, which was founded in 1438 by Henry VI as a memorial to all those who lost their lives in the Hundred Years War. The most recent ceremony was held in 2001 – it takes place every hundred years in the first year of the new century. The Warden, as Head of House, leads a procession carrying lighted torches in search of the legendary mallard. This is said to have flown up out of a drain when the foundations of the college were being laid. If and when they find it, the mallard will be a very old bird indeed. In the meantime, they march round the college singing the 'Mallard Song', a ditty which is also sung at All Souls' gaudies in the intervening years. This must never reach the ears of strangers. While all this is going on, the Lord Mallard is carried round in procession, seated in a sedan chair, with a dead duck suspended from a pole. They march three times round the quad and then proceed up to the roof, still in search of that elusive bird. (Various sources)

JANUARY 15TH

1892: On this day John Burns, alias Robert Shields, 'engineer of no home', was charged with stealing from a shop in Castle Street. He had taken a haddock worth 4*d* from the property of Thomas Shelton. Shelton stated that he was in his shop about 9.30 p.m. that evening when the prisoner had come in and tried to sell him paper and envelopes. The shopkeeper told him that he was not interested, and then 'noticed one end of a haddock sticking out from under the breast of his coat'. When Shelton took the fish back, the prisoner offered to pay for it. Burns pleaded guilty, claiming that he had been the worse for drink when he went into the shop. Superintendent Head said that the prisoner had given the name Burns when he was arrested, but, when he was searched, a pedlar's certificate in the name of Shields was found on him. Apart from the name, the prisoner's height did not agree with that given on the certificate. Mr Shelton said that Burns had threatened him at the police station, telling him, 'If you charge me I'll settle you, I'll swing for you.' Burns was sentenced to twenty-one days' hard labour. (*Jackson's Oxford Journal*)

JANUARY 16TH

1886: The following is a notice from *Jackson's Oxford Journal* of 1886, showing their egalitarian desires:

REDUCTION IN PRICE TO TWOPENCE
IMPORTANT NOTICE

In order to bring this Journal within the means of all classes of readers, and especially for the benefit of the Agricultural Community, with whose interests the fortunes of this paper have been intimately connected for more than a Hundred and Thirty Years, *Jackson's Oxford Journal* is now published AT TWO PENCE

It is believed that the increased circulation thereby ensured with materially augment the value of its Advertising Columns.

A special feature in *Jackson's Oxford Journal* will continue to be the exceptionally high quality of the paper, and the clearness of type and every endeavour will be made to maintain its present reputation as a high-class family and commercial Newspaper.

Our numerous Subscribers in this and the adjoining Counties and the Commercial Community in London and all parts of the Kingdom, who have extended their support to this Journal for so many years are respectfully thanked for the same, and requested to introduce this reduction in price to the notice of their friends.

Subscribers' Orders now received by the Publisher, HUGH HALL, 65 Corn Market Street, Oxford, to whom all Cheques and P.O. Orders should be made payable.

(*Jackson's Oxford Journal*)

JANUARY 17TH

2001: On this day it was revealed that local pigs were enjoying the leavings of some of the top tables in the land. Not only were the porkers enjoying the 'posh nosh', they were also taking part in an unusual recycling project. Every week, farmer Michael Eadle was collecting 3,000 litres of unwanted food from Christ Church, Corpus Christi, St Catherine's, St Peter's and Wadham Colleges, as well as from Headington Girls' School and Oxford Brookes University. He held a licence issued by the Ministry of Agriculture to reprocess the waste by heat treatment before feeding it to his animals. This type of recycling process is good for the environment as food dumped in landfill sites attracts vermin and over time harmful oils resurface. He approached Oxford City Council for help in collecting even more to feed to the 1,500 Large White pigs which he kept at Redways Farm, Beckley. He suggested council-assisted collections from schools, residential homes, and hospitals to get potential pig food that would otherwise end up in the ground, but he claims the council were not interested; however, a spokesman said he was willing to talk further with Mr Eadle. (*Oxford Mail*)

JANUARY 18TH

2001: On this day an Oxford table tennis team achieved a double century with their combined ages, which made a total of exactly 200 years. The three were Terry Strange aged sixty-eight, Peter Simpson, sixty-seven, and sixty-five-year-old Trevor Hookham. Together they made the Old Headington-based Viking Flames, who played in Division 3 of the Oxford & District League. These three old hands had been playing together as a team for around ten years, and until that season had represented the Nuffield Orthopaedic Centre. Peter Simpson, who had been playing table tennis for forty-five years, said that he didn't think that their combined ages was unique or even that unusual as it was a game that players could enjoy well into their older years. Proof of this was given by the fact that their opponents didn't react in any way; indeed, Peter claimed that they didn't know that the trio were that old. Terry Strange, who had represented Oxfordshire at both cricket and hockey, was the second leading table tennis player that season in Division 3; although, they did admit that the team was finding it tougher-going in the lower reaches of the table. (*Oxford Mail*)

JANUARY 19TH

2000: On this day five students were extremely fortunate to escape a fire. Firefighters from the Slade and Rewley Road stations were called to their house in Ridgefield Road, Cowley, after a neighbour noticed flames coming from a bedroom window at 9.30 a.m. The students, who were not named, were rescued from the house and one of them was given treatment for smoke inhalation. Station Officer Kevin Parfitt explained that the bedding had been set alight by a candle at about 4.30 a.m. that morning, but the housemates thought that they had managed to put it out. However, the fire had not been properly extinguished and flames had burst out again five hours later. Fortunately, the person whose bed it was had moved as his bedding was wet from the previous attempts at putting out the fire. Although the house was fitted with fire alarms, the nearest one had failed to sound. Parfitt added that the equipment should have been checked and that firefighters should have been called as soon as the first blaze was noticed. (*Oxford Mail*)

JANUARY 20TH

1969: After an evening of violent protests against Enoch Powell's speech at the Town Hall, six policemen were hurt. One of them suffered a couple of broken ribs, while many other people were treated for injuries at the Radcliffe Infirmary. A local clergyman was charged with using a tin of peas in a string bag as an offensive weapon. A demonstration had started before 5 p.m. and lasted for two-and-a-half hours, during which time protestors assaulted police lines and threw bricks through the windows of the building. However, Mr Powell had already been brought into the Town Hall well before the demonstration had started, and after 90 minutes the meeting finished, whereupon he was smuggled out and taken off to dinner at Woodstock. Frustrated protestors then attacked the police station in St Aldates, and later some 300 students marched the 3 miles up to Cowley where Enoch Powell was addressing the Conservative Club. Mr Powell said that the night had proved a triumph, not only for free speech but also for the Oxford University Conservative Association and the Oxford Conservatives. It was agreed on all sides that police officers had dealt with the situation exceptionally well, and donations for the police fund were left at the police station. (Various sources)

JANUARY 21ST

1998: On this day television history was made when the Oxford Brookes team had to field a virtual contestant when they took on the London School of Economics on *University Challenge*. One of the members of the side from the former Oxford Polytechnic, Jacqui Hill, aged twenty-five, was taken ill a mere 3 minutes before the quiz had finished. She was suffering from high blood pressure and was unable to complete the filming. The producers had to think quickly in order to avoid having to either reshoot the whole programme or continue with only three contestants from Brookes, neither of which was satisfactory. They came up with the answer of making use of a technique known as 'picture-massaging'. In order to paint in the missing contestant, an earlier picture of Jacqui was superimposed. The only clue came at the end of the contest, when sharp-eyed viewers might have noticed that she was the only team member who did not wave goodbye. In the event, said the programme's producer, Peter Gwyn, the manipulation made no difference to the result of the contest as the Brookes students were already lagging behind the LSE with a score of 40 to 245. (*Oxford Mail*)

JANUARY 22ND

1998: On this day an Oxford girls' secondary school announced that they were adopting a Canadian idea aimed at fighting back against bullying. Pupils from Milham Ford Girls' Upper School in Harberton Mead, Headington, were to take part in a special conference with school staff and experts on the subject. Their aim was to explore methods of stopping bullying and smoking in schools. The project followed a nationwide survey which had been presented to David Blunkett, the then Secretary for Education, which showed that eight out of ten schoolchildren were the victims of at least one prolonged attack of bullying during their time at school. The delegates from Milham Ford helped decide what constituted unacceptable behaviour and what punishment was suitable. Anne Peterson, a teacher at the school, had come across the idea during her eighteen years of teaching in Canada. She explained that pupils were given responsibility and would work towards appropriate and viable measures to prevent bullying, and that any potential offenders knew exactly what punishment they could expect. The school already had no smoking and anti-bullying policies which were to be more strictly defined. The girls also had to carry out a survey among fellow pupils regarding their own experiences of smoking and bullying. (*Oxford Mail*)

JANUARY 23RD

1998: On this day *Oxford Mail* readers were saddened to hear of the death of a disabled student who had become something of a local hero. Nick Stephens, an undergraduate at New College, was found dead in his room. When he was nineteen, Nick had gained a place at the college despite being paralysed from the neck down as a result of contracting meningitis when he was eighteen months old. A post-mortem examination to establish the cause of death proved inconclusive and an inquest was ordered. Nick had become well known throughout the University as one of its most astonishing students when, despite not being able to move or even breathe without help, he came to Oxford to read Jurisprudence. Professor Alan Ryan, Warden of New College, described him as 'a free spirit trapped in an unwilling body'. He added, 'The consolation for us is that he died doing what he wanted to do. He had returned to college in tremendously high spirits, just longing for term to start.' The medieval buildings of New College had been specially adapted for Nick, who was able to teach his fellow students valuable lessons in what disabled people are able to achieve. (*Oxford Mail*)

JANUARY 24TH

1998: On this day Malcolm Shotton described being made manager of Oxford United as his dream job. He also said that he would have dropped just about anything else to have taken the position. 'If you could have picked a club to be your first club as manager … well there's no doubt Oxford would have been mine,' he told the *Oxford Mail*, adding that, 'the club is very special to me, the place is very special and the fans are very special to me.' He was also very much looking forward to working with caretaker-manager Malcolm Crosby and Maurice Evans, who had also been a caretaker-manager for several months in 1993. While acknowledging the skills of his right-hand men, Shotton stated that he had his own ideas about the game, which he was intending to put into practice. He had already been told about United's financial difficulties during his interview for the position of manager, but he expected that they could be overcome. He said that he had very good memories of Oxford and that his son had been born at the John Radcliffe Hospital, very close to the Manor ground. In the event, Shotton resigned as manager in October 1999. (*Oxford Mail*)

JANUARY 25TH

1867: On this the day the following notice was circulated as a stern warning to local landowners, farmers and stockbreeders:

CATTLE PLAGUE

The subjoined Circular has been substituted for that of the 17th instant and it is important to observe the corrections –

County Hall Oxford, 25th January 1867

SIR – The Lords of the Council, having found that Pass Masters at Cattle Markets have not infrequently given passes upon improper Licences – I am desired respectfully to draw your Attention to this subject; and to suggest that Cattle and Animals (including in the latter category Sheep, Lambs and Pigs), can only be taken to Market under a Store Stock Licence; and can only be removed from the Market under a Market Pass.

At the same time it is observable that Sheep, Lambs and Pigs may be moved from place to place as heretofore, without a Licence, without a Pass, excepting to or from a Cattle Market.

If the above restrictions be not strictly enforced, the Lords of the Council intimate that it may become imperative to revoke the Market Licences now in force.

I have the honor to be, Sir,
Your faithful Servant,
JOHN M DAVENPORT

(Jackson's Oxford Journal)

January 26th

1895: On this day, this advertisement appeared in *Jackson's Oxford Journal*. It is is surprisingly modern in its aims:

THE MATRIMONIAL HERALD and FASHIONABLE MARRIAGE
Official Organ of The World's Great Marriage Association (Limited) Est. 1883 Recommended by the Clergy Brilliantly successful in negotiations for 1894 Marvellous increase in marriages Exclusively Patronised by the Nobility, Professional and commercial Classes throughout the British Empire Its magnificent and practically illimitable clientè[le] daily augmented by private recommendations from associates happily and advantageously married. Charges merely nominal Strict secrecy In plain sealed envelope 5*d*. – Editor, 40, Lamb's Conduit-street, London WC.

(*Jackson's Oxford Journal*)

January 27th

1967: On this afternoon thousands of people turned out in Cornmarket to get a glimpse of Senator Robert Kennedy as he left the Oxford Union. He had come down from London by train the day before, accompanied by veteran politician and trade union official Lord 'Manny' Shinwell. Mr Kennedy had just made his first speech in Britain and received three standing ovations from the 1,200-strong audience. So much interest was generated that about 500 students who had not been able to get seats in the debating hall gathered outside and banged on the door in frustration. On his way out Mr Kennedy had to pass protestors waving placards against American involvement in Vietnam, but this was the only disruption to his visit. Police and detectives formed a 40-yard human chain along Cornmarket so that he could reach his car in order to get back to an Anglo-American conference at Ditchley Park. Kennedy leant out of the car in order to clasp the hands of his many admirers and a group of teenage girls chanted, 'Oh Bobby! Oh, Bobby!' as the forty-two-year-old politician grinned happily at his pop-star reception. Less than eighteen months later he was assassinated. (*Oxford Mail*)

JANUARY 28TH

2011: On this day an engagement was announced in the press. The engaged couple were the two Corpus Christi college tortoises Oldham and Foxe. By coincidence, the date set for the wedding itself was announced as 29 April, the same day as that of Catherine Middleton and Prince William. Corpus Christi's Junior Common Room stated that the couple, who met at the college six years earlier, would marry in the grounds and then settle down in the Corpus Christi's President's garden. 'Currently the committee are playing around with the idea of lettuce confetti, and inviting the other tortoises in Oxford as bridesmaids, pageboys, and best men,' added JCR Vice-President Sophie Cass. She hoped that the event would 'be an opportunity for the whole college to get together and celebrate both the union of our beloved tortoises and the royal wedding that the rest of the country will primarily be preoccupied with'. Oldham, the bridegroom, who had proposed on holiday in Kenya the previous October, said, 'We are both very, very happy.' Foxe admitted that joining the JCR's royal family was a 'daunting prospect, but added, 'Hopefully I'll take it in my stride.' Her parents said they were 'absolutely delighted' and 'thrilled' by the announcement. (*Oxford Mail*)

January 29th

1985: This was the day that Oxford academics turned out in force to vote against the proposal to confer an honorary Doctorate of Civil Law on the then prime minister, Margaret Thatcher. As a protest against the government's cuts in funding for education, a campaign was launched to prevent her from being honoured. Both the turnout of more than 1,000 people and the vote of 738 votes for, to 319 against, the motion were much higher than anticipated. The result was met with cheers by students, who had handed in a petition with 5,000 signatures. The refusal meant that Thatcher was the first Oxford-educated prime minister since the war not to be awarded the degree. Sir Patrick Neill, the Warden of All Souls College, one of Mrs Thatcher's leading supporters, was disappointed at the decision and said, 'We have never given honorary degrees in the past because we approved or disapproved of someone's policies.' But Professor Peter Pulzer, also of All Souls, who led the opposition, said that he thought the University had demonstrated its 'very great concern, our very great worry about the way in which educational policy and educational funding are going in this country'. (Personal observation)

January 30th

1878: An advertisement in *Jackson's Oxford Journal* in 1878 gave notice of the publication of a new title:

> [A book] Which will considerably interest old Oxford men is about to be privately issued to subscribers by the butler of Brasenose College – name a complete collection of the Shrove Tuesday 'Brasenose Ale Verses' so far as they can be discovered. These verses, which are the only survivors of the old *Terrae Filius* style of composition that are now to be found in Oxford, are annually presented by the butler, together with the strong spiced ale which they ostensibly glorify at the Shrove Tuesday dinner. A copy dating from the end of the seventeenth century has been preserved by Hearne; but unfortunately all those written during the eighteenth century are lost as they were spoken and not printed. The first copy of the verses of this century is Heber's which has recently been discovered.

The composition of these verses came to a temporary end when the college brewhouse was demolished in 1889, but the custom was revived in 1909, despite the fact that the beer was no longer made in the college. The tradition continues to this day. (*Jackson's Oxford Journal*)

JANUARY 31ST

1820: On this day readers of *Jackson's Oxford Journal* were informed that:

[On] The day appointed for the interment of his late Most Gracious Majesty, and the Mayor having issued, in token of veneration for his manifold virtues and exalted rank, a most judicious injunction that the shops should be closed and no business transacted upon that day, the same was universally observed, with loyal and reverent decorum throughout this city. During the hours of twelve and one in the forenoon, and eight and nine in the evening, the bells of the several parishes tolled and threw an air of solemn impressiveness far and wide over the neighbourhood.

One eyewitness, twenty-year-old Miss Mary Latimer of Headington Hous,e recorded the events in her diary:

Today we received news of an event which devastated the whole English Nation and will fill us with deep distress for some time. George III, King of England, died on Saturday the 29th January at Windsor. Born 4th June 1738, he was aged [blank in diary]. My mother, Jane, Caroline and I walked in the direction of Oxford to hear the Bells which tolled from noon until one.

(*Jackson's Oxford Journal*)

FEBRUARY 1ST

1995: On this day, during repairs to the attic floor of the Sheldonian Theatre, a time capsule was discovered. The package, which was hidden behind the ceiling painting, had been deposited there in 1901 by a previous restorer, Robert Nairn of Dublin. The Chairman of the Curators and the University Archivist were alerted and, with bated breath, the package was opened. It contained a letter giving details of the state of the painting when he had started work, and what he had done, with advice for future action. It concluded, 'God bless the Pope and save the King, Robert J. Nairn'. There were also faded photographs, business cards, pamphlets, *Pick-Me-Up* – a magazine with risqué cartoons – a catalogue from May's Drug Stores, No. 132, High Street, and two issues, in fragile condition, of the *Daily Mail*, one covering the death of Queen Victoria. News of the time capsule made the national press, and the *Daily Mail* of Wednesday, 1 March, carried an article with illustrations from the original copy in the time capsule. *The Times* of 28 February showed a small picture of University Archivist, Simon Bailey, displaying a selection of the contents of the package, together with an outline description of its origin and contents. (*Oxford Mail*)

FEBRUARY 2ND

1820: On this day, twenty-year-old Miss Mary Latimer, of Headington House, wrote of her feelings about the future king, George IV, and the loss of his father. She recorded in her diary:

I got up at eight. After breakfast my Mother, Jane, Edward and I walked to Oxford to hear the King proclaimed George IV. The Mayor, Sir W.E. Taunton, and the Herald were on horseback and the other members of the council on foot. The Vice-Chancellor (Dr Hodson), the other Heads of Houses, the noblemen, the Doctors, and various other members of the University were seated upon a platform which had been erected on the roof of St Mary's Church. Sir W.E. Taunton read out the proclamation twice while walking along High Street and afterwards at the five gates of the town. All the windows along the route of the procession were crowded with people wanting to watch the ceremony, but in the midst of the joy which spread across everyone's face, I could not stop myself crying when I thought that we had lost such a good King whose memory will always be treasured by the people over whom he had reigned for almost sixty years.

(Diary of [Elizabeth] Mary [Jones] Latimer, Oxfordshire County Record Office)

February 3rd

2006: This was the day that one young lady's outstanding achievements were listed in the *Oxford Mail*. Kate Pounds, aged twenty-eight, who had been blind since she was a baby, swam for Great Britain in the World Youth Games and as a runner took part in the Youth Championships when she was in her teens. Later, she became the first blind student to go to St John's College, Oxford, becoming an active member of the student body and graduating with a degree in Human Sciences. She also worked to help homeless people in Oxford. Kate was the first person in the country to live on a narrowboat with a guide dog. Other favourite activities included cycling on a tandem with her husband Nick, whom she met at university, and running along the canal at Wolvercote where they live, with her guide dog, a golden retriever named Grant. When she was interviewed by the *Mail*, Kate was living on the same narrowboat where the couple had lived for nearly five years. She was hoping that a new boat would be ready for their baby which she was expecting that April and which, all being well, would be born on the boat. (*Oxford Mail*)

February 4th

1869: On this day PC Joseph Gilkes, recently transferred from the Metropolitan Police, ran into trouble in Blackfriars Road. Gilkes, who was in plain clothes, told a crowd of people obstructing the road outside Axtell's butchers, waiting for cheap meat, to move on. When a Keziah Cox challenged him, he shoved her and she slipped and fell over. She started abusing him and then hit him with her hand. Her husband joined in the attack and knocked Gilkes down. When he got to his feet, Keziah struck him on the head with a dish and the rest of the crowd turned nasty. Gilkes ran off but was chased by the mob and was forced to jump into the Isis. He was carried away by the current and drowned. Later, when a waterman saw his body in the river, it was recovered and taken to the Nag's Head public house. The Coxes were arrested and an inquest was arranged for the following day. A verdict of death due to drowning, rather than from the obvious blows to the head, was returned. Later the pair were charged with 'savagely assaulting' Gilkes. John Cox was acquitted but Keziah was found guilty and imprisoned for seven days. (*Jackson's Oxford Journal*)

FEBRUARY 5TH

1808: The following advertisement appeared in Oxford in 1808:

SHIP INN, OXFORD

The Nobility and Gentry of Oxford and its environs, and the public in general, are respectfully informed that the Royal Shrewsbury Mails, the Birmingham Post Coaches, the Worcester, Ludlow, Hereford, Leominster, and Holyhead Coaches, are removed from the [Golden] CROSS to the SHIP INN in this city, where parcels and luggage will be properly booked and forwarded by all the above Coaches.

N.B., W. D.APPLEBY of the above Inn flatters himself that by a strict attention to the comfort and convenience of the passengers, and by moderate charges, to merit their support and approbation.

(*Jackson's Oxford Journal*)

FEBRUARY 6TH

1998: It was announced on this day that Oxford City Council planned to combine with the University of Oxford in order to propose that Oxford be designated a World Heritage Site, meaning that it would be recognised as one of the 500 most important places on earth. If the bid went ahead and proved successful, Oxford would take its place alongside the Great Barrier Reef, the Taj Mahal, and, much nearer home, Durham Castle and Cathedral, and the city of Bath. The names of only a dozen places in the UK are likely to be submitted to UNESCO each year. UNESCO, the United Nations Educational, Scientific and Cultural Organisation, selects the sites, which are then subjected to very stringent checks by experts. It was pointed out that there were more protected buildings just in the square mile of central Oxford alone than anywhere else in Europe, with architecture ranging from Norman to the twentieth century. There were already seventeen World Heritage Sites in the UK, including Blenheim Palace and Woodstock, both in Oxfordshire. If Oxford had been nominated, there would have been a minimum of eighteen months of examination by UN inspectors before it was designated a World Heritage Site. In the event, however, nothing further happened. (Various sources)

FEBRUARY 7TH

2001: On this day the parents of pupils at the smallest school in Oxford came in for a huge amount of praise for their money-raising efforts. Kate Rule, head teacher of the ninety-pupil Headington Quarry School, said that parents had thrown themselves wholeheartedly into thinking up ways of acquiring enough cash to buy more computing equipment. Their success meant that the number of computers was increased to six, two in each classroom. They were used by pupils to send and receive emails with two young sisters in Mexico, who had attended Quarry School while their parents were working at Oxford University and who had since returned home. Mrs Rule acknowledged that the amount needed was large for such a small school to raise and added that Quarry was one of the last schools to receive money from the National Grid For Learning scheme. The two additional computers had cost between £8,000 and £9,000 and the government had only given £5,000, so any additional money was very welcome. The parents had been very supportive and enjoyed the fund-raising activities. They had organised a fashion show, arranged jumble sales, and held discos and other events, including no less than two Christmas bazaars. (*Oxford Mail*)

FEBRUARY 8TH

1855: This notice beseeching the public for money appeared on this day:

OXFORD FEMALE PENITENTIARY

The Funds of this Institution having been for some years insufficient to meet increasing expenses, there is now an accumulated deficiency of about £70. Moreover, the Committee has undertaken to pay £100 a year to the Wantage Home in return for which ten places are to be continually reserved for penitents sent from the Oxford Home, whose maintenance is guaranteed.

In order to meet both the present deficiency and the increased annual demand, all persons favourably disposed towards the Society are earnestly requested to contribute.

A MEETING (at which the Report for 1854 will be read), in furtherance of this object will be held (by permission) on Monday next, February 19th, at Three P.M. in the Council Chamber; the BISHOP OF OXFORD in the Chair.

(*Jackson's Oxford Journal*)

FEBRUARY 9TH

1863: On this day a new school for girls was advertised:

ESTABLISHMENT FOR YOUNG LADIES

Crescent Lodge, Park Town, Oxford

CONDUCTED by THE MISSES HOOPER,
assisted by a talented Lecturer and the following Masters –

Music & Singing DR CORFE and MR T. GRIZELLE
German Herr BERTRAM

French Mons A. MANIER Académie De Douai, Université de
France

Drawing and Painting Mr RICHARDSON

Latin, Mathematics and Arithmetic Mr NORWOOD

Dancing and Calisthenics Mr WOOD

The domestic arrangements are on a liberal scale, and every
attention is paid to the health and comfort of the Pupils.
Prospectuses of terms (which are moderate) on application
to the Principals. The Classes are open to young Ladies not
residing in the Establishment.

(*Jackson's Oxford Journal*)

February 10th

1355: On this St Scholastica's Day, a terrible event took place which affected Oxford life for the next five centuries. Starting ordinarily enough with a dispute over the quality of the ale served in the Swyndlestock Tavern in Carfax, it turned into a massacre and went down in local history as one of the blackest days on record. The brawling, pillaging and firing of property continued unabated for two days and nights. At the end, sixty-three students and about half that number of townspeople had lost their lives. The king, Edward III, involved himself in the clash with the result that a charter was granted in the University's favour, to the great humiliation and mortification of the Town. The Mayor and burgesses were forced to attend a church service annually in St Mary's, on the anniversary of the massacre, and hand over a fine of 1*d* for each student slain. The penance continued until 1825 when the Mayor rebelled and refused to submit any longer to this centuries-old edict. It is pleasing to relate how, in 1955, on the 600th anniversary of the massacre, the current Mayor was given an honorary doctorate by the University as an olive branch. (Various sources)

FEBRUARY 11TH

1779: On this day an exotic gargantuan bird visited Oxford:

PIDCOCK, The Proprietor of the GRAND CASSOWAR from the Island of Java, in the East-Indies, which has been exhibited at Oxford for near a Fortnight past, to the great Satisfaction of the University &c, begs leave to inform the Public, that he shall be at Abingdon on Monday next; on his Way to London, through the Towns of Wallingford, Reading, Windsor &c – This Bird is the only one of the Species alive in England; and is most singularly curious as she has neither Tongue, Wing nor Tail, is six Feet high, and weighs 200lb. She laid an Egg at Warwick on the 14th of January last, which was blown at Oxford on the 5th of February inst and also another, rather larger, on the 9th of February. These eggs are excessively beautiful, being an elegant Mixture of White and Green.

Admittance to Ladies and gentlemen One Shilling each

(Jackson's Oxford Journal)

FEBRUARY 12TH

1942: On this day Reserve Constable Albert Alexander, who was in his mid-forties, became the first patient to be treated with injections of penicillin. In December, Albert, who was in the Oxfordshire police, had been accidentally scratched in his mouth by a thorn from a rose bush. By the New Year, the scratch had become badly infected with both staphylococcus and streptococcus bacteria, which led to his being sent to the Radcliffe Infirmary. Despite being given a variety of treatments, Constable Alexander was in a very bad way – his head had become covered in abscesses and one of his eyes had to be removed. As a last resort, he was given an intravenous infusion of 160mg (200 units of penicillin). Within twenty-four hours his temperature had dropped, he began to want to eat once more, and the infection started to heal. Unfortunately, because of penicillin's instability and the wartime restrictions on the laboratory run by Howard Florey and Ernst Chain, only a small amount had been administered, and, despite some being taken from the patient's urine, they had none left by the fifth day, with the result that Constable Alexander died on 15 March. (Various sources)

FEBRUARY 13TH

1865: On this day a very determined suicide succeeded in hanging himself. George Burdett, aged forty-nine, was a coal dealer and agent for Leicester coal merchants Ellis & Sons. He made the first attempt by hanging himself from a beam in his stable in Jericho, but was discovered almost immediately by his servant, who untied the rope and helped him down. The man then stayed long enough to ensure that Burdett went back indoors in apparent safety. He then hurried off to the White Hart Inn in Cornmarket Street where Ellis' traveller was staying prior to his meeting with Mr Burdett, and told him what had happened. In the meantime, however, Burdett had picked up his rope and gone next door to St Sepulchre's Cemetery in Jericho, where he hanged himself on a willow tree. He was found soon afterwards but, by then, he was beyond help. The coroner, Mr W. Brunner, heard that George Burdett had been in financial difficulties and that for this reason the meeting which had been arranged with the traveller from Ellis & Sons had been playing on his mind. The coroner's verdict was 'death due to temporary insanity'. (*Jackson's Oxford Journal*)

FEBRUARY 14TH

2006: On this Valentine's Day, just before midnight, an arsonist set fire to the Scout hut in William Kimber Crescent, Headington. After initial enquiries, the police described the fire as suspicious and began an investigation into the cause. Inside the hut were most of the sets and props which had been made over the previous six months in preparation for that year's Gang Show, sponsored as usual by the *Oxford Mail*. With only four weeks until the opening night at the New Theatre, the organisers contacted the paper in desperation. After reading about the Scouts' problem, a huge number of businesses and individuals offered their help in a mammoth effort to make sure that the show would go ahead. The Oxford Gang Show Chairman, Graham Ledger, soon had three A4 pages full of contact details for volunteers, including builders and carpenters, all eager to be involved in rebuilding the stage sets. All sorts of materials were donated, along with a cheque for £100. He said that his phone had been ringing non-stop and described the support the Scouts had received as phenomenal. Although there were probably more volunteers than were needed, every one of them was contacted and thanked. The next job was repairs to the hut itself. (*Oxford Mail*)

FEBRUARY 15TH

1840: On this day, representatives of Oxford City Council extended their congratulations on the marriage of Queen Victoria:

We, your Majesty's dutiful and loyal subjects, the Mayor, Aldermen and Burgesses of the city and borough of Oxford, in council assembled, humbly beg permission on the present joyful occasion of your Majesty's alliance with his Royal Highness Prince Albert of Saxe Coburg and Gotha, to approach the throne of our Sovereign with unfeigned expressions of our devoted attachment to your royal person and family and to offer our cordial congratulations to your Majesty and your Royal Consort. Firmly and unalterably attached as we are, and our predecessors have ever been, to those invaluable principles of civil liberty which are the chief glory and civil inheritance of Britons and which happily prevailed when your Majesty's illustrious ancestors were first called upon to wield the sceptre in these realms, we hail, with feeling of unmingled satisfaction, the choice made by your Majesty of a Protestant Prince … it will be our constant prayer that your reign may be long and prosperous – that you may have grace to govern with justice and mercy – that your people may live in peace, contented and happy – and that your Majesty and your Royal Consort may be blessed with mutual affection and experience domestic felicity without limit or alloy.

(Jackson's Oxford Journal)

FEBRUARY 16TH

1889: On this day Charles Turner, a worker at the Weirs paper mill, discovered something strange and unpleasant in the mill's pool – a human corpse. When it was examined back in the mortuary it was described as looking like a dilapidated statue. Decomposition had been stopped early by petrifaction, which had caused the flesh to take on a stone-like quality due to the lime in the water of the pool. The body had a hole in the stomach, some fingers missing and the features were indistinguishable. Its height was about 5ft 6in and the few shreds of clothing which remained included a black stocking on one leg and a glove on the right hand, all of which suggested that the corpse was that of a woman. It was thought that she had been in the water for three or four months; all the hair had been washed off the head. The body must have been washed up as it contained no gas which would have caused it to float. The inquest was adjourned for a fortnight in order for some identification to be attempted. The body was to be checked for clues such as broken limbs or gold fillings in the teeth. (*Jackson's Oxford Journal*)

FEBRUARY 17TH

1998: On this day the *Oxford Mail* interviewed a member of Oxford University who had been born in a canoe in the Amazonian rainforest of Peru. His home was a hut made with palm leaves, and he had fished for piranhas and hunted armadillos and monkeys. However, when he was thirteen, Miguel Hilario had read about New York in *National Geographic* magazine. He said, 'It made me realise there was a whole new world outside. I decided I would like to see these places with my own eyes.' He studied at a seminary run by missionaries in Lima. Young Hilario was so poor that he lived on scraps from restaurants and read by street lights. Eventually, he won a scholarship to study Theology in Texas and then another to study Politics and Economics at Mansfield College. He told the *Mail*: 'It's the dream of anyone in the world to come to Oxford. But for someone from the Amazon rainforest it is a chance in 5 million. Being here is extraordinary and I'm really honoured.' However, he never forgot his origins and set up a Peruvian Amazon Indian Institute to help other members of his tribe and to act as an ambassador for them. (*Oxford Mail*)

FEBRUARY 18TH

1998: Oxford's groundbreaking electric bus service became a victim of cuts in the county council's budget in 1998. It had survived a threatened closure the year before, only days after the Council Chairman, David Buckle, had been presented with an environmental award by Tony Blair who was, at the time, Leader of the Opposition. However, the council's environmental committee agreed to end the contract in order to save the running cost of £100,000 a year. Roger Williams, chief transport planner, said that the council had been forced to do so by the economic climate and the 'lack of generosity of the Government'. The service, believed to be unique, linked the railway station with the University Science Area and was introduced as an experiment in 1994 to cut pollution. It was subsidised by the council and used eighteen-seater electric minibuses provided free by Southern Electric and run by Stagecoach, who had taken it over from Oxford Bus Co. It was pointed out that any service subsidised by the county council would be running at a loss, otherwise one of the bus companies would be doing so. It was felt that the government should have made some provision for new technology and encouraged such projects. (*Oxford Mail*)

FEBRUARY 19TH

1966: On this day a very successful week-long run of Christopher Marlowe's *Dr Faustus* came to an end. Staged at the Playhouse Theatre by the Oxford University Dramatic Society (OUDS), the production had been exceptional as it starred Richard Burton, with a 'special guest appearance' by Elizabeth Taylor as Helen of Troy, three years after her legendary appearance as Cleopatra. Burton took the lead, and although Miss Taylor's was a non-speaking role, the reviewer from the *Oxford Times* reported that her presence imparted 'a splendid radiance', very much in keeping with Marlowe's famous quotation, 'Was this the face that launched a thousand ships?' The director of the play was Nevill Coghill, the distinguished literary scholar and translator of the *Canterbury Tales*, who had been Burton's tutor at Exeter College. In 1943, at the age of eighteen, Burton had come up to Oxford to read English for a special period of six months, made possible because he was an air force cadet. The critics wrote that student members of OUDS gave creditable performances, with Maria Aitken getting a mention in the part of the Good Angel, while the Seven Deadly Sins mask received a special commendation. (*Oxford Mail*)

FEBRUARY 20TH

1998: On this day mathematician Martin Soper claimed that Oxford had been planned to resemble a giant spaceship some 4,000 years before, by people inspired by visiting Martians. He claimed that nomadic tribes constructed Oxford to correspond with the star group Orion – the great hunter – possibly in an attempt to communicate with aliens. He stated that he was convinced that interplanetary flight took place and that the earth was changed in very ancient times to make it habitable. The mathematician was a member of the UFO society, Contact International, and had spent seven years developing his theory. He said that Oxford was built around 1500 BC, along with Stonehenge and Maiden Castle, to mirror one of the three stars making up Orion's Belt. He added that the design of Oxford as a giant UFO matches the blueprint of a flying saucer allegedly handed to author George Adamski by aliens in 1951. County archaeologist Paul Smith said, 'It is a nice little fantasy, but the design of Oxford comes from the fact that it is a medieval walled town. Oval shapes are the norm for medieval walled towns. His theory about Oxford does not have any foundation at all. This is pie in the sky.' (*Oxford Mail*)

FEBRUARY 21ST

2002: This was the day that actor John Thaw, star of the hit series *Inspector Morse* and *The Sweeney*, died at the age of sixty. He died at home with his wife, Sheila Hancock, and his three daughters around him. On 19 June John Thaw had made a public announcement, which shocked the country and made front-page headlines, saying that he was undergoing treatment for cancer of the oesophagus. He added that he intended to get back to work when the course of treatment was completed. He hoped he could film two further episodes of the legal drama *Kavanagh QC* in the spring. Ms Hancock, who married Thaw on Christmas Eve 1973 in Cirencester, had herself overcome breast cancer thirteen years previously. Her first husband had also died from oesophageal cancer in 1971. She stated that everybody, from the media to Thaw's thousands of fans, had been 'wonderful during this difficult period'. It was his role as Inspector Morse that had brought him cult status and worldwide fame. Some 13 million people watched the final episode, during which Morse was killed off. (Various sources)

FEBRUARY 22ND

1711: On this day the foundation stone was laid for the Clarendon Building, designed by Nicholas Hawksmoor. It was financed by the proceeds of the sales of the Earl of Clarendon's *The History of the Great Rebellion*, a biased but nevertheless valuable account of the English Civil Wars, which was published posthumously in 1702–4. His son gave the copyright of the work to the University to help finance the Clarendon Press. It was not until the third edition appeared that the money was forthcoming; the proceeds from the first two runs had been misappropriated. The printing press of the University was moved from the Sheldonian Theatre and remained until 1830, when the present building was opened in Walton Street. On the west wall of the Clarendon Building is a statue of the Earl, clutching a copy of his work and surrounded by pigeons; it was carved by Francis Bird in about 1721 and cost £55. The building was completed in 1724. (Various sources)

FEBRUARY 23RD

1864: On this day among the places to eat and drink in Oxford were:

R.S.ABBOTT

DINING ROOMS AND EATING HOUSE

2, PARK END STREET, OXFORD

(2 minutes' walk from the railway stations)

RESPECTFULLY informs the public that he has commenced business as above, and hopes by cooking MEAT &c. of the best quality, and selling at moderate prices, to receive a share of their patronage, which it will be his study to deserve.

NB CHOPS and STEAKS on the shortest notice.

*** Ham, Beef, German Sausages and Collared Head, Sausages, &c always on hand and sent to any part of Oxford.

Excellent accommodation – Private Dining Rooms – All Orders punctually attended to.

———◆———

OXFORD

WANTED – A few more CUSTOMERS to the WELLINGTON INN, CORN MARKET,
Where they will get a good Dinner for *7d*, an excellent Likeness for *6d*, or 12 Carte de Visite Portraits for *7s.6d*.

(Jackson's Oxford Journal)

FEBRUARY 24TH

1999: On this day it was reported that an astonishing suggestion had been made that Lewis Carroll, or Charles Lutwidge Dodgson to give him his real name, was a viable suspect for Jack the Ripper. The accusation appeared in *Jack the Ripper: Light-hearted Friend*, a book expounding a greatly flawed theory on the unsolved murders which took place in the autumn of 1888 in Whitechapel in London's East End. Its author, Richard Wallace, makes the Christ Church lecturer in Mathematics a prime suspect. He claims that Carroll suffered a mental breakdown after being the victim of a homosexual assault when he was twelve and felt a need for revenge on society as a consequence. As part of his evidence, he points out that Carroll's diary was kept in purple ink apart from the days that the murders took place, when he used black. Furthermore, Carroll had no alibi on the nights that the Ripper was at work. 'Quite simply, Carroll was a psychopathic killer,' said Dr Wallace. Apparently, a clue to Carroll's mind can be found in the 1872 nonsense poem 'Jabberwocky', which contains the lines: 'The vorpal blade went snicker-snack! He left it dead, and with its head; He went galumphing back.' (*Oxford Mail*)

FEBRUARY 25TH

1999: This was the day that Ian Yeung of Trinity College got his name in the papers for all the wrong reasons. He had been stupid enough to wander round his hall of residence holding a replica gun. When he was spotted, the police were called and officers in bulletproof vests pounced on him and pinned him to the floor, ordering him to drop the plastic replica weapon. Yeung was said to belong to a fantasy role-playing club called the Oxford Guild of Assassins. The twenty-year-old medical student was questioned at the scene and a report was sent to the Crown Prosecution Service in order to decide whether or not charges would be brought. A police spokesman said that the matter was being treated very seriously. The Trinity College Dean said that Yeung was 'scared to death' when he went to reprimand him and kept asking if he would be sent to prison. The *Oxford Mail* also reported that a taxi driver had informed the police that a man was brandishing a handgun in a car in the High Street that Monday. They called at a house in Ridgefield Road and removed a replica weapon. A nineteen-year-old man was given a verbal warning. (*Oxford Mail*)

FEBRUARY 26TH

1998: This was the day that a bulletin was published regarding the condition of Nigel Wesson. Mr Wesson had lost part of his arm after an attack by a big cat belonging to Chipperfield's Circus, which was spending the winter at its usual venue at Heythrop near Chipping Norton. Rajah, a 500lb Bengal tiger, ripped off Mr Wesson's left arm at the elbow after he had put his hand into the cage, thereby breaking an 'unwritten rule'. Mr Wesson was airlifted to the John Radcliffe Hospital in Oxford where his arm was amputated above the elbow. A spokesman for Chipperfield's Circus told reporters that Mr Wesson was an experienced keeper who had joined them from another circus just over a fortnight previously and that he was 'a very experienced, methodical person'. He went on to say that, 'The accident happened in seconds and we are heartbroken about it.' It was stressed that there was no question of Rajah being destroyed for having behaved like a normal tiger. That morning he was playing happily with his two sisters in an open-air compound, totally oblivious of his wrongdoing. The four-year-old tiger, which had been bred by the Chipperfield family, had appeared in television advertisements for Esso. (*Oxford Mail*)

FEBRUARY 27TH

2009: Then prime minister Gordon Brown visited the University of Oxford in 2009 to announce ambitious targets aimed at increasing the number of pupils studying mathematics and the sciences in state schools. In the afternoon, he was shown round the new £109 million cancer centre at the Churchill Hospital, which he said was an excellent example of how new investment could provide a great deal of comfort for its patients. A spokesperson for Oxford Radcliffe Hospitals said, 'We are delighted that the Prime Minister has chosen to come here. We have had an opportunity to show him how well public money is being spent.' Mr Brown also visited a biochemistry laboratory in South Parks Road, before delivering the prestigious Romanes Lecture in the Sheldonian Theatre. He stressed that investment in science was essential to Britain's ability to compete in the future and promised that the sciences would not be allowed to become 'a victim of the recession'. He announced incentives to encourage science, maths and IT graduates who had lost their jobs to retrain as teachers, as part of a drive to make sure that within five years the majority of state schools would offer physics, chemistry and biology as separate subjects. (*Oxford Mail*)

FEBRUARY 28TH

2005: On this day that the *Oxford Mail* carried an obituary for the founder of the human rights organisation Amnesty International. On 25 February, Peter Benenson, who lived at Nuneham Courtenay, died aged eighty-three in Oxford's John Radcliffe Hospital after a long illness. Mr Benenson, who read History at Balliol College, started a campaign called 'Amnesty 61' after reading about two students in Portugal who had been thrown into prison after drinking a toast to liberty. That same year, Mr Benenson founded Amnesty International, and wrote a book called *Persecution 1961*, which told the stories of eight men and a woman who suffered for their principles. During Amnesty's first few years, Mr Benenson provided much of its funding and was involved in all aspects of its running. In 2001 Mr Benenson, who had already declined a knighthood, was given a special place at the *Mirror*'s Pride of Britain Awards in London. By the time of Mr Benenson's death, Amnesty International was in its 44th year and had become the world's largest independent human rights organisation. Today it has more than 3 million members worldwide. A public memorial service in tribute to its founder was held by Amnesty International later that year. (*Oxford Mail*)

FEBRUARY 29TH

2012: On this day, the *Oxford Mail* made an announcement that a number of red-haired celebrities had agreed to help raise funds for the Oxford charity SOS – the Sumatran Orang-utan Society. Leading names included: Hollywood star Nicole Kidman; BBC Radio DJ Chris Evans; Girls Aloud singer Nicola Roberts; comedian Tim Minchin; actress-turned-cake-maker, Jane Asher; and local band Radiohead. Each of them donated items for an online Jungle VIP Auction. Other celebrated redheads taking part were Spice Girl Geri Halliwell; snooker player Steve Davis; musician Mick Hucknall; and presenter Anne Robinson. Ways of raising cash included selling T-shirts on the Internet, and auctioning off fashion items, memorabilia and handwritten song lyrics. The future of the orang-utans of Sumatra (who share 96.4 per cent of human DNA) is critical as they could become the first species of great ape to become extinct. The charity SOS work among local communities whose members live near orang-utan forest habitats, and helps and advises on a sustainable future for man and ape. Three years earlier, comedians, including dark-haired Marcus Brigstocke, put on a show at Oxford's New Theatre and raised about £10,000 for the charity based in the Cowley Road.(*Oxford Mail*)

MARCH 1ST

2003: On this day a memorial service was held in the University Church for the Rt Hon. Lord Jenkins of Hillhead, Chancellor of the University. David Steel and his wife arrived early and were later joined by Shirley Williams. Sitting behind them were Lord Heseltine and his wife and Lord Hurd and his wife. The organ played gently away in the background as the guests took their seats, and then suddenly changed tune as the long procession snaked into the church. The staves of each of the six Bedels were covered with black cloth. The procession was made up of the Vice-Chancellor, the Proctors, the Assessor, the Registrar, and the Pro-Vice Chancellors; all of whom wore black edges round the bands at their necks. Other University officials, predominately the Heads of Houses, past and present, were also in attendance. The Vice-Chancellor's address was moving and he obviously meant every word he said. The speech contained an amusing anecdote about the late Chancellor's aspirations towards losing weight, and finished with the words 'and I miss him sorely'. The occasion finished with tea in the cloister of All Souls College and there was also an opportunity to look round the College's newly refurbished Codrington Library. (Personal observation)

MARCH 2ND

1959: This was the day when the notorious Cutteslowe Walls were finally demolished. In December 1934, the Urban Housing Co. had put up two 7ft-high walls to prevent residents of the council estate at Cutteslowe from walking through to the private development that lay beyond. This involved a detour of about a mile to reach the Banbury Road and the estate residents were understandably annoyed. Not only were they physically inconvenienced, they also felt that they were being treated as inferior citizens because they did not own the houses they lived in. The Cutteslowe residents' first attempt at demolition was in May 1935, when their case was taken first to court and then to Parliament. Oxford City Council demolished the walls on 7 June 1938 but a High Court injunction led to them being rebuilt. During the Second World War a tank demolished one wall and a car damaged the other, but both were rebuilt. Finally, the City Council purchased the strips of land on which the walls were built and started to pull them down. The ensuing celebrations included the Cutteslowe residents going to and fro at will, which they had been unable to do for many years. (*Oxford Mail*)

MARCH 3RD

1998: The whereabouts of the head from the corpse of Oliver Cromwell had remained a mystery for nearly 300 years. But on this day in 1998, it seemed that this conundrum might have been solved. There had always been a question over the exact location, but three possible venues had been championed. A very strong contender had been a skull given to the former Master of Balliol, Benjamin Jowett, but comparisons with a death mask in the Ashmolean Museum, taken of the Protector, ruled this out. It was decided that Cromwell's head was the one that had been buried in a biscuit tin in his old Cambridge college, Sidney Sussex, in 1960. The burial place of the head, which had been given to the college by the Wilkinson family of Suffolk, was kept secret for fear of it being stolen or mutilated. Dr Louise Scheuer, Honorary Senior Lecturer in Anatomy at the Royal Free Hospital in London, carried out tests on the head owned by Jowett after it was brought from Canterbury and compared with the death mask in the Ashmolean. She said dimensions of the skull were very different from those of the mask and, in fact, the skull and its lower jaw had not belonged to the same person. (*Oxford Mail*)

MARCH 4TH

1966: On this day, the Cowley Road branch of Parslows the bakers was fined £60 for selling a chocolate eclair which contained a piece of metal. The lady who found it said that she had bought four eclairs. When she gave a piece to her two-year-old son, she noticed that there was metal in it from a wire cake tray. Parslows had already been guilty of five such convictions in Oxford in the previous two years.

A Public Health Inspector had discovered an infestation of 'American drugstore beetles' in the warehouse of well-known Oxford grocers. These beetles feed on pharmacological products, including prescription drugs. They have very eclectic tastes which include spices, dried food, hair, leather, books, and museum exhibits. They can bore into furniture and even tin foil and lead sheeting. In this case they settled on a Fry's 'Punch' bar, which had been bought in the shop. The purchaser offered some chocolate to a friend, who noticed a small hole in the wrapper; investigation revealed a maggot inside the bar itself. The infestation was said to be confined to one room of the warehouse and only one bar of the infected chocolate had been sold. (*Oxford Mail*)

MARCH 5TH

1964: On this evening in 1964, two teenage pop fans in central Oxford could scarcely believe their eyes. The girls were strolling down the High Street, near Carfax, when two beautifully dressed men came walking towards them. As they came closer, the girls thought that their faces looked very familiar, but it was their distinctive hairstyles and the long coats with the velvet collars which really drew their attention. After they had gone past, they looked at each other in silence, and then told each other that it couldn't possibly have been John Lennon and Paul McCartney. It was not until the following day that they knew it to be true when they read in the *Oxford Mail* that The Beatles had been in the city as part of a campaign by then student Jeffrey Archer to raise £1 million. The Fab Four had dinner at Brasenose College followed by drinks at the exclusive Vincent's Club. One of the girls commented that lucky as they had been to see John and Paul, it was George and Ringo who were their real favourites. (Personal observation)

MARCH 6TH

1901: One this day an Irish worker, part of a team repairing the ceiling panels of the Sheldonian Theatre, was overcome by the urge to commit himself to paper. Not only did he leave a letter for posterity, he also hid a pair of his working trousers and some tools under the attic floor. Although a very comprehensive authorised time capsule compiled by the chief restorer had been found in February 1995, this unofficial one remained undiscovered until October 2004. The stained trousers were found to be in a bad state of repair. The letter, which was rolled up in a cigar tube, read:

> Sheldonian Theatre
> March 6 1901
>
> Dear Friend –
> When you have inspected these trousers please hand them over to the Curator of the Taylor Buildings for the Museum as they were worn by Frank Morrill Chief Assistant to John C. Nairn and Son who restored the ceiling of the building.
> Hope you will enjoy yourself when you have found this valuable treasure. I expect I will have fed the worms by that time, however I will have a good time before I do so.
> Goodbye old chap good bye
> Yours in ashes (?)
> Frank Morrill.

(Personal observation of package)

MARCH 7TH

2001: On this day the hearings concerning protests staged by students at Oxford University were in progress. The Students' Union had led a protest against the actions taken by the Proctors, the senior members of the University who are in charge of discipline. More than fifty students, among them William Straw, the son of Home Secretary Jack Straw, demonstrated at Somerville College and outside the Proctors' Office in Wellington Square. The Proctors responded by setting up a court to deal with thirty students of the 300 or so who had occupied the Divinity School from 7–11 February. The students' protest was in reaction to the University's treatment of those students who had refused to pay tuition fees following, what the students felt, was an unreasonable increase in the price. The President of the OUSU said that the demonstration had been successful and showed student solidarity. She was quoted in the *Oxford Mail* as saying: 'The Proctors have absolute power to discipline all students in Oxford. The procedure is completely illegitimate because the Proctors act as prosecuting counsel, judge, jury and executioner. It's a kangaroo court reminiscent of some tin-pot dictatorship.' (Various sources)

MARCH 8TH

1966: On this day Oxford City Police released a photograph showing what happened to the illegal substances they confiscated. In the picture, one of their officers was in the process of destroying thousands of 'purple hearts' (heart-shaped purple tablets containing a combination of amphetamine and barbiturate), and several ounces of hemp, all of which had been seized in raids in and around the city that January and February. The tablets were disposed of by firstly crushing them and then dissolving them in water. The officer in the picture was surrounded by other illegal items which had been seized in raids, including: syringes, opium, cocaine, cannabis resin, morphia and marijuana. After they had been found and removed, these substances were sent off for analysis at the Forensic Science Laboratory in Birmingham. On their return to Oxford, they were kept safely under lock and key at the City Police Station in St Aldates until all prosecutions involving them had taken place and they were no longer needed as evidence. A police spokesperson stated that most of these illegal substances were then burnt in incinerators. (*Oxford Mail*)

MARCH 9TH

1825: On this day Oxford citizens had an amazing choice of headgear available at Jarvis' London Water-Proof Hat Warehouse in St Ebbe's. This included 'an extensive and fashionable assortment of superior SILK and BEAVER HATS of every description'. Mr Jarvis' 'undivided attention being devoted to the hat business', his 'determination' was to offer 'every article of the best quality upon terms calculated to ensure him a distinguished share of the patronage of a discerning public'. Ladies were catered for with beaver bonnets of all qualities and in the latest fashions. The boys and youths of the town could purchase 'seal, sable, cloth and other caps in great variety' and there were also:

Hat covers, umbrellas, whalebone for stays, &c. The following low prices will powerfully evince his claims to public attention boys', youths' and men's stout hats from 1s 4d to 2s 4d, boys', youths' and men's beavers 4s 6d, 5s 6d to 6s; fine ditto 7s, 8s, and 9s each; a large assortment of waggoner's dogs' hair hats 5s, 6s, and 7s each, fine water-proof beavers 18s, 20s, and 22s; the best that can be manufactured 24s each; umbrellas beginning at the low price of 5s, – Hats, beavers, bonnets and seal caps cleaned and altered.

(*Jackson's Oxford Journal*)

MARCH 10TH

1900: On this day, the whole of Oxford went mad with joy at the news that Ladysmith had been relieved. Military bands and amateur musicians patrolled the streets, flags were waved everywhere, processions formed and marched round the city, soldiers were carried shoulder high, 'Rule Britannia' was sang and, occasionally, the premises of those who failed to join in the fun were raided. Bonfires were set alight from the Cowley Road to Walton Street, the most spectacular of which was outside the Indian Institute, fed by anything that would burn; much of it was pillaged from Wadham College. Fortunately, despite the alcohol consumed, there were few skirmishes and no serious injuries were sustained. From the balcony of the Town Hall, the Mayor addressed a vast crowd which packed St Aldates as far as Carfax and overflowed into Cornmarket, along Queen Street and down the High Street. He led patriotic cheers for British victories and the singing of the National Anthem. Celebrities such as Buller, Roberts and Kitchener were cheered by name and then the crowd moved off to other parts of the city. The excitement continued until long into the night, some bonfires being kept alight until 2 or 3 a.m. (*Jackson's Oxford Journal*)

MARCH 11TH

1681: In the spring of 1681, with the plague in London, the courts and Parliament moved to Oxford, the country's second capital. This had also been done during the Civil War some forty years previously. Anthony à Wood describes the event:

This day arrived his Majestie's carriages, laden with bedding, tapestry, hangings and other necessaries to furnish lodgings [at Christ Church] for his reception as likewise for her Majesty at Merton College where she is to reside; also abundance of goods by water and land appertaining to the several Embassadors and Peers insomuch that the City seemed like a great mart or fair. On Monday his Majesty is expected to make his entrance, against which time all preparations are making for his joyful reception, the bells through the City being ordered to be rung and several bonfires will be made, the gentry having promised to give very liberally; so that it is expected the better to compleat the general joy, several hogsheads of wine will be bestowed on the people if the conduit do not run with it. A great party of the worthy Members elected to serve in Parliament are already here and express their great zeal for the speedy settling of affairs.

(*Life and Times of Anthony à Wood*, ed. Andrew Clark, OUP, 1961)

MARCH 12TH

1829: On this day the first world-famous boat race took place between Oxford and Cambridge. It was the result of a challenge issued to Oxford by Cambridge. Oxford wore dark-blue jerseys, later to be adopted as the famous Oxford Blue, while Cambridge sported pink sashes. On this occasion Oxford were both more skilful and stronger. In 1836 Cambridge dressed in white outfits, with a light blue ribbon decorating the bow of their boat, so adopting the lighter Cambridge Blue. This first race was rowed at Henley-on-Thames and, according to the press, was watched by about 20,000 people. Even though this was the only time that the race was at Henley, the residents were so taken with the idea that they later decided to start a town regatta, which in time became the prestigious Henley Royal Regatta. Subsequent University boat races took place at Westminster, a venue which became so overcrowded that, in 1845, a course was decided upon between Putney, then out in the countryside, and Mortlake. From 1856 onwards this became the established course for the annual event. It is 4½ miles long, much longer than an Olympic course. (Various sources)

MARCH 13TH

1998: On this day workers at the Unigate Dairy in Kidlington received a special order for 100 pints of Breakfast Milk to be sent to an Irish baby giraffe. The ten-day-old calf called Aoife, who had been rejected by her mother at birth, was being hand-reared by staff at Belfast Zoo on the special high-fat milk. The milk was similar to that of a giraffe and was able to be frozen, thus it could be stored in bulk for Aoife. However, with Aoife guzzling her way through fourteen pints a day, she had soon exhausted all the stocks of the milk in Northern Ireland. Her keepers were very worried about her future, especially when they discovered that the only supplier of the milk was the Unigate Dairy in Oxfordshire. On receipt of the order, workers rallied round and within hours had sent off a special consignment from Oxford Airport. The Oxford-based air-taxi firm Air Med provided an aircraft and Unigate's customer service manager, Bernie Palmer, flew with the milk to Belfast. He helped to give Aoife a very welcome feed, with the compliments of the cows of Oxfordshire. The 7ft-tall calf was later said to be thriving. Mr Palmer described the 'tall order' as the most unusual that they had ever received. (*Oxford Mail*)

MARCH 14TH

2002: On this day a rail traveller 'went berserk' just after 12.30 a.m. at the idea of being obliged to spend the night in Oxford train station. He had reached Oxford on a service from London with his girlfriend, but had intended to get off at Reading. He was carried on to Oxford, where he discovered that the first train back home to Reading was not until 4 a.m. that morning. Both the passenger and his girlfriend were drunk when they got off the Great Western train in Oxford. The girl did try to calm him down but with no success; in his rage, the man picked up an aluminium wheelchair ramp and started to smash windows at the station. Terrified station staff were forced to take refuge from his rampaging and hid in an office for safety as they watched the man break five large glass panels in the sliding doors which divided the platform from the foyer. The panels, which would cost thousands of pounds to replace, were taped up after the incident. Staff managed to call the police, who arrived and arrested the furious passenger. (*Oxford Mail*)

MARCH 15TH

2003: This was the second and final day set for the election of a Chancellor of Oxford University. A replacement was needed following the death of Lord Jenkins of Hillhead that January. This election differed from previous ones as any person holding a degree from the University was now eligible to vote. This was done by marking one's chosen candidate on a ballot sheet, and the election, which took place in the Divinity School, was presided over by the Proctors. Three candidates remained: Lord Bingham of Cornhill, High Steward of the University; Lord Neill of Bladen, who, as Sir Patrick Neill, had been Warden of All Souls College and Vice-Chancellor; and Mr Christopher Patten (later Baron Patten of Barnes), Governor of Hong Kong, and the incumbent Chancellor of the University of Newcastle. Another candidate, Sandra (Sandi) Toksvig, television personality and Cambridge graduate, had been eliminated in the first round according to the newly introduced single transferable vote system. Chris Patten was elected, having received 1,730 more votes than the runner-up, Lord Bingham, who polled 2,303; Lord Neill of Bladen only received 1,470 votes. The newly elected Chancellor, the seventh member of Balliol College to hold the office, was installed as part of that year's Encaenia. (Personal observation)

MARCH 16TH

1998: On this day it was revealed that Oscar-nominated actress Kate Winslet had paid a secret visit to a film set based in the former Oxford Prison site in order to be with her boyfriend, film director Jim Threapleton. Extras on the six-part ITV drama called *The Jump* looked on in surprise as the *Titanic* star kissed and cuddled Threapleton during breaks in the filming. The *Oxford Mail* was told:

> They were obviously very much in love and were making no effort to hide it. Nobody realised who she was at first. She didn't look like a film star – she had camouflage trousers and a stripey woolly hat on. She and Jim looked like love-struck teenagers. None of us could believe our eyes. Even though she had nothing to do with the show, she was walking around and chatting to everyone openly – she seemed very nice. She came and met Jim during the lunch break and they kissed in front of us all. Then they disappeared into a corner together.

During the four days of shooting, the programme's cast and crew stayed in North Oxford at the Linton Lodge and the Cotswold Lodge Hotel. (*Oxford Mail*)

MARCH 17TH

1900: This St Patrick's Day was celebrated as it never had been previously. Other years, only two or three shamrock-wearers would have been spotted, even if one walked through the city streets all day. That year there were queues of eager buyers at the gates of the Covered Market when it opened at 8 a.m. The real shamrocks soon sold out and many purchasers had to make do with 'various other forms of vegetation'. The emerald-green Irish flag could be seen flying all over Oxford on both public and private buildings, and such was the demand that many drapers sold out of the cloth to make them. According to *Jackson's Oxford Journal*: 'The universal "wearing of the green" showed unmistakeably the sentiment of the mother country for the "land of the West" and the question of whether the leaves were true or false matters not a jot.' The reason for this sudden urge to wear 'the dear little plant' was the fact that the Queen had expressed a wish for the Irish regiments to wear the shamrock on that day in recognition of their gallantry on the battlefields of South Africa. (*Jackson's Oxford Journal*)

MARCH 18TH

1899: This extract is taken from a suicide letter written by a Miss Helen Bickford of No. 221 Iffley Road to her brother:

> I am not to be buried, Alfred. You stayed away through life, and the hideous mockery of following me to the grave must be prevented. And again, and the must be done, and the best way that I should prefer followeth, and that is that my body by accepted by any hospital in return for which I require to be dissected and examined as to my having led a pure life, such confirmation to be forwarded to you and to Dr G. Batten, MD, Lordship-lane, Forest Hill.

It finishes: 'No ceremony of any kind over my body; they are but idle words when acts have failed during life and it is in the power of many around me to act, but they will not – with love, Nellie.' The next-door neighbour told the coroner that he had noticed 'a most offensive smell emanating from the house'. Miss Bickford was discovered in her nightdress in front of a gas fire which had been turned full on. 'The body presented a dark brown appearance and seemed to have been tanned by heat.' (*Jackson's Oxford Journal*)

MARCH 19TH

2009: On this day in 2009, the authenticity of a portrait said to be the only known painting of William Shakespeare to have been made during his lifetime was called into question. The painting has hung on the walls of Cobbe family homes in Hampshire and Surrey for the last three centuries or so, and appeared on the front page of *The Sunday Times* as an authentic representation of the Bard as a handsome young man, a claim backed up by the Shakespeare Birthplace Trust. Unfortunately for its owners and supporters, Professor Katherine Duncan-Jones, of Somerville College, pointed out the similarities between the Cobbe portrait and one of a lesser-known Elizabethan, Sir Thomas Overbury, who met a mysterious end in the Tower of London. She believed it to be a copy of a portrait of him which is in Oxford University's Bodleian Library. Among the clues which made Professor Duncan-Jones come to this conclusion was the fact that by the time the painting was completed in 1610, as claimed, Shakespeare would have been forty-six. In addition, from his dress, the sitter appears to be a nobleman and of a much higher social status than that which Shakespeare ever attained. (*Oxford Mail*)

March 20th

1895: A notice appeared on this day calling to arms the Oxfordshire Hussars:

QUEEN'S OWN OXFORDSHIRE HUSSARS

The Regiment will assemble for permanent duty at Oxford on Wednesday May 1st. The first two days, Thursday and Friday, will be devoted to troop and squadron drill. The inspection will take place on Thursday, May 10th. Pay will not be allowed to any man who does not complete six squad drills, recruits twelve squad drills, the annual course of musketry and the two days troop drills on 2nd and 3rd of May … The rates of pay and marching allowances are the same as last year. Officers commending squadrons are requested to make their own arrangements for the march to Oxford, so as to arrive on May 1st. The officers' mess will be at the Randolph Hotel. The Regimental competition to select the three best men (in tent pegging, lemon cutting and head and posts) will compete for the Brigade challenge cup and gold medal, will take place at Oxford before the 10th of May and the Brigade competition at Buckingham on the 11th May. Sections entering for the volley matches for 1895 may fire during permanent duty if in the opinion of the section commander his section has had enough practice.

(*Jackson's Oxford Journal*)

MARCH 21ST

1556: On this day Thomas Cranmer, Archbishop of Canterbury, was the third of the Oxford Martyrs to be burnt at the stake. He had been told that he would have the opportunity to make a final recantation in public in the University Church. However, the onlookers were stunned when, after saying a prayer and urging his listeners to obey the King and Queen, he renounced his previous recantations, proclaiming that the hand that had written them should burn first. He went on, 'And as for the Pope, I refuse him, as Christ's enemy, and Antichrist with all his false doctrine.' This was too much to be tolerated and he was pulled from the pulpit and dragged round to Broad Street where he was tied to a stake and burnt outside Balliol College in the same place that Latimer and Ridley had met identical deaths six months previously. A cross made of cobblestones marks the site today and a wreath of flowers is placed there on the anniversary of his death. Scorch marks from the flames which burnt Cranmer can be seen on a pair of gates which now hang inside the college between the Front and Garden Quadrangles. (Various sources)

MARCH 22ND

1880: On this day in 1880, the Oxford and Cambridge boat race generated a huge amount of interest in the city, despite the fact that it was taking place some 60 miles away on the Thames in London. A great number of people had taken advantage of the train to London, which had been laid on especially for the boat race and which started early in the morning to give them the opportunity of seeing the race for themselves. However, a great deal of disappointment was caused by the fact that the train that they had got up so early to catch was postponed. On the following Monday, back in Oxford, a huge crowd gathered in Carfax, anxiously awaiting the result to be announced. In those days, before the advent of radio and television, they had no idea of how the Dark Blues had got on and had to spend the Sunday in suspense. A telegraph had been sent immediately after the end of the race to say that the Oxford crew were the victors, and when the loyal crowd heard this good news, a great cheer arose. (*Jackson's Oxford Journal*)

MARCH 23RD

1839: The following appeal to the charitable public which appeared on this day:

This Appeal is made on behalf of FOUR ORPHAN CHILDREN, three sons and a daughter of the late R.H. Guest, for many years landlord of the New Inn in Oxford who expired after a painful illness on 26th February last, under most distressing and heartrending circumstances, which if generally known would excite the charity of all charitable and humane persons – having had the whole of his furniture &c distrained on the 19th of December last for a small sum due for rent, since which day he with three of his children (until within a week of his death) lay on the floor with scarcely any thing to cover them and without the common necessities of life. The object of this appeal to the public is to raise a sum sufficient to place the children at school for a limited period during which time it is hoped that masters will be found for them, and thereby prevent the necessity of these unfortunate orphans becoming inmates of a workhouse. Mr T. Mallam, High-street; Mr W. Thorpe, Holywell-street; and Mr T. Dry, Pembroke-street, have kindly consented to receive subscriptions and apply them for the benefit of the children.

(*Jackson's Oxford Journal*)

MARCH 24TH

1998: A survey revealed that, far from being elegantly clothed examples of a *Brideshead Revisited* lifestyle, students at Oxford University were definitely sartorially challenged – Evelyn Waugh's Hooray Henrys and Henriettas had disappeared from the scene long before. The survey, which covered nineteen universities in Britain, showed Oxford in bottom place as regards keeping up with the latest fashions. Students, both male and female, were said to spend a mere £72 a term on clothes, compared with their counterparts in London and Glasgow who paid out nearly double that amount. The number of Oxford students who were car owners was far below the average; one third of all final-year students at other universities owned a vehicle. It came as no shock, though, to learn that the city had some of the highest accommodation costs in Britain at around £58 a week. Members of Oxford were said to work harder than at other universities, putting in a typical thirty-plus hours of study a week. The President of Oxford University Student Union commented that he didn't think that the results would come as much of a surprise to any Oxford student. (*Oxford Mail*)

MARCH 25TH

1834: On this day the following 'insolent anonymous' letter was printed, having been sent in the post by a 'liberal scribbler' to the wrong person. The subject is the then recent controversial walkout by the Bible printers at the University Press, which provoked strong feelings:

Sir, – I have been in the habit of dealing at your shop but do not intend to do so for the future, because in the *Oxford Journal* of last Saturday, your name is attached to an advertisement from a number of men who have struck for an advance of wages. You are therefore an abetter and supporter of men who (by their own showing) were receiving at the reduced rate 33*s* per week, and who are conspiring to oblige their employers to continue their high wages when the productions of their labour are at a lower price. What makes the case more atrocious is that the wages of only a part have been reduced. My custom is small and may not be missed; but it may have the effect of convincing you that society will no longer tolerate the interference of impertinent and meddling persons in supporting illegal combination.

I am

Cato Censor

(*Jackson's Oxford Journal*)

MARCH 26TH

2009: On this day, an East Oxford man gave a press interview about his plans to cycle through Zimbabwe dressed as a clown, with cycling partner Asher Mupasi, a Zimbabwean living in Birmingham. Father-of-three Richard Pantlin explained how he intended to make the 373-mile bike ride from Bulawayo to the capital, Harare, in order to present President Robert Mugabe with a postcard which he had bought in the country during his one and only visit twenty years previously. Mr Pantlin wore a battered topper and red nose at the interview but his juggling balls, comedy horn and oversized boots were packed away ready for the flight from Heathrow. His aim was to raise enough money to complete an orphanage in central Zimbabwe for the charity Health Education and Learning Programme, and to remind Mugabe of how very different the situation had been twenty years before, when happy, smiling people represented to Mr Pantlin all that the country then stood for. He said that he was still waiting to hear back from the Zimbabwean regime but that he had spoken to the Chargé d'Affaires at the embassy, who called it 'a noble project'. (*Oxford Mail*)

MARCH 27TH

1879: On this day John Sanger & Sons' Mammoth Circus, Hippodrome and Menagerie, from Sanger's Grand National Amphitheatre in London, was visiting Oxford. It was, claimed the posters, the largest, most carefully selected and by far the best equestrian company ever organised in any country. The entire programme was of that 'varied, novel and high-class character which had gained the proprietors a worldwide reputation'.

The major attractions were 220 Horses; 50 Ponies; 7 Elephants; 6 Camels and Dromedaries; 2 Zebras; 4 Peruvian Gold Horses (the only ones ever seen in England); 16 Lady Riders (the best of the day); 10 Gentleman Riders; Gymnasts; Acrobats &c, and 'the 6 Great Clowns that caused so much laughter last Winter to the largest Audience ever known in London'. The Grand Procession which began at 1 o'clock was on no account to be missed, said the posters, as Mr Burke, the Master of the Horse and Champion Whip, would drive 50-in-hand without any assistance whatsoever, and would be a spectacle quite unequalled for magnificent display. Afternoon performances began at 2.30 and evening ones at 7.30. Reserved seats (select) cost 3/-, First Class 2/-, Second ditto 1/- and Third ditto 6d.

(*Jackson's Oxford Journal*)

MARCH 28TH

1899: On this day, at an inquest held into the death of four-year-old William Edward Ivings, the coroner heard how the boy had eaten sardines for breakfast on the Thursday morning. When his father had come home for dinner that afternoon, William had been shaking as if he had a cold, and had said that he felt sick. When Mr Ivings returned from work that evening, the boy was about the same, but he was sick later that night. The doctor was called, and he found that William was suffering from sickness and diarrhoea. He left a prescription, but as there was no improvement, he returned on the Friday evening. The child's condition worsened as the days went by until, on the Sunday, he died at about 4.45 p.m. The doctor suggested that the sardines might have been the cause. Mr Ivings had only eaten half of one because he disliked the taste of the oil which they were in, but he hadn't noticed any unpleasant or unusual smell, and nobody else in the house had eaten any. The sardines came from a small 3½*d* box bought from a shop in the Iffley Road. The doctor said that, although undetectable by taste or smell, ptomaine might have been present in the fish. (*Jackson's Oxford Journal*)

MARCH 29TH

2011: On this day, at 11 a.m., what might have been an exceptionally high-profile wedding took place at Oxford Registry Office. The ceremony cost just £167 and there were only a few guests. Nevertheless, they were a fairy-tale couple, an aristocratic English rose and her prince. The bride, Lucy Cuthbert, was a niece of the Duke of Northumberland and the groom was Prince Bandar Bin Khalid Bin Faisal al-Saud of Saudi Arabia. The bride wore a white thigh-length dress and cream jacket, while her husband wore a classic British grey three-piece suit. The couple dispensed with the conventional limousine or horse and carriage, and arrived at the registry office in a chauffeur-driven Land Rover. The bride's uncle owns Alnwick Castle, the building used as Hogwarts in the Harry Potter films, and her father is the owner of Beaufront Castle. The groom is the grandson of the Crown Prince of Saudi Arabia and heir to a billion-pound oil fortune. The family Airbus, painted in the colours of his favourite Dallas Cowboys American Football team, is at his disposal and he is permitted to land at RAF Brize Norton, not far from Glympton Park, his 2,000-acre estate near Woodstock. (*Oxford Mail*)

MARCH 30TH

1899: The following advertisement was made for a new medical officer for the city in 1899:

> The Guardians of the Poor within the City of Oxford intend shortly to appoint a MEDICAL OFFICER for the District of the United Parishes. The gentleman to be appointed must possess the usual qualifications (both Medical and Surgical) and will be required to perform the duties specified in the orders of the Poor Law Board and Local Government Board. The salary will be £100 a year with extra fees as directed by the said order. Both salary and fees will be subjected to the statuary deduction under the Poor Law Superannuation Act 1896. The Medical Officer will not be appointed Public Vaccinator. The successful candidate will be obliged to take up his residence within the Boundary of the District not later than two months after the date of his appointment. Applications stating age and accompanied by copies of testimonials must be sent to me under cover subscribed 'Appointment of Medical Officer', on or before 15th April prox. Selected candidates will have notice when to attend. Canvassing the Guardians directly or indirectly is strictly forbidden and will be deemed a disqualification but this does not apply to sending copies of testimonials to members of the Board by post. Adolphus Ballard, Clerk to the Board.

(*Jackson's Oxford Journal*)

MARCH 31ST

1999: This was the day that the *Oxford Mail* announced the engagement of the winners of the paper's Valentine's Blind Date at the Races competition. Paul Allday and Lorraine Bonner, who had only known each other for a month, had met on the day-long blind date which had taken place on Newbury racecourse. The couple fell in love the minute that their eyes met across a crowded paddock, and they became practically inseparable. Twenty-five-year-old Paul, a chef from North Hinksey, said that if it hadn't been for the competition they would never have met and that they were very much in love and extremely happy. As the champagne corks popped, twenty-year-old Lorraine from Witney looked the picture of happiness. She confided that they had known from the first day that they were made for each other, as they had so much in common – the strangest coincidence being that they both had mums and stepdads called Sue and Kevin. The couple had ordered the engagement ring a few days previously, and were holding an engagement party in Cumnor the following month. They even had the church booked for a May wedding in Witney. Paul and Lorraine planned to live in the town and have two children. (*Oxford Mail*)

APRIL 1ST

1998: On this day commuters discovered a novel way to avoid Oxford's notorious traffic jams on their way to work – by parachute. More than fifteen leading executives and academics signed up for the exercise pioneered by a local parachute club. The intrepid parachutists took off from an airfield near Bicester and aimed to land in Christ Church Meadow. They found refreshment stalls waiting for them, as well as first-aiders. Banker Ivor Cash told the *Mail*, 'I can't wait to tell the rest of the office how I got to work. They'll never believe me.' The return trip cost commuters £40 a day, but the club said that it was considering the introduction of monthly travel cards in order to attract tourists and shoppers. Child discounts would also be made available, with parents being asked to hold their youngsters' hands tightly on descent. Clinical psychologist Dr Onmi Couch believed senior executives would be more prepared for dismissal as a result of parachuting to work. Dr Ian Vention, from a Jet Pack Working Party dealing with inner-city pollution, said the attic in an ordinary house would become the garage of the future. Environmentalists welcomed the move but feared an increase in bird casualties. (*Oxford Mail*)

APRIL 2ND

1879: On this day in 1879, an inquest was taken at the Tree Inn, Iffley, on the body of a tailor's wife, Mrs Harriet Piper, aged fifty. Witnesses described how during the previous few months 'she had been very strange in her manner and appeared to be wrong in her head'. A couple of days before her death, Mrs Piper had expressed a wish to go to the Albion pub in Littlegate to view the body of a Mrs Henry Piper, who was lying dead there. She went upstairs, kissed the corpse and then said, 'Don't tell John' – her husband – and fled out of the house. Her husband went out after her, but he was unable to find any trace of her despite enquiring all night. When Henry Cordrey, the lock-keeper at Iffley, was clearing out an obstruction to the sluice gates near Iffley Mill, he found a woman's body. When they finally managed to release the body, it was found that the clothing had been torn away, but a brooch with photos of the deceased and her husband was discovered, along with a gold ring and a key to their house. A verdict of 'Found drowned' was returned. (*Jackson's Oxford Journal*)

APRIL 3RD

1954: On this day the 100th University boat race was rowed on the Thames in London. The Dark Blues beat the Light Blues by 4½ lengths, despite the windy conditions along the 4¼-mile course between Putney and Mortlake. Oxford, who had only won the race eleven times in the previous thirty-eight years, must have hoped that their winning time of 20 minutes 23 seconds marked a change in their fortunes. At 12st 4lb versus 12st 11lb, the Dark Blue crew had a lighter average weight than their opponents. They won the toss, chose the Surrey station and started off in the lead. It was a close contest until about halfway along the course when Oxford surged ahead. Even the increasingly bad weather could not put off the Dark Blues. By the time they reached the Chiswick Steps they were 11 seconds ahead and the outcome of the race seemed almost certain. However, for a second, by Duke's Meadow, Cambridge threatened to make a last push, but Oxford managed to hold them off and crossed the finish line at thirty-four strokes a minute after an average of thirty throughout. (Various sources)

APRIL 4TH

2000: On this day a report highlighted the conflicting faces of East Oxford, the most multicultural and trendy part of the city. Its twenty-first-century regeneration, with ethnic restaurants and shops, and the mix of students, shop, office and factory workers, was noted. The sizeable Asian population and the food shops which cater for it have made East Oxford one of the country's leading centres for curry, with award-winning chefs in abundance. Not only has the price of houses shot up, suggesting that it might be a desirable place to live, but its nightlife, in the form of cinemas, pubs, bars, musical venues, restaurants and nightclubs, has attracted young people away from what is considered to be the more upmarket parts of Oxford. However, the cool façade hides the depressing fact that government statistics show that the East Ward, St Clement's in particular, is the third most deprived area in the South East of England. It has the highest number of people claiming income support, one of the worst sectors of private housing and the largest ethnic minority. For this reason, the Ward was given a £3 million grant towards improving its housing and environment and general quality of life. (*Oxford Mail*)

APRIL 5TH

1881: On this day, to mark the funeral of Benjamin Disraeli, the Earl of Beaconsfield, the bells tolled, flags were flown at half mast, blinds were drawn and shop shutters were lowered. As soon as the news of the statesman's death reached them, some residents of North Oxford came up with the idea of organising a subscription to buy a wreath for the funeral. The amount to be given was strictly limited to a penny per person, and in a remarkably short time they had collected more than 400 pennies, mainly from working men. In fact, the organisers had some difficulty in preventing donors from contributing more. Also, had there been more time, scores more people would have made donations. This inscription accompanied the wreath:

Oxford, 5th April 1881 My Lord, the Oxford Working Men's Conservative Association (St Giles' branch) beg you to kindly accept the enclosed small wreath and lay the same upon the coffin of the Earl of Beaconsfield as a slight token of their profound sorrow at the loss that England has sustained on the death of one who was so deservedly the chief of the great Constitutional Party of the State.

(*Jackson's Oxford Journal*)

APRIL 6TH

1752: This was the day that Miss Mary Blandy was hanged at Oxford Castle. Well aware that some of the crowd had gathered to look up her skirt, she begged of those carrying out the execution, 'Gentlemen, don't hang me high, for the sake of decency.' Mary became famous for all the wrong reasons. Firstly, her trial and subsequent execution for the poisoning of her father, Francis Blandy, the Town Clerk of Henley-on-Thames, was one of the most sensational of the eighteenth century and is still well known in legal circles today. It is listed in the *Newgate Calendar* and has all the ingredients that sell newspapers today. It was a riveting case not only of murder but also of scandal, snobbery, intrigue and above all sex. The deed was done at the instigation of 'Willie', Mary's married lover, Captain William Cranstoun. Secondly, her ghost is one of the most persistent in Oxfordshire, sightings having been reported at Oxford Castle, where she is said to flit across the mound at dusk. She has also been seen at several other venues in her hometown, even as recently as 2004, when she put in an appearance at the Kenton Theatre. (Various sources)

APRIL 7TH

1999: An Oxford pub was ordered to remove cult cartoon figures from its windows in 1999. The South Park pub (which was formerly called the Ampney Cottage) in the Cowley Road was rejuvenated by taking advantage of its new title. It was turned into a sort of shrine to the American cult television cartoon show of the same name, even though the Oxford pub was initially so called because of its proximity to the city's South Park on Headington Hill. Wychwood Breweries of Witney were dismayed to be sent a letter from the show's London lawyers demanding that they remove the cartoon figures from the pub's windows. However, the bosses of the American South Park were not able to prevent them from using the name. The brewery said that the characters were only a bit of fun and were removed as soon as the letter was received. The name South Park has confused many people who don't know Oxford, and the City Council commented that it has received thousands of irrelevant enquiries on its website from fans of the show who didn't realise that a real park of that name exists. (*Oxford Mail*)

APRIL 8TH

1999: On this day, it was suggested that a book war might break out in Oxford and Cambridge after the American-based book chain Borders announced that it had plans to move into both university cities. Borders, which already had 250 stores in London, Brighton and Glasgow, as well as Australia, Singapore and the United States itself, announced that it was going to move into Cambridge as family booksellers Blackwell's signed a deal to purchase Heffers, another family business with a long history in Oxford. The academic marketing manager at Blackwell's said that they were not complacent, but they were not 'desperately worried' either as they were catering for different markets. In any case, Blackwell's had the advantage of a 120-year-old connection with shops in the heart of Oxford and a branch at Oxford Brookes University. As with other Borders shops, the Oxford branch, in the redeveloped Debenhams site on Magdalen Street, included coffee shops and music departments ,and allowed visitors to sit and read the books on sale there. In the event, the Borders presence in Oxford turned out to be short-lived as the shop closed in 2009 and has been converted into a Tesco Metro. (*Oxford Mail*)

APRIL 9TH

1680: On this day, the *Gazette* included an account of how Great Tom, the bell with a chequered history, was finally born. Great Tom, who resides in Christopher Wren's Tom Tower at Christ Church, is a symbol of Oxford worldwide, and once hung in the central tower of the enormous abbey at Osney. When the abbey was suppressed by Henry VIII, Tom moved to the cathedral, was rechristened Mary and was hung in the steeple. After three abortive attempts at recasting, the present Tom was finally born and put into his own tower. The article relates how 'all the bells of the steeple immediately rang with joy at the birth of their elder brother'. Songs were written about Tom and his siblings: 'Hark! The Bonny Christ Church Bells' and 'Great Tom is Cast'. Today Tom booms out 101 times at 9.05 p.m., once for every one of the original 100 scholars, plus an extra one who arrived according to the Thurston bequest in 1663. Nine o'clock was the time by which the scholars had to be home at night. At the time, Great Tom would have kept Oxford local time (5 minutes slower than Greenwich Mean Time), so today it is sounded at 9.05 p.m. in keeping with tradition. (*London Gazette*)

APRIL 10TH

1875: 'A painful situation prevailed in Oxford on Wednesday morning last when it became known that one more name has been added to the list of unfortunate persons who have lately come to [an] untimely end at their own hands.' This was in relation to twenty-four-year-old Edwin Hill of High Street, who shot himself at his father's home on this fateful morning in 1875. At the inquest, when the jury went into the bedroom to view the body:

> A shocking sight presented itself. The body of the deceased lay partly undressed on the bed and a breech-loading Snider rifle laid pointing to his breast and the trigger of which was fastened to one of the rails of the bedstead by a necktie. Just below the region of the heart, on the left side, was a hole where the bullet had entered and the shirt was burnt for some distance round while his body was blackened and scorched with the powder. The bullet did not appear to have gone through the body and there was no flow of blood from the wound.

After hearing that the deceased had suffered from rheumatic fever, heart disease and severe depression, and had killed himself while intoxicated, the jury returned a verdict of 'temporary insanity'. (*Jackson's Oxford Journal*)

APRIL 11TH

2000: On this day, the main news item was that Swindon's former Page 3 girl, actor and television presenter Melinda Messenger had given birth to a baby in the city's John Radcliffe Hospital. The glamour model's pregnancy ended two weeks early after she was rushed into the Women's Centre following a routine antenatal check-up. The baby, who was delivered by emergency Caesarean section, weighed in at a little less than 6lb. Melinda and her husband, Welshman Wayne Roberts, named him Morgan Kelly. Megan Turmezei, spokesperson for the John Radcliffe Hospital, said that all was well with mother and baby, and announced the same day that she could guarantee that the Women's Centre would not be closing, despite the national shortage of trained midwives. Representatives of three of the royal medical colleges stated that the NHS was 1,600 specialists short of the number needed to keep its services running at full capacity, and that the shortfall in midwives could result in the closure of eighty maternity units throughout the country. Mrs Turmezei said that the unit at the JR would avoid this fate with a strategy to recruit more staff. (*Oxford Mail*)

APRIL 12TH

1880: On this day the residents of Oxford could visit the:

WHITE HOUSE GROUND, OXFORD

MYERS' HIPPODROME

From Paris and Crystal Palace & Agricultural Hall, London

SIXTY HORSES DRIVEN IN HAND BY ONE MAN!

THE Name of MYERS throughout the world is a guarantee of the Performance which has stood the test of all the Critiques and the Press of Europe. The Lions and Elephants trained and performed by John Cooper surpass anything of the kind ever seen. Myers' Elephant pulling against 50 Men in every Town they visit will be a great feat and well worth the price of admission.

The Proprietor of this Establishment can safely say that with the above Artistes, Horses and Animals, he can guarantee to the Public that the best satisfaction shall be given.

NB Two Performances each day – at Two o'clock in the afternoon and half-past Seven in the evening.

PRICES – Two shillings, One shilling and Sixpence

Superintendent of the Zoological Department, Mr John Cooper; Costumier, Mr E.N. Poll and Assistants; Conductor of the Orchestra, Herr Emile Scholz; Masters of the Horse, Messrs and August; Equestrian Director, Herr Blennow; Agent in Advance, Mr J. O'Connor; Sole Proprietor, Mr James Washington Myers.

(*Jackson's Oxford Journal*)

APRIL 13TH

1880: On this day a great deal of excitement was generated by the visit of Prince Leopold to lay the foundation stone of the City of Oxford High School for Boys. Notices to this effect were placed in *Jackson's Oxford Journal*:

THE FOUNDATION STONE WILL BE LAID by HIS ROYAL HIGHNESS PRINCE LEOPOLD on TUESDAY the 13th April instant at Twelve o'clock

Ladies' and Gentlemen's Tickets of admission to the Site may be had of the following gentlemen The Mayor, Ald. Carr, Ald. Hughes, Ald. Cavell, Ald. Eagleston, Professor Green, Mr Jenkin and Mr Saunders at the Town Clerk's Office.

There will be a PUBLIC LUNCHEON at the Town Hall at Two o'clock on the same day, at which Prince Leopold will be present.

Several distinguished guests have been invited.

Tickets for the Luncheon may be obtained from the same Gentlemen as those for admission to the Site.

Gentlemen's Ticket £1 1s; Ladies 10s 6d

JOHN GALPIN, Mayor

(*Jackson's Oxford Journal*)

April 14th

1662: On this day:

[John Nixon] alderman of Oxon and founder of the free-schoole there, departed this life at the hour of eleven in the morning. He was born at Bletchington com. Oxon and the son of John Nixon, labourer there. He built a free schoole and when he died he left speciall order in his will that no priviledged man's sons should be educated there – malitious – he had got all his estate from the University and so he requited. When he grew rich he was a bitter enemy to scholars and being a justice of the peace put into the stocks Thomas French, a minister, for being drunk. He had a smooth flattering tongue and [was] verie hard in his dealings, in so much that it was a comparison amonge scholars 'like alderman Nixon, hard and smooth like any sleick stone'.

Anthony à Wood's criticism refers to 'Privileged Persons of the University', meaning that they were local tradesmen in its service, but they were not necessarily wealthy. Nixon's Free Grammar School, situated behind the present Town Hall, was opened in 1659, and finally closed its doors in 1894, after providing education to the youth of the city for 235 years. (*Life and Times of Anthony à Wood*)

April 15th

1912: This was the day that the ship that couldn't sink fell victim to an iceberg with a loss of more than 1,500 lives. One of the lesser-known heroes was cellist John Wesley Woodward, aged thirty-two, from Windmill Road, Headington who was part of an orchestra that continued to play hymns on deck while the *Titanic* sank. When she heard the news of her son's death, his mother was so distressed that she arranged to have a séance held in Oxford, and she claimed that she succeeded in getting in contact with him. A plaque in Woodward's memory can be seen in All Saints Church. It states that the deceased 'nobly performed his duty to the last when the ship sank after collision with an iceberg on April 15 1912'. However, the collision actually took place at about 10 p.m. on the evening of 14 April and records state that the ship sank at 2.18 a.m. on the 15th, as presumably did Mr Woodward. Two Oxfordshire passengers who did survive were twenty-four-year-old Amy Stanley of Wolvercote, who was travelling to the United States to become a children's maid, and *Titanic* steward George Moran, who was landlord at the White Horse in Abingdon for many years. (Various sources)

April 16th

2002: On this day Oxford bibliophiles heard that, far from being threatened by competition from rivals moving into the city, Blackwell's itself was to put in a bid of about £5 million for a chain of academic bookshops in Scotland. The company's flagship shop in Oxford is one of the largest in the world and it was planned that the newly acquired Edinburgh shop would be transformed into the Scottish equivalent at a cost of more than £1 million. The businesses for which Blackwell's were bidding had formerly been part of James Thin, which had gone into liquidation the previous January, leaving the jobs of about 450 employees in jeopardy. In March of that year, the administrators, PricewaterhouseCoopers, had sold eight of James Thin's general bookshops to the Ottakar's chain for £1.64 million, so saving 141 jobs.

Blackwell's shop in Broad Street, founded in 1879, was named Chain Bookshop of the Year in the British Book Awards; the award was a coup for its manager John Thwaites, who had come to Oxford from Waterstones in Gower Street, London, two years beforehand. (Various sources)

APRIL 17TH

2000: On this day an undeniably mature student explained how the dream of a lifetime was about to be realised. Anne Ballard had always wanted to be a student at Oxford University, despite having already taken a degree in Psychology and Philosophy at St Andrews University. Her twin daughters were both at Oxford, one of them reading English, and Anne followed her course, but found that it was nowhere near as good as actually being an Oxford student in her own right. The pinnacle of her ambition was to become a reader of the Bodleian Library, and to be allowed to order any book she pleased. Fifty-seven-year-old Anne was about to give up a well-paid job to take up a place at Harris Manchester College, which specifically caters for older students, to read English. She was given the idea of applying when she read an article about mature students in a national newspaper and sent away for information about how to become one. Having passed her interview and entrance exam she then had to think about how she would finance the course, deciding that she might have to find a part-time job or dip into her savings. (*Oxford Mail*)

APRIL 18TH

1664: On this day, the bedmaker to a Canon of Christ Church lay dying of a fever. At 10 a.m., a physician called and took her pulse. As he did so, he saw something as big as a bat hovering or flying over her face and breast. The room she was in was quite dark but the anomaly left an even darker shadow on her breast and bedclothes. At about 3 p.m. she became light-headed and talked much of the Devil and expressed the belief that she was going to hell. When her brother visited, she called him 'Devil'. (*Life and Times of Anthony à Wood*)

1900: On the same day, at the annual sale of work at St Matthew's there was a very varied selection of items.

> On one stall I noticed a number of little packets labelled with a mysterious word, and the legend 'A Cure for Wrinkles'. This struck me as such a frivolous and unbecoming type of label for so sober and well-conducted a parish that I felt bound to investigate. To my intense amusement, on careful scrutiny I found the mystic word was 'Sretrag' and inside the packet were a pair of garters!

('Notes by an Oxford Lady' in *Jackson's Oxford Journal*)

APRIL 19TH

1895: On this day, the final vestry, or meeting of parish officials, was held at St Martin's Church, Carfax, to hear what the rector, the Revd C.J.H. Fletcher, had to say about its closure after nearly 1,000 years. The reason for the closure of what had been the City Church, and the amalgamation of the parish with that of All Saints, was the widening of the road to allow traffic to pass more easily. Only the famous tower with its chiming clock was to be spared. The rector described the union of the two as a sort of marriage ceremony, which would take place on the following Easter Monday. The font, communion table, plate and other furnishings were to be stored away until the bishop announced what was to be done with them. Those attending heard that the portion of Holywell Cemetery allotted to the parish was almost full, whereas their partner's had plenty of room left for burials. The rector concluded by saying that they 'would sometimes see, haunting the vacant site of St Martin's, the ghost of their last Rector, who outlived his church and parish, but who would never outlive the happy memories associated with both'. (*Jackson's Oxford Journal*)

APRIL 20TH

1986: This was the day that Oxford United managed to get to Wembley and win its first major knockout trophy, the Milk Cup, under manager Maurice Evans. In front of 19,396 spectators, they defeated Queens Park Rangers by 3–0. In January 1982, when the club had been teetering on the verge of bankruptcy, it was rescued by the Oxford-based millionaire publisher, and boss of the Pergamon Press, Robert Maxwell, who became something of a local hero when he saved the club. It was while Maxwell held the purse strings that United managed to claw their way up from the Third Division to the First under the management of Jim Smith. When the team won the Milk Cup, supporters turned out to welcome and congratulate them as they did a tour of honour round the city in an open-top bus. The club colours, blue and yellow, were everywhere and there were photographs of the team (and Maxwell) in shop windows. However, it did not take long for him to blot his copybook when he came up with the suggestion that Oxford should merge with Reading as part of a club which would take the name Thames Valley Royals. (Various sources)

APRIL 21ST

1956: On this day thousands turned out to give a 'boisterous' welcome to Soviet leaders Marshal Bulganin and Mr Khrushchev. They were received by the Vice-Chancellor outside the new Bodleian Library following a guided tour of AERE Harwell. The crowds, mainly students, clung to every available viewpoint, including window sills and the roofs of cars. They greeted the visitors with renderings of 'Old Black Joe', the 'Song of the Volga Boatmen', and 'Rule Britannia'. Banners reading 'Stalin for Prof' and 'We want Grace' were also very much in evidence. The Russians were behind schedule, as a reception and speeches in the Town Hall took up more time than planned, so Christ Church was taken off their itinerary. A chair which had been looted by British soldiers during the Crimean War was given to them by St Peter's Hall, to be returned to Russia. Other highlights of their visit included New College, the Sheldonian Theatre, and Addison's Walk in the grounds of Magdalen College. As they left Magdalen, one of the students said 'Goodbye' to them in Russian, and received a pat on the cheek from Bulganin as a reward. (*Oxford Mail*)

April 22nd

1998: On this day, a stopwatch used to time Roger Bannister's breaking of the 4-minute mile was prevented from leaving the country after being auctioned at Bonham's London salerooms. It had been owned by Charles Hill, the timekeeper of the historic run in 1954, but he had sold it twenty-five years previously to Norman Simons, the vendor who put it up for sale. The Nero 1/10 split-second timer was expected to fetch something between £400 and £600, but reached £8,855 when the auction house's 15 per cent commission had been added. The buyer was the novelist Jeffrey Archer, who had been President of the Oxford University Athletics Club in 1965 while he was at Brasenose College. Lord Archer donated it to the athletics club, saying that he wanted to make sure it came back to Oxford rather than leave the country. Lord Archer did not attend the sale, but there were loud cheers when the buyer's name and intentions were announced. It was only right, he said, that the club should be given the watch. He added that he had very fond memories of his presidency and the gift was his way of saying thank you. (*Oxford Mail*)

APRIL 23RD

1900: In this extract, an Oxford resident laments the lack of patriotic spirit on evidence in the city:

> There was no very great demonstration here on the anniversary of our patron saint's day, as far as I could see. A few enthusiasts wore roses, but our national flower was not much in evidence which is not to be wondered at this time of year. If St George had grasped the situation, he would no doubt have contrived to be born or die – I don't know what special event in the saint's existence is commemorated on the 23rd – when the roses were in full bloom. But it is something to know that April 23rd is St George's Day, for until the last year or so I don't believe that one Englishman in a hundred had the least idea on the subject. It seems we share our saint with Portugal. We are all well aware that St George is generally represented on horseback, fighting a dragon, but it is difficult to find out anything definite about him. Some historians, unable to prove his existence, fall back on the convenient myth theory and tell us that the saint is merely a symbolic device for victory.

('Notes by an Oxford Lady' in *Jackson's Oxford Journal*)

APRIL 24TH

1801: University Bedel G.V. Cox notes in his *Recollections of Oxford* (1868) that a serious fire broke out in Oriel College on this day:

> … which for a while threatened great destruction; but by the great exertions of Academics and others it was extinguished, after the complete gutting of two or three sets of rooms and a great amount of injury to books and furniture. The Provost's Lodgings were for a time in danger, the fire being in rooms over the passage from one quadrangle into the other.

As was only too common in Oxford and indeed elsewhere, the fire seems to have been started by a candle which had been left unattended. One can just imagine the panic and chaos which ensued as both senior and junior members of the college rushed to and fro rescuing what belongings they could and throwing them out of a window into the quad below, 'not only heedlessly, but in a great degree, unnecessarily'. An Irish undergraduate was particularly anxious to return to his lodgings in order to collect a valuable mirror, which he then tossed out of the window along with other looking-glasses and pictures. (*Recollections of Oxford*)

APRIL 25TH

1878: This was the day that Keble College opened 'a Hall to accompany the gorgeous chapel'. The ceremony was performed by the Marquis of Salisbury, the Chancellor of the University. Anticipating the general opinion about the appearance of the college, *Jackson's Oxford Journal* wrote:

> We are not disposed to go into raptures about Keble College. The great charm as well as the great value of our English Universities is that they have originated great religious and intellectual movements, not that they have been originated by them … But there are sanguine persons who hope that Keble may ultimately shake off the trammels of its present condition and take rank with the other foundations which now, and not unjustly, regard it as something of an interloper. A College which has supplied an oar to the University Eight has by that feat taken itself out of the ranks of mere seminaries and theological forcing houses. The embellishments which have been lavished on Keble are moreover a gain to the University at large, though in some respects a dubious one. However, in the 'Light of the World' Keble holds a work which has more than individual and intrinsic interest.

(*Jackson's Oxford Journal*)

APRIL 26TH

1859: The marriage register of the church of St Michael at the North Gate states that on this day in 1859, William Morris married Jane Burden. Jane was a local girl, whose father Robert was an ostler living in St Helen's (Hell's) Passage, which runs between Holywell Street and New College Lane; and where there is now a blue plaque to her memory. William Morris was a graduate of Exeter College and a founder member of the group of artists known as the Pre-Raphaelite Brotherhood. In October 1857, on a visit to the theatre with her sister, Jane had been noticed by Dante Gabriel Rossetti and Edward Burne-Jones. The artists, who were in Oxford painting the murals in the Oxford Union based on the legend of King Arthur, asked her to pose for them as she struck them, as the ideal model for Queen Guinevere. Later she modelled for Morris and they became engaged, after which she concentrated on extending her education to the extent that she became sufficiently accomplished to move in any social circle. Jane had a close relationship with Rossetti and in 1871 he and Morris took the joint tenancy of Kelmscott Manor where the three of them lived together. (Various sources)

April 27th

1809: On this day an advertisement appeared in *Jackson's Oxford Journal* which shows how close the country came to the centre of the modern city. It is impossible to imagine livestock stabled in traffic-ridden St Giles as we know it today, but for centuries the parish was a suburb outside the city walls:

TO be LET, and entered on immediately. The following PREMISES, situated on the West side of St Giles', near the churchyard – A very large and commodious YARD, with stabling, waggon, and cart houses, ox pens, pig sties &c. with a large slated barn. Also – another compact and well-sheltered barn leading into the Workhouse lane with some stabling and out-building. Also – two TENEMENTS, formerly the farm house, with a very spacious brew-house and out-house, and rooms over, easily convertible into a distinct tenement, and a good garden. The above yards and houses are so situated that they may be occupied separately or jointly, and the premises are not merely suited for the farming business but would afford excellent accommodation for any trade or manufacture where much room is required.

For further particulars apply to Mr Phillips at Mr Allom's, baker, New Inn Lane.

(*Jackson's Oxford Journal*)

APRIL 28TH

1883: On this evening, HRH the Prince of Wales arrived at the GWR station at about 6 p.m., where he was met by authorities from both the University and City, and by a guard of honour made up of the City Companies of Rifle Volunteers and a brass band. He then proceeded to Christ Church where he was met by the Dean and Mrs Liddell (parents of the more famous Alice) and, after dining, he went to the new Examination Schools in the High Street for a concert held in aid of the Royal College of Music, which started at 9 p.m. The concert was followed by a conversazione, during which all the rooms in the various schools were opened for the company to view, and refreshments were served. The following day, after a breakfast hosted by the University Chancellor, the Marquis of Salisbury, in Christ Church Hall, the prince performed the ceremony of laying a memorial stone at the Indian Institute, with full Masonic honours, in front of a very distinguished gathering. The crowd included the Chancellor and Vice-Chancellor, various Heads of Houses, a selection of earls, marquises and viscounts, leading Oxford masons and the Secretary of State for India. (*Jackson's Oxford Journal*)

APRIL 29TH

1899: Exciting details about the forthcoming visit of Barnum & Bailey's show were announced on this day. The parade, scheduled to begin between 9 a.m. and 10 a.m., consisted of a platoon of:

Mounted Police; Mounted Officers; Grand Military Band; Stupendous Forty-Horse United Team; Open Den of Tigers and Trainer; Open Den of Lions and Trainer; Open Den of Leopards and Trainer; Open Den of Panthers and Trainer; Open Den of Hyenas and Trainer; Open Den of Bears and Trainer; Open Den of Wolves and Trainer; Novel Melechoir Chimes, drawn by Six Horses; Lady Performers and Side-Saddle Experts; Mounted Ladies of the Hippodrome; Gentlemen Hippodrome Riders; Two 2-Horse Roman Chariots, Lady Drivers; Two 4-Horse Roman Chariots; Band Chariot 'Euterpe' drawn by Ten Horses; Eight Golden Chariots containing rare wild beasts; Triumphal Chariot with queer musicians and comic heads; Caravan of Camels with Asiatic Riders; Twenty Performing Elephants; Two Elephants with Howdahs and Oriental Beauties; Blue Beard Chariot drawn by Six Zebras; Japanese Dragon Chariot with performers; Cinderella's Fairy Coach; Little Red Riding Hood Chariot; Mother Goose Chariot; Blue Band Chariot 'America' drawn by Ten Horses; Seven Golden cages containing rare animals; Mammoth Organ Chariot and a Grand Triumphal Float.

(*Jackson's Oxford Journal*)

APRIL 30TH

1999: This was the day that Oxonians who fancied boasting a diamond on one of their teeth, just like Mick Jagger, were told just how to go about it. Other choices were a gold tooth, like Sporty Spice's, or a ruby one, like Simply Red's Mick Hucknall. By this time, local dentists, like the one in St Clement's, were offering a whole range of tooth jewellery at less than millionaire prices. Ready-made jewellery was coming onto the market, from 15- and even 18-carat gold, sometimes set with diamonds and rubies. In St Clement's, one could choose from twenty-three designs, which each cost about £50, the same amount as dentists would charge to fit them. Going by the name of Twinkles, they were semi-permanent and could be removed in a matter of minutes if the wearer changed his or her mind; the gem was glued in place so that the surface of the tooth would not be damaged in any way. An amusing story is told about why Jagger swapped his original emerald for a diamond – apparently it was frequently mistaken for a piece of spinach which had become stuck between his teeth. (*Oxford Mail*)

MAY 1ST

1998: On this day police erected barricades to seal off Magdalen Bridge prior to the time-honoured May Day celebrations. It was closed from 4 a.m. until 6.30 p.m. to prevent revellers from jumping off into the Cherwell beneath. In previous years, daredevils had been seriously injured and even killed leaping from the bridge. At the time, the Cherwell was said to be running ten times faster than usual after a heavy rainfall. Police officers, mounted police and riot vans formed cordons on each side of the bridge, which prevented a group of students from gaining access through the adjacent Botanic Garden. One man did manage to get into the river from the bridge but he was hauled out by officers in a boat. The operation involved 120 officers and the University's own police force. Superintendent Cressida Dick said, 'The celebrations passed peacefully. We believe the success of the event vindicated the decision by the Magdalen Bridge Safety Committee to close the bridge. There were no injuries and no-one was arrested.' An estimated 5,000 people turned up, about half the usual number, and some students said that they were disgusted by the spoilsport tactics and the cessation of centuries of tradition, which ruined the atmosphere. However, the closure was backed by Oxford University Student Union. (Various sources)

MAY 2ND

2001: The intermittent search to find the body of an Oxford University student who lost his life attempting to climb Mount Everest was renewed on this day in 2001. Andrew Irvine, who rowed against Cambridge in 1922 and 1923, gained climbing experience by scaling the walls of his college, Merton, to the annoyance of the Dons. The last time that twenty-two-year-old Irvine, known as Sandy, was ever seen was when he and George Mallory disappeared into clouds on the mountain on 8 June 1924. In 1999 Mallory's body was found preserved in ice. A frozen sock and mitten thought to have belonged to one of them was also found, but nothing was found of Irvine or his camera, which might have contained photographs which would provide evidence of whether or not they had succeeded in reaching the summit. It is believed that they did do so, in which case they got there almost three decades before Sir Edmund Hillary and Tenzing Norgay, but this cannot be proved. Sir Edmund Hillary had commented that, at any rate, he and Sherpa Tenzing, who accomplished the feat on 29 May 1953 in the week of the Coronation, were certainly the first climbers to reach the summit and come back down again. (*Oxford Mail*)

MAY 3RD

1860: The following report appeared in *Jackson's Oxford Journal* on this day:

> Holman Hunt's Painting 'The Light of the World' – This celebrated painting which Mr Ruskin describes as 'one of the noblest works of sacred art ever produced in this or any other age,' has been on view at Mr Wyatt's Picture Gallery in the High Street during the week and may be seen until the afternoon of this day. A more beautiful specimen of high art, or a more solemn subject, full of meaning and touchingly conveyed, has never emanated from the mind of man, or been so powerfully rendered by his skilful hand. It is a painting which all should see who can do so, for it is one that will leave behind an impression that will not easily be eradicated.

Wyatt's advertisement read:

> 'Mr J Wyatt has much pleasure in announcing that this deeply interesting masterpiece of sacred Art, having been lent him for a few days, will be on view at his Gallery commencing Thursday next, the 26th inst. Hours of exhibition Ten to Five, and in the evening from Six to Eight. Admission by card only, which can be obtained at Mr Wyatt's, 115 High-street.'

(*Jackson's Oxford Journal*)

May 4th

2004: This day's rain was not able to put a damper on celebrations when the Earl and Countess of Wessex arrived in the city to open the John Henry Newman School at Littlemore in 2004. It was raining when the royal couple arrived at the school for their first public engagement since the birth of their daughter, Lady Louise Windsor, but there were smiling faces all around when they were met by Year One pupils waving Union Jacks at the school in Grange Road. Prince Edward, who was wearing a grey suit and a yellow tie and Sophie, who had on a cream suit with a matching coat, were escorted by head teacher Jenny Lee and accompanied by various local dignitaries. The first person to whom the Countess spoke was eight-year-old Jake Belcher and his teacher, Tina Parsons, who told her about the special programme the school were using to help children with learning difficulties. Jake thought that Sophie was really nice and very pretty, and said that he couldn't wait to get home to tell his parents about it. The Earl and Countess were shown round the school and then joined 350 pupils in the sports hall where the Countess unveiled a plaque and received a posy. (*Oxford Mail*)

MAY 5TH

2006: On this day glorious sunshine greeted the Queen as she arrived at Oxford Castle to open it formally following its £40 million redevelopment. The site, which dates back to 1071, includes numerous restaurants, a heritage centre and the Malmaison Hotel, a £20 million conversion of part of the former Oxford Prison. On arrival inside the complex, Her Majesty, looking radiant in pink, was greeted by the 500 people who had been lucky enough to have been sent an invitation. She was given a tour of the site by a former prison governor, which included one of the hotel's bedrooms that had been made from three former cells, and then she unveiled a commemorative plaque. Earlier in the day, well-wishers were out in force by 9 a.m. to catch a glimpse of the Queen as she met pupils from Pegasus Primary School, Blackbird Leys, and New Marston Primary School. The Queen went on to have lunch at Christ Church, where the cathedral bells rang out as her maroon Bentley swept into Tom Quad. The choristers sang and a play which had been specially written in her honour was performed. After lunch she inspected the Oxford Dictionary of National Biography at the Oxford University Press. (Personal observation)

MAY 6TH

1954: On this day a crowd of about 1,000 people watched Roger Bannister, a twenty-five-year-old Oxford medical student, attempt to run a mile in less than 4 minutes at the University Sports Centre in the Iffley Road. For weeks before the attempt, Bannister had set himself a punishing training schedule, which paid off as he crossed the finishing line with a time of 3 minutes 59.4 seconds. Two of his friends, fellow Oxonian Chris Chataway, and former Cambridge University steeplechaser Chris Brasher, were running with him. Immediately after crossing the finishing line Bannister dropped to the ground exhausted, 'It was only then that real pain overtook me,' he said. 'I felt like an exploded flashlight with no will to live; I just went on existing in the most passive physical state without being unconscious.' The spectators went quiet and then crowded round him as he was supported by two track officials. Then his time was given, 'Three …' The rest of the announcement was drowned out by the cheers as everyone realised that Bannister had achieved his goal. He ran across to Brasher and Chataway and hugged them, and then the three ran a lap of honour round the track. (*Oxford Mail*)

MAY 7TH

1920: On this day, shortly before his twentieth birthday, Kenneth Grahame's son, Alastair, dined in Hall at Christ Church as usual. At the end of the meal, as usual, he requested a glass of port. Then the second-year undergraduate took an evening stroll from his college to a level crossing between Wolvercote and Oxford. The following morning his body was found on the railway line running through Port Meadow. His head had been severed from his body by a train. The inquest returned a verdict of accidental death, although there seems little doubt that Alastair meant to commit suicide, as it could be seen from the position of his body that he had lain face-downwards across the rails. It was recalled that he had always found it difficult to fit in with his classmates at school and that he had been under considerable pressure to keep up with his academic work. Less than a week later, on 12 May, Mouse, as he was called by his father, was buried in Holywell Cemetery next to St Cross Church. His father, the author of the children's classic *The Wind in the Willows*, scattered lilies of the valley on the coffin. (Various sources)

MAY 8TH

1894: A court report from *Jackson's Oxford Journal* in 1894:

On this day at the Oxford City police court, the Mayor, Deputy-Mayor, two Aldermen and five Justices heard that William Reynolds, a casual inmate of the Workhouse, was charged with refusing to undertake the work allocated to him by those in authority there. The morning after his admittance, Reynolds was given 3 cwt of stones to break. William Carter, the deputy relieving officer, told the bench, that he absolutely refused to do this. When he was questioned about this, Reynolds replied that the Workhouse officials had taken away his food. The bench decided that Reynolds should be sent to prison for seven days ... with hard labour. At the same court, Richard Chesterman, a labourer of Friars Wharf, was charged with being drunk and disorderly in Queen Street at 11.10 that morning, when he was 'holloaing and waving his arms in the air'. The prisoner, who stated that he was very sorry for what had taken place, was sentenced to one day's imprisonment. Also, Richard James Manion of Jericho was summoned for leaving his butcher's cart in Jericho Street overnight and thereby causing an obstruction. He was fined a shilling, with six shillings costs.

(*Jackson's Oxford Journal*)

MAY 9TH

1843: This was the long-awaited day in 1843 when the celebrated lion-tamer Van Amburgh arrived in town. An 'immense multitude' lined Abingdon Road, and St Aldates was packed from Folly Bridge to Carfax. When the procession entered the city at 11 a.m. precisely, it was led by Mr Van Amburg driving eight cream-coloured horses which were drawing elegant open carriages that contained a splendid brass band. Five other carriages followed, containing the animals in the exhibition. The elephant had arrived the previous night and had spent it in a stable in the Star yard. The procession came up St Aldates, went down the High Street, turned round at the Plain and then made its way back again, rounding Carfax corner very skilfully, before continuing along Cornmarket and Beaumont Street to Walton Place, behind which was a field belonging to St John's College, where it stopped. There, a spacious pavilion, large enough to hold 2,000 spectators, had been erected. The show included 'the laughable tricks of the monkey and pony, the sagacity of the elephant, and above all, the daring feats of Mr Van Amburgh with the lions, tigers and leopards filled the vast company with astonishment and delight'. In all, more than 7,000 people attended the show. (*Jackson's Oxford Journal*)

MAY 10TH

1666: On this day, at about 5 p.m., great claps of thunder were heard and soon thereafter a great deal of rain fell. Shortly before this, two undergraduates from Wadham College, who were out on the river by themselves without a waterman, had set off from the boat station at Medley en route back to town. As they were standing near the prow of the boat, there was a flash of lightning which catapulted them both into the river. They were pulled out of the water after about a minute but by then it was already too late to save the one who was 'stark dead'. The other was found stuck fast in the mud – luckily for him in an upright position – and, apart from some numbness, he had come to no harm. However, even though he was put straight into a warm bed, he had not recovered from the shock by the following night and could not remember what had happened to make him end up in the river. Other students in a boat a few yards away had felt a disturbance and one fell off his seat, but little else. (*Life and Times of Anthony à Wood*)

MAY 11TH

2001: On this day, the Oxford Language Race began. Competitors were charged with learning a foreign language from scratch in only a month, and the event started when University students and staff drew the name of the European language they had to master out of a hat. They were all languages which are not normally taught in schools, such as Bulgarian, Catalan, Finnish, Ukrainian, Polish and Lithuanian. The idea was that the learners would not have any prior knowledge of their chosen language. The learners were to make use of books, cassettes, videos and the Internet at the University's Language Centre in the Banbury Road to give them a chance of outdoing their competitors. In all, thirty people were taking part in the contest. At the end of the month participants would be expected to hold a 10-minute conversation with a fluent speaker of the target language and also be able to recite a poem in that language. The unique challenge was organised by the Language Centre as part of the European Year of Languages, and to raise money for the local charity Reading Quest, which helps young people who have difficulty reading. The winner's prize was a pair of return air tickets to any European destination served by British Midland Airways. (*Oxford Mail*)

MAY 12TH

1897: When the Town Hall was opened by the Prince of Wales on this day in 1897, the undergraduate body turned out in force. The Metropolitan Police had sent along a mounted detachment and, when these two groups met, the trouble started. The newcomers saw the students as a threatening mob and panicked. They thrashed about with their batons and several students were badly beaten, while others were ridden down by police horses. The crowd retaliated by pulling a policeman from his horse and trampling him underfoot before moving on into other streets where they met up with the local police. Among the mob was a well-known Oxford character, F.E. Smith, 1st Lord Birkenhead and Fellow of Wadham College, who saw the police manhandling his college scout. F.E. rushed to help him and was himself arrested and sent to the cells for the night, being charged with obstructing the police in the lawful execution of their duty. Smith's cell was a brand new one and, as he was shown into it, he raised his hand for silence and said, 'I have great pleasure in declaring this cell open.' With this, he walked inside and slammed the door behind him. At the court hearing he was found not guilty. (*Jackson's Oxford Journal*)

MAY 13TH

1998: On this day, the *Oxford Mail* reported how seventy-one-year-old Professor Terry Willis had come to the rescue of a canoeist stuck in a bush with no paddle. The canoeist had got into difficulties on the River Cherwell, crashing into a fence and bushes on the riverbank at the bottom of Professor Willis's garden. He managed to pull the young man out of harm's way with a rope and hook. However, this kind action came at a price to the rescuer. Four police divers and an annoyed ambulance crew, all called by worried passers-by, arrived at his door. The canoeist was severely reprimanded by the police for having gone on the river when it was dangerously high. Feeling sorry for him, the professor gave him tea and some dry clothes before helping him to search for his missing paddle and agreeing to take care of his canoe until he could come back for it. Five weeks later he was still stuck with the canoe but was minus his trousers which he had lent to the landlubber. He had heard nothing from the young man, who had said that he was from Oxford Brookes University, and was now asking for help to find the mystery man. (*Oxford Mail*)

MAY 14TH

1998: On this day, protestors against the decision to remove the old LMS station building from its site near the station and to reassemble it at Quainton railway centre in Buckinghamshire were given a chance to air their views. The proposed move was to facilitate the widening of the junction as part of the Oxford Transport Strategy, but the eco-warriors stepped in to prevent it happening by squatting in the old building. Their concern started with the fate of nearby trees but soon included the station itself. One protestor, Sushila Dhall, leader of the Green Group, was quoted as saying, 'I would lie in front of a bulldozer sooner than see a six-lane road built.' However, those in favour of the move pointed out that saving the LMS building by dismantling it and reassembling it at Quainton was preferable to leaving it to fall apart *in situ*. In addition, pedestrians would benefit from a footbridge at platform level connecting the station to the south side of the junction and a signal-controlled pedestrian crossing at the lights which would give them priority over traffic. Eventually, the old station was successfully relocated, the roadway widened and the pedestrian facilities installed. (*Oxford Mail*)

MAY 15TH

1999: On this day, Aziz-Ur-Rahman, owner of the Aziz Indian Cuisine restaurant on Cowley Road, had a very good reason to be proud. His establishment had been included in the list of the country's Top 30 restaurants by the *Real Curry Restaurant Guide*. This came as no surprise to the stars who ate there. Among the best known were the British band Radiohead, who would frequently drop in when they returned home to the city. And they were not the only ones; Arsenal defender Martin Keown, who lived nearby in Wheatley and who had gone to school in Oxford, came in for a takeaway regularly. Other diners included John Thaw and top French chef Raymond Blanc. Such was its reputation that people were said to visit the Aziz from all over the country and bookings even came from abroad. Mr Rahman said, 'I'm very proud to have received that award. We are with the elite.' He added, 'Radiohead are a regular customer. They regard it as one of the best restaurants they have ever been to. When they come back from abroad they will come straight here as they think so much of it.' (*Oxford Mail*)

MAY 16TH

1998: Academics at Oxford Brookes University in Headington were celebrating the news that it had become the first of the ex-polytechnics to be rated above any of the traditional British universities in *The Times* newspaper's *Good University Guide* in 1998. Oxford Brookes was listed as the top new university for the third year in succession, and fifty-second of Britain's ninety-six universities. This result was expected to help crush the myth that polytechnics were in the second division of academic institutions. This placed it above the Universities of Bradford, Ulster, Lampeter and Salford for the first time. Among the factors by which universities were assessed were qualities of teaching and research, and prospects of employment for its graduates. The Vice-Chancellor of Brookes, Professor Peter Fidler, said that he was delighted that its standards had been recognised and expressed his gratitude to the local community for the support given by schools, councils, charities, hospitals and businesses. As for the University of Oxford, in the *Good University Guide*, which covers all the universities in the country, it finished in second place overall, behind Cambridge admittedly, but displacing Imperial College London. (Various sources)

MAY 17TH

1860: On this day, Rarey's Circus (which in reality seems to have been an exhibition of horse-breaking skills) attracted about 900 people, including Dean Liddell of Christ Church and Mrs Liddell, the Vice-Chancellor, the President of Corpus Christi College, and the Mayor and Sheriff of Oxford. The first animal to be broken, a two-year-old thoroughbred filly described as being 'of a most vicious and savage nature', was brought in. At first it seemed to be in a good mood but then it suddenly dashed off into the audience, dragging Mr Rarey along behind it. The three front rows of half-crown seats were broken and more than thirty people fell off their seats. One lady was taken home in a carriage, but fortunately there were few casualties, most people being more frightened than injured, and the animal was eventually secured. Rarey stressed that this was the first accident of any kind that had taken place. At a later performance attended by the Prince of Wales and his suite, 'a very vicious animal from Wheatley was in attendance', but Mr Rarey said that after the then recent episode he would not perform until stronger barriers had been put in place. (*Jackson's Oxford Journal*)

MAY 18TH

2010: This was the day when a brass plaque (removed when Oxford High School for Boys in George Street closed in 1966) was returned home to what is now the University's History faculty. The plaque, which had been unveiled by Sir Winston Churchill, commemorated a former pupil, T.E. Lawrence of Arabia. It was moved to the newly opened Oxford School in Cowley, but due to its poor condition it was sent off to the County Council's museum store at Standlake for conservation work to be done on it. Old Boys of the school requested that the plaque be brought back to George Street and raised £2,400 towards the cost of repairing it and mounting it near the bottom of the main staircase. It was unveiled by the Professor of Modern History, Robert Gildea. T.E. Lawrence's family lived in Polstead Road in North Oxford, and he was a pupil at the High School from 1896 to 1907. He went on to read History at Jesus College before going on to make history himself during the First World War. In 1919, he was elected to a seven-year fellowship at All Souls College. (Various sources)

MAY 19TH

1870: The *Independent*, Sheffield, reported what it called 'University Rattening' or the 'Christ Church Outrage' on this day. 'We notice with extreme regret a circumstance which has just occurred immensely to the discredit of the undergraduates of Oxford.' Some young men had removed a number of busts and statues, some of them very valuable, from Christ Church Library and had taken them into Peckwater Quadrangle. Another 'wild lot' had come along and made a bonfire on which they put the statuary, destroying it. The paper said that high spirits may be forgiven for some pranks, but when actions are fuelled by alcohol as well, stupid things are done which can be bitterly regretted afterwards. Indeed, 'those who can remember their own youth can conceive of young men bringing themselves to act with no more consciousness of right and wrong than the inmates of an asylum.' The article said that Britain had prided itself on the fact that the 'lower classes' show 'scrupulous care' towards priceless treasures, which makes it doubly shocking that it was members of the 'first families in the land that have caused so much damage'. To make matters worse, they did not even appear to have had any regrets. (*Jackson's Oxford Journal*)

MAY 20TH

1870: A jury made up of townsmen and members of the University heard of the 'melancholy' suicide of Favour James Gregg, of Balliol College, on Port Meadow. A close friend stated how the deceased had been very depressed because his mother had been confined to an asylum, but that he had been noticeably more cheerful of late. A witness explained how he had been crossing Port Meadow with a horse and cart when he noticed something black lying under a hedge. On closer inspection, he saw that it was a man lying on his side and said, 'Halloa, governor; what's the game now?' but got no answer. The mystery man drew his legs up. 'I went over to his side. I saw his eyes work. He raised his head a little way, and the blood began gulping out.' The witness drove off and found a policeman at Wolvercote station and, with assistance, they took him in the cart to the infirmary. 'He tried to speak but there was only a rattling in his throat. There was a wonderful lot of blood about where he lay.' A blood-covered razor was discovered at the scene. Gregg died at the infirmary on the Sunday night. (*Jackson's Oxford Journal*)

MAY 21ST

1999:On this day, the *Oxford Mail* reported on University College's celebrations:

The Queen and the Duke of Edinburgh visited Oxford, principally to take part in University College's year-long celebration of its endowment 750 years ago. Founded by William of Durham, 'Univ' is claimed to be the oldest college in the English-speaking world. The Royal visitors were met by the Chancellor, Lord Jenkins of Hillhead, at the University Church, where they met officials from Town and Gown before a Thanksgiving Service. It was almost fifty-one years to the day since the then Princess Elizabeth visited the College, when the University awarded her an honorary degree. In the Bodleian Library, as part of an exhibition 'University College—the first 750 years' Her Majesty was shown a letter sent by Charles I to the Master and Fellows of Univ in 1643 seeking cash to pay his army. College Archivist Robin Darwall-Smith thought that they would have contributed. The Royals went on to Univ and met students, Fellows and staff. After a reception in the Master's Garden, Members of the College demonstrated a range of student activities. Her Majesty said that she believed that it was the first occasion that a sovereign had visited Univ since the Crown became College Visitor over 270 years ago.

(*Oxford Mail*)

MAY 22ND

1939: On this day, the one millionth Morris car rolled off the production line at the works at Cowley. The Morris car company had developed out of a bicycle repair business in Longwall Street, which made its first car in 1913. This was the first British car company to produce a million vehicles. Lord Nuffield, wearing a trilby and with a cigar clenched between his teeth, turned up in person for the event and congratulated the works manager, Mr A.E. Keen. About a year previously the Nuffield Organisation had agreed to build, fit out and manage an enormous new factory in the Midlands at Castle Bromwich, with the express purpose of making Supermarine Spitfires. When an air raid damaged the Morris Bodies factory, the plant changed to the production of jerry cans, making millions of these containers for use during the rest of the war. The Cowley plant was converted for repairing aircraft and the production of Tiger Moth machines for training pilots, as well as mine sinkers which were based on a design which the factory had produced during the First World War. Another British car 'first' came in 1961, when the one millionth Morris Minor was built. (*Oxford Mail*)

MAY 23RD

1998: Politician and Philosophy, Politics and Economics graduate, Ann Widdecombe, expounded the belief held by many that Oxford was as perfect a spot for romance as anywhere. The virginal MP announced that during her three years at Oxford, she was in love with fellow student Colin Maltby, and it is just possible that the ancient mellow stones, dreaming spires and punts on the river may have made a contribution. As she put it herself, 'I think it's very difficult to go to Oxford and not fall in love. Most people do – it's such a dreamy place; punts on the river, commemoration balls. There were a few gnomy types who stayed in their rooms and worked, but not many.'

But not everyone agreed with Ms Widdecombe that Oxford is a place for dreams of love and romance. Sarah Fitzpatrick, captain of the Magdalen College team that won *University Challenge* that year, said, 'I don't think Ann Widdecombe is right. In fact, I think that Oxford can be particularly bad for romance – but I don't know why. It's just my impression. I suppose that the setting works for some, though not for everybody – and for others, it doesn't work at all.' (*Oxford Mail*)

MAY 24TH

1999: Oriel College was served with a $100 million (£70 million) writ by a former student, who alleged that it had infringed on his human rights because he was not allowed to continue studying there after failing his exams, thereby causing him 'unnatural distress and mental cruelty'. American Tong Park gained admittance to the college during the 1980s by using a false name and passport. The University Chancellor, Lord Jenkins of Hillhead, the Vice-Chancellor, Colin Lucas, and the Provost of Oriel, Ernest Nicholson, along with two former provosts, were all served with the writ, which had been issued by a Californian court and served by Oxfordshire county bailiffs. James Methven, the Dean of Oriel College, stated that he was shocked and amused when he was served with the writ, and that he didn't know much about Park as it was well before he was Dean. 'I was just minding my own business when two Oxford County Court bailiffs burst into my room.' The case was put into the hands of the University solicitors but the authorities were not worried unduly about the writ because the law would have had to have been changed in order for Park to win the case. (*Oxford Mail*)

MAY 25TH

2001: On this day, former President of the United States, Bill Clinton, officially opened the Rothermere American Institute. He was welcomed back to Oxford by the Chancellor, Lord Jenkins of Hillhead. Then Lord Rothermere spoke of his father's dream to create an institute for American Studies. In his speech, Mr Clinton stressed the importance of the special relationship between both Britain and America and America and Europe. Quoting Martin Luther King, he stated how all the people of the world are bound together in an 'inescapable web of mutuality' and had to work together to overcome the global AIDS pandemic, poverty and Third World debt. He also spoke of threats to the environment as a global issue, needing the cooperation of all nations. Julian Harris, an American Rhodes Scholar, sang songs – including the 'Star-Spangled Banner' – before Mr Clinton unveiled a plaque and declared the institute officially open. After the speeches, he toured the institute and admired a glass sculpture depicting the relationship between Britain and America by Julian Stocks. Before having tea at Rhodes House he met many of Oxford's 245 Rhodes Scholars. Mr Clinton's visit finished with a formal dinner at New College. (*Oxford Mail*)

MAY 26TH

1998: Oxford student Ed Sheldon was over the moon after winning £40,000 at roulette in Australia. It began when he bought a vodka and coke in the Chequers Inn off High Street and won the prize of a trip Down Under. Ed, a second-year History student from Corpus Christi College, flew with a friend to the Gold Coast in Queensland and placed a very large bet at the exclusive Jupiter's Casino. The stake of $50,000 AUD was part of the prize donated by Smirnoff. Ed explained how the adrenalin 'was really pumping'. Because most of his friends had put their chips on black, he followed their example. 'Once the wheel started spinning I was overwhelmed with both fear and excitement. I can't believe that I actually won 100,000 Australian dollars – my mind is still spinning with ideas of what I am going to spend the money on.' A spokesman from Smirnoff said that Ed was shaking when he won and that the cash meant that he was no longer dependent on his student grant. The firm advised him to keep on with his studies and, on completing his degree, Ed planned a career as a television producer. (*Oxford Mail*)

MAY 27TH

1871: This was the day that the citizens of Oxford heard that parliamentary approval had been obtained for the removal and rebuilding of the parish church of St Peter-le-Bailey. The building was to be demolished on its site on the corner of New Inn Hall Street and Queen Street, the present Bonn Square. The church's unusual name came from the fact that the original church, which had already been replaced in 1740, once lay in the bailey of Oxford Castle. The new Victorian church was built further along New Inn Hall Street to allow for the widening of the road leading to the railway stations. The position of the existing church, which jutted out into the road, had caused accidents, some of which had been fatal. The new site, which cost about £1,500, was purchased and donated by the rector of the parish and the estimated cost of the church was £5,000. This was to be offset by the £500 which it was hoped would be obtained from the sale of the furnishings and fabric of its predecessor. The Local Board was contributing £1,400, which left the remaining £3,100 to be raised 'by private and public bounty'. (*Jackson's Oxford Journal*)

MAY 28TH

1989: Traffic in West Oxford ground to an unexpected halt and chaos ensued when the temporary traffic lights in Botley Road were tampered with on this day. A man who had had too much to drink was held at Oxford police station after he had succeeded in twisting the light sensor round on a set of lights near the railway station. After the sensor was put out of action, the lights remained on green for several hours, leading to huge traffic jams in that part of the city as cars met head-on with no means of getting round each other or reversing. Fortunately, there was only one minor crash, in which both cars were slightly damaged. A police inspector said that the thirty-four-year-old man had been too drunk to be interviewed but in the morning he was released with a caution. The drink made him decide that it would be 'a bit of a laugh' to turn both sets of lights to green at the same time. He was taken in as drunk and disorderly because a person of a similar description had been reported as having interfered with the lights, but there was no concrete evidence with which to charge the man. (*Oxford Mail*)

MAY 29TH

2003: On this day, *Oxford Mail* readers learnt that the man who had attempted to make a success of the notorious Millennium Dome had pledged his support to the city in its bid for the title of European Capital of Culture. Frenchman Pierre-Yves Gerbeau had taken up the challenge of increasing the number of visitors to the national white elephant attraction three years before. His prediction for the latest accolade was Oxford first, followed by Birmingham in second place. Other shortlisted cities were Cardiff, Newcastle-Gateshead, Bristol and the eventual winners, Liverpool. Monsieur Gerbeau's opinions lost value when he showed his ignorance of the fact that the winner would have to be one of these cities when he added, 'I think Britain has a very good chance of getting the Capital of Culture 2008.' All of the member states in the European Union take it in turns to hold the title for a year and that year was Britain's turn. Next day, two BBC Radio Newcastle presenters broadcast from Broad Street to tell Geordies that Oxonians weren't interested in the bid. (*Oxford Mail*)

MAY 30TH

1878: On this day the following letter, which shows how Victorian charity worked at ground level, was written to the editor of the *Oxford Journal*:

> Sir, some account of the robbery of Mr Stanley, on his way from London to Oxford, has already appeared in the local papers. The Charity Organisation Society having satisfied themselves by careful enquiries of the truth of his statement, will be much obliged if you will allow them to make an appeal to the public on his behalf through your columns. Mr Stanley, who is a native of the West Indies, began life as a mason and presently rose to be a small builder and contractor. Having saved a little money, he sailed for England in order to complete his professional education; but on his way from London to Oxford within a few days of his arrival, he was robbed of all his savings, £188 in notes and coin and a watch and chain worth £25. We appeal to the public to give Mr Stanley a fresh start. Subscriptions will be received by the Secretary to the Society, 6 Church-street, St Ebbe's. I am Sir, yours faithfully, FH Peters, Chairman.

(*Jackson's Oxford Journal*)

MAY 31ST

2000: This was the day that Oxford archaeologists announced that they had discovered what they believed to be the country's very first roadworks. Traffic jams around rush hour are a fact of twenty-first-century life but, according to the Oxford Archaeology Unit, this is not a modern phenomenon. They believe that men working on Roman roads caused just as much of a nuisance on the 16-mile stretch between Gloucester and Swindon 2,000 years before. Four years of research on Ermine Way, undertaken by eighty archaeologists, has shown that the road has been resurfaced seventeen times during its existence, eight times in the Roman period alone; at one point it is 5ft higher than it was when first constructed in around AD 50. The main cause of damage was from the wheels of chariots and stagecoaches. Findings along the length of the road included a hipposandal, or Roman horseshoe, and a complete farming settlement dating from the Iron Age. Ermine Way, a very important Roman road running from London to South Wales, joins the M4 and M5 motorways nowadays. The Archaeology Unit's findings have appeared as a 600-page report called 'The Road over the Hills', which has been handed to English Heritage. (*Oxford Mail*)

JUNE 1ST

1754: On this day, a sweep's boy called Joseph Holloway died from a shotgun wound, despite receiving prompt treatment from a surgeon. Some days beforehand, just before an important local election, a Whig procession had been passing over Magdalen Bridge when a shot rang out and Joseph was found to be fatally injured. The inquest held the day after he died returned a verdict of 'wilful murder by person in a post-chaise drawn by grey horses'. This person was identified as a Captain Turton. When Turton appeared at the Assizes on Wednesday 24 July, a true bill was found against him in regard to Joseph's murder. At the Assizes in July 1755, however, he was found not guilty for some reason.

There have been curious consequences of the killer's escaping justice. A man was returning home over Magdalen Bridge when, in the mist, he saw a dark shape that seemed to topple over the bridge into the river beneath. He told the police what he had seen, but they were not particularly concerned as they had received numerous reports of a 'black man' falling from the bridge. They had, in fact, dragged the river on several occasions, but nothing suspicious had ever been found. (Various sources)

JUNE 2ND

1870: An advertisement from Littlemore Asylum::

Contacts for Littlemore Asylum. The Committee of Visitors invite Persons for Tender for the supply of Six Dozen Pairs of Men's Leather Boots. A sample of the Boots may be examined at the House Steward's Office at the Asylum. Also for the supply of the following Provisions for three months from the first day of July next namely:

1 Tea, Sugars, Rice, Cheese, and other Groceries, Bacon, Cork Crane inspected Butter, new, and of the best quality; Soap, Candles and Oils.

2 Household Bread in loaves, weighing (when cold) 4lbs each

3 Flour

4 Butchers' Meat

5 Fresh Eggs

A printed form of Tender shewing the Provisions to be supplied, may be obtained either at the Asylum or at the County Hall

And Parties are at liberty to tender either for all or a portion of the Articles enumerated under any of the Items

The Tenders to be delivered at the Asylum (with samples – as to the items 1, 2 and 3) on or before Wednesday the 22nd instant

The Committee do not bind themselves to accept the lowest or any Tender

John M Davenport
Clerk of the Committee of Visitors, County Hall Oxford

(*Jackson's Oxford Journal*)

JUNE 3RD

1907: This was the final day of the Oxford Historical Pageant. The event was held from 27 June to 3 July that year. It was made up of fifteen scenes plus 'an Interlude or Masque'. The Pageant Committee included such experts as the poets Robert Bridges, Laurence Binyon, and the historian Professor Charles Oman. Postcards showing the various events were published and survive in collections today. The performance started with the town's patron saint, Frideswide, and continued through the centuries depicting such events as the massacre of St Scholastica's Day in 1355. It also celebrated persons associated with the Oxford area such as philosopher and scientist Friar Bacon, and Henry II and his paramour Fair Rosamund. The masque was an interpretation of the 'Medieval Curriculum' written by a modern Sir Walter Raleigh, the Professor of English Literature.

The second part showed Henry VIII and Wolsey; the funeral procession of Amy Robsart, who is buried in the University Church; the state progress of Elizabeth I, James I, and Charles I's court; the 'Surrender of Oxford'; James I and Magdalen; and a 'Scene in the eighteenth century'. It concluded with 'The Secret of Oxford' by distinguished writer and critic Sir Arthur Quiller Couch. (Various sources)

JUNE 4TH

1998: On this day details were given of an idea which had proved an unexpected hit in a city centre pub – topless pool. Female models had been stripping off during matches at the Castle Tavern in Paradise Street. The games, which took place every week on Friday nights, were so popular that the pub's takings had more than doubled since they started. The pub's manager thought up the idea so that the Tavern could compete with larger pubs in the town. He reported, 'The pub's full. We've been turning people away it's so busy.' The rules of the game were very straightforward. The girls, who usually worked as strippers, began playing with their tops on, but if they lost a game they had to take them off. The manager said these matches would continue as long as they remained popular and that the Castle was considering other attractions, such as a Miss Wet T-shirt competition. The Chairman of the City Entertainments Licensing Panel believed that topless pool did not contravene the pub's licence. He said, 'Some would see it as tacky, others enjoyable but I do not think the council needs to get involved.' (*Oxford Mail*)

JUNE 5TH

1975: An ode to a dearly beloved tortoise, Christie of Corpus Christi College written by her closest friend, Alan Stokes:

To Christie

Her golden shell lies buried in the soil,
Her patterned back lies hid from human view,
More than a hibernation is her sleep
As Christie's corpus settles down at last

She was a fighter, with a well-placed butt
All-comers would be tackled, all except
The virile tortoise from across the street
Who in the television tortoise race
Pressed his attentions on her, it was clear
That Christie was a maiden, pure and chaste
And chased about she was, she grew so tired
That in the finals Christie took a Third

The garden will not be the same again
For Derek is obedient, He won't run
Across the lawn to halt a game of bowls
And then be set down in the flower-bed
Only to clamber back across the path
Onto the green to join in with the game
Older than all, she watched for 90 years
Contented as she basked upon the lawn,
A grand old lady; she is sadly missed.

(Oxford Mail)

JUNE 6TH

1974: On this day a unique ceremony took place in the Sheldonian Theatre to welcome back two of the nine statues known as the Muses to the roof of the Clarendon Building. The statues were erected in 1717 but by the mid-twentieth century two of them, Melpomene (Tragedy) and Euterpe (Music), had become unsafe and there was a real danger that they might fall onto passers-by. They were therefore removed.

Their story is told in a poem by Ernest Sabben-Clare which was read at the ceremony. In it, Richard Blackwell, coming out of his famous bookshop opposite, looks along Broad Street and notices the missing Muses. Dismayed, he rushes off to the Vice-Chancellor, and offers to pay for replacements.

The new statues are made of fibreglass and covered with a mix of lead powder and resin instead of plain lead like the originals. They were executed by Richard Kindersley in consultation with Robert Potter and were designed to look identical to the originals. The poem's conclusion is an update on the situation in which Euterpe complains about modern-day pollution and wonders if she might have ended up in Cambridge, but Terpsichore (Dance) reminds her that the enduring glory of the University is all that matters. (Programme of the event)

JUNE 7TH

1851: This was the day that sixteen Oxfordshire men played an All England XI at cricket on the Christ Church ground.

Oxfordshire went in first against the bowling of Wisden and Clarke, and up to the time of going to dinner had succeeded in scoring 39 runs, with the loss of only one wicket. After dinner, Messrs H. Wyatt, Parker and Yonge gave additional life and spirit to the game by their splendid batting, for they hit both the fast bowling of Wisden, and the slow bowling of Clarke to all parts of the field and had it not been for the heavy state of the ground, hits that told for one only would have been marked on the score paper two and three. Independently however, of this drawback, when the stumps were drawn for the day the number of runs obtained was 90, with six wickets down. Mr Greenwood of the Maidenhead Inn set up 'a spacious booth where "creature comforts were liberally dispensed" in the most effectual manner and at a moderate charge.' At the end of the match the following day the Oxfordshire side were judged very worthy opponents of some of the best bats in the world.

(*Jackson's Oxford Journal*)

JUNE 8TH

1994: On this day the honorary degree of Doctor of Civil Law was conferred on William Jefferson Clinton. The national anthems of both England and the United States were played before the Chancellor of the University, Lord Jenkins of Hillhead, opened the Congregation. The Public Orator read out an address in Latin, which stated the reasons why the then President was worthy of this honour, the first of which was that 'he has worked to cherish and increase the friendship between our two nations'. Another was that 'he has a powerful collaborator in his wife, especially in questions of the health of the citizens'. This was a graceful compliment to Mrs Clinton, who was in the audience. The statement 'he has pursued his studies among us at Oxford' acknowledged that he had been at University College on a Rhodes Scholarship, but declined to mention that Mr Clinton had not taken an Oxford degree. The Chancellor admitted the former President to the degree with a format that concluded with: 'Acting upon my own authority and that of the whole University and by the power and force of this Diploma, I admit you to the degree of Doctor of Civil Law.' He then presented the diploma and gave a short speech. (Personal observation)

JUNE 9TH

1834: On this day both Town and Gown went mad with joy as they welcomed the Duke of Wellington when he came to be installed as Chancellor of the University. In the morning 'carriages arrived without intermission', packed with the great and the good, to take part in the celebrations.

> At half past three o'clock, the new sovereign of Alma Mater entered the city followed by a body of equestrians waving hats and raising loud cheers in concert with the acclamations of the inhabitants. Not less than a thousand of the Under Graduates of the University, and a considerable number of the Gentry of the city and neighbourhood had gone out to meet the Noble Duke, but they missed him and this prevented his being attended by an immense cavalcade.

Wellington was noted to appear in excellent health and spirits as he made his way up the High Street, bowing to left and right, until he arrived at his lodging in University College. All eyes were on the Iron Duke and nobody noticed the Duke of Cumberland who was in the carriage in front. Cumberland strolled up and down the High Street several times, before attending a reception at University College. (*Jackson's Oxford Journal*)

JUNE 10TH

1834: This was the day of the installation ceremony of the Duke of Wellington. The ladies in the audience arrived at the Sheldonian Theatre at 9.30 a.m. and were seated in a section which was partitioned off 'for their exclusive accommodation'. It is a section which is sometimes still called the Ladies' Gallery. Senior members of the University and ticket-holding members of the public were allowed in at 10 a.m. and, half an hour later, the relative peace was shattered by the arrival of the undergraduate audience in the Upper Gallery. Shortly before Wellington himself appeared, numerous members of the aristocracy took their places and the new Chancellor, resplendent in his gown, was escorted in to tumultuous applause. The academic robes and gowns, the noblemen's robes, the military and naval dress uniforms, as well as the ladies' summer finery combined to make an unforgettable spectacle and, as one eyewitness put it, 'joy beamed on every countenance.' Twenty-one honorary Doctorates of Civil Law were then conferred, the Creweian Oration was delivered and recitations were given by the winners of University prizes. The new Chancellor closed the congregation at 1.30 p.m. and left the theatre in procession to applause which equalled that which was heard when he entered. (*Jackson's Oxford Journal*)

JUNE 11TH

1959: On this day James Hugh Calum Laurie, the youngest of four children, and son of medical doctor and 1948 London Olympic rowing gold medallist Ran Laurie, was born in Oxford. Better known as Hugh Laurie, the famous actor was brought up in the city and went to the Dragon School before going on to Eton and then Selwyn College, Cambridge, where he read Archaeology and Social Anthropology. During his time at Cambridge, he was a member of the Hermes Club and the Hawks' Club, as well as the world-famous Footlights Club, of which he was President in 1981. Following in his father's footsteps, Hugh rowed at school and university and represented Britain. He gained a Blue for Cambridge when he took part in the University boat race in the crew which lost by 5ft. Unfortunately, glandular fever put a stop to his rowing career, but he was introduced to his future acting partner Stephen Fry at the Footlights Club by Emma Thompson. With Fry, Thompson and Ben Elton, Laurie took part in the spoof on *University Challenge* as a team from Footlights College, Oxbridge, in an episode of the comedy programme *The Young Ones*. (Various sources)

JUNE 12TH

1872: This was a day of assorted jollifications all over the city as part of Commemoration Week. The annual Encaenia, or honorary degree ceremony, took place at 11 a.m., preceded by a procession leaving from Christ Church. The fete organised by members of the University Masonic Lodge was held in the grounds of New College, where the band of the Coldstream Guards and the Orpheus Glee Union had been hired for the occasion. However, by far the most remarkable event was the feast held in the evening by University College as part of its millennium celebrations. The college claimed to be the oldest foundation in Oxford, but this was dismissed by other colleges as the Aluredian Myth. This myth held that the great educationalist and patriot, King Alfred, was the college's true founder. Based on some documents forged in 1381 during a dispute over property, it predated the accepted one belonging to William of Durham by nearly four centuries. One distinguished academic sent his regrets at being unable to attend the banquet, accompanied by a box of burnt cakes. That evening there was also a concert at Magdalen College and the day of festivities concluded with the University Ball in the Corn Exchange. (*Jackson's Oxford Journal*)

JUNE 13TH

1893: On this day Dorothy Leigh Sayers was born at No. 1 Brewer Street, off St Aldates and christened in Christ Church Cathedral. Her father was headmaster of the Cathedral School where a blue plaque marks her birthplace. When she was four, her father became rector in Bluntisham, Huntingdonshire. However, Dorothy returned to study Modern Languages at Somerville College. David Coombs writes how she took pleasure in 'unashamedly talking in the Bodleian, cutting lectures, none too surreptitiously, smoking cigars, wearing a badly fitting wig, and proclaiming to all who would listen (and those who wouldn't) that she was an agnostic and proud of it'. She was very popular and spent a lot of time socialising and singing with the Oxford Bach Choir. Despite this, she took first-class honours in Modern Languages, although she had to wait until 1920 before Oxford started admitting women to degree courses. Dorothy's first job was a short stint at Blackwell's, who published her first book, a volume of poetry, in 1916. She left Oxford for London in 1920, but fifteen years later Somerville featured as the fictitious Shrewsbury College in Sayers' novel *Gaudy Night*, in which she calls Oxford 'City of life, city of my dreams'. (Various sources)

JUNE 14TH

1863: A report from *Jackson's Oxford Journal*:

This was the Sunday of Commemoration Week and a great variety of sermons were preached throughout the city. St Mary's was packed with those wishing to hear Dr Pusey speak on the superiority of Christianity over all other religions and the need to treasure it. At the Cathedral there were 'as usual, crowded and fashionable congregations' who heard the Beethoven anthem 'Great God of All', while Dr Corfe 'presided at the organ with his accustomed ability'. The college services attracted large congregations, that at Merton including full choral services and collections for the choir. At Carfax, the annual sermons for the benefit of the Blue Coat Boys' School raised £27 *os* 9*d* while special ones were preached at St Aldates 'towards the liquidation of the debt consequent on recent restoration,' which produced £47. Later, the time-honoured custom of promenading in the Broad Walk was observed in the evening. The weather, although gloomy, was tolerably fine, and from seven to nine o'clock that splendid walk was thronged. The greatest crowd was at about half-past 8, but before Great Tom boomed forth its 101 [strokes at 9.05 p.m.] the numbers had considerably diminished, and by dusk the walk was virtually deserted.

(*Jackson's Oxford Journal*)

JUNE 15TH

1814: On this day, following the defeat of Napoleon, the victorious Allied sovereigns and commanders were feted in Oxford by both Town and Gown. This was in celebration of the Peace of Paris, and the abdication of Napoleon Bonaparte the previous April. The Prince Regent, the Prussian Field Marshal Blucher, King Frederick William of Prussia and Czar Alexander of Russia, were all given honorary degrees in the Sheldonian Theatre. In the course of the tour of the University which followed, the Prince, who was noted as being handsome but also very stout, 'groaned audibly' as he struggled up the staircase in the Bodleian Library. Their visit finished with a gala dinner in the Radcliffe Camera, which was suitably decorated for the occasion. The Prince stayed in Christ Church Deanery, the Czar was lodged at Merton College and the King of Prussia at Corpus Christi College. 'Prinny' dined in Christ Church Hall on 15 June, and afterwards his name was entered into the list of members of the college but with 'barbarous Latinity'. It reads: *Regia celsistudo Georgii Principis Walliae Regentis.* Even then the writer had to have several attempts at it, with Georgii altered from Georgius. (*Jackson's Oxford Journal*)

June 16th

2008: Details were released of a luxury train journey organised on the *British Pullman* by Orient Express from London to Oxford on this day in 2008. About 200 rail fans had already booked for the ride, which cost about £350 or £2.65 a mile. The cost of the fare was to include a three-course supper with champagne, and brunch with Bellini cocktails. Optional extras included Sevruga caviar at only £90 for 50g, bouquets of flowers at £45 and French crystal champagne glasses at £80 a pair. The luxury in which passengers would travel was in stark contrast to the conditions about which regular commuters usually complained. Departure was to be from London Victoria at 9 a.m. They were to first travel by a steam locomotive as far as Didcot, and then by diesel into Oxford. There were to be eleven dining cars, all of which were constructed between 1927 and 1938; parlour cars to look out for included Perseus, which formed part of Sir Winston Churchill's funeral train, and Zena, which appeared in the film *Agatha*. Up to 252 passengers were tended by twenty-five stewards. Such a train was a magnet for trainspotters. They lined the route in advance of the train for a chance to see it pass by. (*Oxford Mail*)

JUNE 17TH

1892: On this day the vicar and parishioners of St Paul's Church in Jericho held a farewell party for the Revd Marsh Kirby. He had been their assistant curate for the previous three years, but he was leaving Oxford to work in Cape Town in South Africa. After the annual tea came a concert which consisted of a variety of items, and among the performers was a Mr Beaney, 'an old man of ninety who sang, "Here we meet, too soon to part"'. The vicars of St Paul's and St Barnabas' parishes made emotional speeches about how the residents of Jericho had taken the Revd Kirby to their hearts and how much he would be missed. A presentation was made of a souvenir album bound in red Moroccan leather which contained photographs of many of the parishioners. It was inscribed: 'Presented with a purse of gold to the Revd Marsh Kirby MA, as an expression of the affectionate best wishes of the congregation of St Paul's, Oxford, 17th June 1892.' The evening ended with Miss Campion singing 'Auld Lang Syne', which the audience joined in with most enthusiastically. Last of all, three cheers were raised for Mr Kirby. (*Jackson's Oxford Journal*)

JUNE 18TH

1998: On this day patients at Oxford's John Radcliffe Hospital were involved in what the *Oxford Mail* termed a 'pillow fight'. Patients had to 'face a daily fight for pillows, with nurses filling pillow cases with blankets to ease shortages'. In the emergency ward, few patients had proper pillows, even though nurses were constantly ordering a new supply. A senior nurse was quoted as saying, 'We never have enough pillows. We use blankets. At the moment we have got nineteen patients and none of them have got pillows.' It was believed that regulation NHS pillows went missing when patients were transferred; nobody accused the patients of stealing them, indeed pillows might even have been 'stashed away in general wards'. It was alleged that at the John Radcliffe genuine NHS pillows had become prized possessions, with nurses grabbing them from spare beds to give to their patients. 'It is frustrating for nurses when they want an extra pillow for a patient and there are none around, with people taking them from other beds.' A report stated that far from being a new inconvenience, the pillow crisis had been 'simmering for many months, coupled with the well-publicised shortages of beds and nurses'. (*Oxford Mail*)

JUNE 19TH

1998: On this day an outraged shopper chased after a Stagecoach bus in central Oxford and attacked it after the driver nearly ran him over. Oxford magistrates heard how the twenty-two-year-old lost his temper and ran along, swearing at the driver and banging on the window with a bag full of shopping. A pane of glass was broken, costing £70 to replace, and the accused admitted causing criminal damage. A witness for the defence had told the attacker that the bus 'could have killed him'. Magistrates heard that after a row with the driver and the bus company's controller, the accused walked into Allders store and stole a pair of jeans, despite having £45 in cash on him. He was apprehended by the security guard and, when subsequently arrested, pleaded guilty to theft. The defence claimed that, 'In his anger and frustration, he simply picked up the jeans and walked out of the store.' Magistrates warned the man, who was already on licence from prison, that he was 'within a whisker' of being returned there. However, he escaped with a conditional discharge but was made to pay £70 compensation to Stagecoach, £15 to the driver for loss of earnings and £40 court costs. (*Oxford Mail*)

JUNE 20TH

1899: The Duke and Duchess of York spent the second day of their first visit to Oxford touring University and college buildings on this day in. They started at Magdalen, where they were received by the President, and were especially interested to see the set of rooms occupied by Prince Christian when he was a member of the college. After seeing the chapel and Addison's Walk, they were driven to All Souls, where the Warden acted as guide. Next was the Radcliffe Camera, where they had a splendid view from the rooftop and saw all the principal buildings of the city. In the Bodleian, they visited Duke Humfrey's Library and the picture gallery, where the Duke remarked on the poor condition of the portraits of William IV and Queen Adelaide; they were told it was due to the lack of heating there. Lunch was taken in Christ Church and then the Warden of New College showed the party round. A tour of the Taylor Institute followed and, in the Ashmolean, the royal couple were very taken with the Alfred Jewel. Concluding the day, they visited St John's, Merton and Oriel, before attending dinner in Christ Church Deanery, where they met Cecil Rhodes and Lord Kitchener. (*Jackson's Oxford Journal*)

JUNE 21ST

1899: On this day a large crowd gathered in Oriel College 'in the double expectancy of seeing' the Duchess of York and the procession leave Christ Church. The procession, which included the Vice-Chancellor, the Duke of York, Heads of Houses, and honorands, made its way from Corpus Christi College to the Sheldonian Theatre. Much of Radcliffe Square was roped off, but many people managed to cram themselves in to cheer. 'The tedium of waiting was relieved to some extent by the preparations of some cinematograph operators who took a series of views of the proceedings.' That year was notable for the fact that a few tickets had changed hands in the manner of modern touts, an offer of £20 being made for a seat in the Ladies' Gallery. Another was the 'seemingly unpatriotic attempt' by some members of the University to prevent Cecil Rhodes from having the honorary degree, which he had been unable to accept in 1892, conferred on him at the ceremony. In the event, the 'Empire Maker' was enthusiastic as he entered the theatre, and apart from the Proctors and Bedels being greeted by the student body with hissing, barking and 'various other canine sounds', the ceremony went very well. (*Jackson's Oxford Journal*)

JUNE 22ND

1895: Concerning the Professorship of Poetry, on this day:

> Mr Robert Bridges who, as was lately announced, was invited a short time back to become a candidate for the Chair of Poetry lately vacated by Professor Palgrave, has intimated to his friends that while recognising the weight of the support offered and the value of the compliment thus paid him, he did not wish to come forward on the present occasion, or to oppose Mr Courthope, whose name was favourably received in the previous vacancy of the chair. Among those who expressed their intention of supporting Mr Bridges were the Bishops of Peterborough and Chichester, the Heads of Worcester, Corpus, Trinity, Balliol, Wadham, Brasenose and Magdalen, the Provost and Head Master of Eton, the Regius Professors of Medicine and History, Sir John Stainer, Professor Butcher, Mr Andrew Lang, Mr T.G. Jackson ARA, Dr Ogle, Canon Gore, Mr A. Sidgwick, Messrs Thursfield, St John Thackeray &c.

In the event, William John Courthope was duly elected to the four-year appointment. All holders of an MA or above, who make up the 1,000-strong body of the University's convocation, are eligible to vote. (*Jackson's Oxford Journal*)

June 23rd

1900: This day was Oxford's first 'Lifeboat Saturday' when the boat, which had been bought by contributions from the residents, was launched. It had been paid for by a whole range of collections and donations, large and small, from all round the city. One of the more unusual collectors was Guest, an enormous ex-circus dog owned by the landlord of the Plough pub in Cornmarket. A 6-mile procession that included bands, boat club members, fire brigades and floats, a 'Grace Darling', a Baden-Powell, some Ancient Britons, a company of Druids, and members of the Royal Antediluvian Order of Buffaloes, who won first prize, preceded the launch itself. While the huge crowd was waiting for the lifeboat to arrive, they were kept amused by music coming from a large gramophone playing in a nearby house. When it finally did come there was considerable difficulty in negotiating its passage down to the water, but eventually it was launched near Salter's boat yard at Folly Bridge to the accompaniment of a band and loud cheers. It set off, preceded by the steamboat *Kohinoor*, which was gaily decorated with flags and Chinese lanterns, and upon which the post office band was stationed aft. (*Jackson's Oxford Journal*)

JUNE 24TH

1646: Of Midsummer Day, Anthony à Wood wrote:

The garrison of Oxon, which was the chiefest hold the king had, and wherein he had mostly resided while the civil war continued, was surrendered for the use of the parliament, as most of his garrisons were this yeare, occasion'd by the fatal battle of Naisby which hapned in the last yeare, wherein the king and his partie were in a woful manner worsted. In the evening of the said day, many of the king's foot-partie that belonged to the said garrison came into Thame and layd downe their armes there, being then a wet season. Some of whome continuing there the next day A[nthony] W[ood] went into the towne to see them. He knew some of their faces, and they his, but he being a boy and having no money, he could not then relieve them, or make them drink yet he talked with them about Oxford and his relations and acquaintance there; for the doing of which he was check'd when he came home.

Anthony and his brother Christopher had been sent from Oxford to be educated at Lord Williams's Grammar School at Thame (where John Hampden had been a pupil) two years previously. (*Life and Times of Anthony à Wood*)

JUNE 25TH

2003: This was the day that Lord Patten of Barnes, better known as politician Chris Patten, was installed as the 294th Chancellor of the University of Oxford. He was succeeding Lord Jenkins of Hillhead, who had died that January. The previous March, Lord Patten, who had read Modern History at Balliol College and who was already Chancellor of the University of Newcastle, had beaten Lord Bingham of Cornhill, Lord Neill of Bladen, and comedienne Sandi Toksvig to the post which dates back to 1224. Senior members of the University, in full academic dress, escorted the Chancellor-elect in procession to the Sheldonian Theatre where the installation was due to take place. The route was lined by Chinese students and tourists, all of whom were full of praise for Lord Patten's tour of duty as the last Governor of Hong Kong. After he had been installed through a format which dates back centuries, the new Chancellor began his first official duty, that of conferring honorary degrees at the annual Encaenia. The honorands included the world-famous tenor Plácido Domingo, who was made a Doctor of Music. The position of Chancellor of the University is unpaid and is normally, but not necessarily, held for life. (Personal observation)

JUNE 26TH

1998: This was the day that the world was told about the exploits of what was described in the *Oxford Mail* as 'a bird-brained cockerel'. His story began two nights before, when his owner, farmer John Goodey of Mill Lane, Marston, put his chickens away for the night in their shed. The one-year-old cockerel refused to go in with his wives, preferring to spend the night wandering round the farm and crowing as he usually did at about 5 a.m. Mr Goodey did not give him another thought and set off for Cheltenham market without realising that the stupid bird had decided to get underneath his van. The cockerel managed to cling on to the axle as the van dashed from Oxford to Cheltenham and back at 60mph, a round trip of some 100 miles. Nobody thought to look for him until one of Mr Goodey's friends heard a crowing sound coming from under the van, and even then they assumed that it was a new anti-theft device. When they all got down on their hands and knees and peered under the van, they discovered the cockerel still clinging like grim death to his unusual perch. (*Oxford Mail*)

JUNE 27TH

1843: On this evening, thousands of people turned up on the banks of the river near Folly Bridge to watch the procession of racing boats in which nearly thirty eights, representing most of the colleges, rowed up and down the river for nearly an hour. The University College boat, as Head of the River, was saluted by all the other crews as they passed. After this display of rowing, a fireworks demonstration followed in the meadow opposite the club barge. It started with two balloons being released and then:

> … an immense number of rockets, Roman candles and other devices, too numerous to mention, concluding with a device exhibiting in its centre a variety of colours, and finishing with a flight of one-pound rockets, shells, mines, sausissons, &c. &c. the whole conducted by Mr C. Horn, artist in fireworks in this city. We understand the expences [*sic*] of this great treat to the strangers and the company assembled were defrayed by a subscription amongst the junior members of this University.

Also on offer on that and the following evening were 'Scottish Entertainments' in a packed Holywell Music Room, where 'the whole of the performances appeared to afford the highest gratification'. (*Jackson's Oxford Journal*)

JUNE 28TH

1887: This was the day that the Queen's Golden Jubilee was celebrated in Oxford, in 'really Royal' weather and with no hitches. It had not been possible for 21 June, the official day, to be observed, because of existing Commemoration arrangements. Flags, banners, and Chinese and Japanese lanterns were particularly evident in the northern part of the city as a prelude to the fair held on Port Meadow. Bonfires were lit and the pubs were given an extension due to it being a general holiday, but everybody was in such good humour that the extra policemen who had been drafted in from Bath proved unnecessary. The Mayor, Alderman Hughes, paid for very distinctive commemorative medals to be given out. These medals were in the form of a Maltese cross, at the centre of which was a picture of the Queen, and on its branches were a crown, a rose, a shamrock and a thistle, coupled with the words, 'Born 1819', 'Crowned 1838', 'Married 1840' and 'Jubilee 1887'. On the back were the City arms and *Civitas Oxoniensis*, and at the top 'Oxford June 28th 1887', while written at the bottom was 'James Hughes, Mayor'. The medals came in three types of metal, according to the status of the wearer. (*Jackson's Oxford Journal*)

JUNE 29TH

1886: On this day, an attempt at a double murder was made in St Clement's. Hiram Bowell of Dovers Row had become suspicious of the repeated visits of a man named Simmonds to his house while he was out at work. On being told that Simmonds was in the house on this occasion, Bowell rushed home and, on finding him, attacked him with a bread knife, wounding him on the throat and hand. When the handle fell off the knife, Simmonds was able to escape. Bowell, however, pulled out a pocket knife and attacked his wife, cutting her throat so badly in two places that he left her for dead. As he left the house, he was followed by Simmonds, who informed a police sergeant who then arrested Bowell. Both stab victims were taken to the Radcliffe Infirmary where Simmonds' wounds were dressed, and Mrs Bowell received stitches to hers which, although bleeding profusely, were not life-threatening. Simmonds stated that he had been to the house on several occasions to see another man, but this man had not been there this time. He added that he had been eating bread and cheese with Mrs Bowell's sister and her husband when Bowell rushed in and attacked him for no apparent reason. (*Jackson's Oxford Journal*)

JUNE 30TH

1838: On this day, Queen Victoria's Coronation was celebrated in Oxford. It began with the peal of bells and the streets were soon alive with activity. Although there was no official dinner held for the poor, both Town and Gown made sure that they were able to celebrate. Dinner was provided for about eighty of the workmen from Tawney & Co. and their wives. And in the afternoon, tea was given to the womenfolk. Children were invited to tea and entertainment in the schools, and souvenir medals were distributed. Dinners were donated by various benefactors, mainly clergymen and leading employers, including Brasenose College, who welcomed those from St Ebbe's parish. All the poor parishioners of Holywell were invited to a substantial dinner of traditional roast beef and plum pudding, in a marquee erected on the Archery Ground, near the church. The Revd Tyndall presided, having paid for wine and negus (wine with hot water, spices and sugar), to drink the health of the new young monarch. The sweeps of Mr Buckland's establishment were entertained by Mrs Tawney with beef and pudding 'and while they testified their loyalty, were not unmindful of their benefactress'. (*Jackson's Oxford Journal*)

July 1st

1903: This was the day of the inauguration of the Rhodes Scholars. The Rhodes Scholarship is the oldest and arguably most prestigious international programme in the world for graduate scholars. Under the terms of the will of Cecil Rhodes, eighty-three Scholars are selected annually to study at Oxford. These are not confined solely to the United States; people also come from Australia, Bermuda, Canada, Germany, Hong Kong, India, Jamaica, the Commonwealth Caribbean, Kenya, New Zealand, Pakistan and Southern Africa (which includes South Africa, Botswana, Lesotho, Malawi, Namibia, Swaziland, Zambia, and Zimbabwe). Rhodes' aim in setting up the scholarship programme was to prepare exceptional world leaders who would 'esteem the performance of public duties as their highest aim', and thereby promote peace and understanding throughout the world. His will states various criteria to be considered in the election of Rhodes Scholars: 'literary and scholastic attainments; energy to use one's talents to the full; truth, courage, devotion to duty, sympathy for and protection of the weak, kindliness, unselfishness and fellowship, and moral force of character and instincts to lead, and to take an interest in one's fellow beings.' Former Scholars include penicillin pioneer Howard Florey, former US President Bill Clinton, and singer and songwriter Kris Kristofferson. (Various sources)

JULY 2ND

1998: On this day residents of Oxford learnt that the bold head of one of the colleges had challenged no less a person than the Mayor of Bath to a duel, the outcome of which would decide the possession of a medieval sword. The Provost of Oriel, Dr Ernest Nicholson, issued the challenge after hearing that the authorities of the City of Bath had decided to claim the 6ft ceremonial sword, which is dated 1423 and which hangs in the college hall. Bath claimed it as an important item in the city's heritage, as it was said to have been discovered in a roof in nearby Swainswick, which once belonged to Oriel, at the end of the nineteenth century. Although the city owned a replica sword, the Mayor wanted the original to be either loaned or returned to Bath, although he admitted that there was no legal entitlement. Dr Nicholson joked, 'Maybe if he brings his replica and I have the original, we could have a duel in the quad and the winner takes all. He must in any event come and have dinner.' He added, 'It's been in possession of Oriel for a long time. We wouldn't give it up.' (*Oxford Mail*)

July 3rd

2001: It was revealed on this day that more people would prefer to own the copyright to the Bible than to any other book or piece of music, according to a survey carried out by Marks & Clerk, of Oxford. The Beatles' hits came second, followed by the works of Shakespeare, then the Harry Potter series, while the works of Beethoven came in fifth. Mr Julian Asquith, a partner at Marks & Clerk, said that copyright lasted only seventy years after the death of the writer or composer; alternatively it could last for seventy years from the first publication of the work protected. While it would be impossible to own the copyright to the Bible or the works of Shakespeare today, it was important for anyone producing a new work to protect it by copyright and there are some golden rules to avoid one's ideas being filched. Firstly, when submitting a script one should obtain an obligation of confidentiality and secondly, when submitting a script for a book or television show, one should put as much of it down in writing as possible. He added, 'You need to get a lot down on paper if you want to be the next J.K. Rowling, and not just rely on a good idea.' (*Oxford Mail*)

JULY 4TH

1862: On this day Charles Lutwidge Dodgson, a mathematics tutor at Christ Church, took a party of children, one of whom was Alice Liddell, the daughter of the Dean of Christ Church, out on the river. He entertained them during the trip to Godstow by telling his passengers a story which he made up as they went along. It began: 'Alice was beginning to get very tired of sitting by her sister on the bank and having nothing to do … when suddenly a White Rabbit with pink eyes ran close by her …' His audience was so enchanted with the story that they begged him to write it down when they got back to Christ Church. He did so, and gave it the title 'Alice's Adventures Underground'. When he finished it the following year, his friends insisted that he publish it. The book, which was given the new name *Alice's Adventures in Wonderland*, appeared in July 1865, under the name of Lewis Carroll. However, it was withdrawn from circulation straightaway due to the inferior quality of the print. An improved edition came out that November and soon became a children's classic. The second part, *Through the Looking Glass*, followed in 1871. (Various sources)

JULY 5TH

1791: On this day the famous composer Joseph Haydn was made an honorary Doctor of Music. Nowadays, the 'D Mus' is one of the main attractions in the Encaenia procession, with honorands of the calibre of Sir Simon Rattle and Plácido Domingo. It is strange to think that in Haydn's time the degree was considered by senior academics to be something of a 'Mickey Mouse' qualification. It was so inferior to the other honorary degrees, that holders were sometimes expected to sit apart during meetings and ceremonies. Fortunately, Haydn's English was not of a sufficiently high standard to realise this. Indeed, he was so delighted that he insisted on wearing his gorgeous ivory- and cerise-coloured silk gown for the rest of the time that he was in Oxford. He was frequently seen parading proudly round the streets in it. As an exercise for his doctoral 'thesis', Haydn wrote a short piece of music which can be played from end to beginning, and this is preserved among the treasures of the Bodleian Library. His 'Oxford Symphony' was so named because it was first played in the Sheldonian Theatre in commemoration of Haydn receiving his award there. (Various sources)

JULY 6TH

1887: The inmates of the Oxford County Asylum certainly enjoyed themselves celebrating the Queen's Golden Jubilee over two days in 1887. Union Jacks and the flags of all nations were everywhere and the entertainments included men dressed up as females, which seems to have been somewhat avant-garde. The women's games were held on the first day, and the female attendants astounded the onlookers with the speed and endurance which they displayed. A treat for the children was 'Colborn the dandy darkey and his big and bewitching sweetheart', who paraded the ground beating a drum, followed by a gang of twenty or thirty youngsters. There was a baby show, entry to which was confined to offspring of employees of the asylum and the judges of which were two single gentlemen. After an *al fresco* meal was served on the lawn, dancing started to the accompaniment of the Asylum Band and this went on until about 9 p.m., when 'brilliant and lovely illuminations spread all over the ground of revels'. The moon joined in 'at her full calmly and peacefully looking on, meanwhile shedding her soft rays on the scene, and a picture more like those described in Oriental stories met the eye'. (*Jackson's Oxford Journal*)

JULY 7TH

1845: On this day the *Sporting Post* reported that there had been an:

EXTRAORDINARY SUICIDE AT OXFORD. Between eleven and twelve o'clock, Mr Sheard, one of the most respected traders in the High Street, Oxford, threw himself from the top of his house on the pavement. He was immediately carried into the house and almost instantly attended by a medical man but life was extinct. His skull was found to be fractured above the ear and his neck broken. A coroner's inquest was shortly after summoned and from the evidence of several witnesses it appeared that the deceased had shown decided proofs of insanity for several days but had that morning appeared so much recovered that it was not thought necessary to watch him so strictly. The deceased was greatly respected by all who knew him. He was a member of the Town Council, had served the office of sheriff and was treasurer to a charitable institution. He has left a widow and six children.

The deceased had a successful tea and grocery business at No. 21 High Street. The business was carried on by his widow, Hester, until 1871, after which their son Thomas ran it until 1894. (*Jackson's Oxford Journal*)

JULY 8TH

1899: On this day a plea was made by the people of Jericho to their neighbours:

> We the undersigned residents of Jericho, are of the opinion that the time has arrived when we may favourably approach you to do all in your power either to affect some alteration in the time and process of boiling putrid fat at the Jericho Tallow Factory or to order it to be closed. For many years outbursts of feeling respecting this abominable nuisance has arisen and the people of this unhealthy neighbourhood have rightly been called a floating population. Only those who are obliged, remain any length of time, together with those who have lost any sense of smell. As the compulsory removal of pigs from this densely populated district was effected some years ago, we implore you to remove this greater nuisance without delay as it is proved dangerous to the general health. About 100 signatures are already appended, and those wishing to sign can do so at 50 Cranham Street. Mr George Alder, who is well-known among Oddfellows, is obtaining signatures, a task which he finds in no way onerous, everyone in the district who has been approached being eager to take some part in the suppression of what is felt to be an intolerable nuisance.

(*Jackson's Oxford Journal*)

JULY 9TH

1669: On this day John Dryden described in his diary the formal opening of the Sheldonian Theatre: the ceremonial hall of the University and the first major building by Christopher Wren. In those days it was known as the New Theatre, and Dryden notes how it cost £26,000 to build. It was largely financed by Gilbert Sheldon, later Archbishop of Canterbury. Dryden describes it as being 'in truth a fabrick comparable to any of this kind of former ages, and doubtless exceeding any of the present', and its opening was 'celebrated with the greatest splendor and formalitie that might be', which attracted 'a world of strangers and other companie to the University from all parts of the nation'. When the Vice-Chancellor, Heads of Houses and Proctors had taken their places in the theatre, the ceremony was opened by the Registrar, who read out the founder's grant and gift. A long and somewhat controversial speech by the Orator followed, and then various declamations were given and some excellent music, both instrumental and vocal, was played. The celebrations went on from 11 a.m. until 7 p.m. and finished with the ringing of bells and 'universal joy and feasting'. (*Life and Times of Anthony à Wood*)

JULY 10TH

1998: On this day, after years of poisoning and general persecution, the buzzard returned to Oxfordshire; something that Ron Smith of Cowley was to find out for himself in a very unpleasant way. Pensioner Ron had to wait for 20 painful minutes with the talons of one of the large birds embedded in his thumb before an ambulance crew arrived. He had tried to catch the bird by trapping it in a fishing net as it was raiding his daughter's goldfish pond. His attacker must have been a captive specimen which had escaped and therefore had no fear of humans, otherwise he would have had no chance of getting near it. A spokesman from the RSPB said that buzzards were in fact the third most common type of bird of prey in the UK, after kestrels and sparrowhawks, and that there were 100 breeding pairs living in the wild in Oxfordshire. He added that the buzzard's remarkable comeback in the county was a cause for celebration, but that it was wiser to leave them to make their own catering arrangements. Mr Smith's buzzard would have been unused to fending for itself and so had taken to scavenging. (*Oxford Mail*)

July 11th

1912: On this day Oxford celebrated its own millennium with a pageant. It was held to mark the city's appearance in the *Anglo-Saxon Chronicle* under AD 912, when Edward the Elder, son of Alfred the Great, took the town and surrounding area into his own hands. The pageant was divided into seven episodes; those featuring St Frideswide and Rosamund had already been performed in 1907. Other important events which were portrayed included: the wedding of Robert d'Oilly, Governor of Oxford and builder of the castle, in about 1074; the Provisions of Oxford in 1258; and Edward IV's visit in 1461, when he made the Mayor his cup-bearer at coronations. The Mayor is made to say: 'We do offer you in token of our gratitude the best cheer of our poor town, to be served to you by our own hands; and in my office as Chief Magistrate I do humbly crave the right to be your Majesty's cup-bearer.' To this, the King drinks to Oxford and states that 'whensover a King of England shall come to his crowning, then shall the Mayor of Oxenford be there, besides the Mayor of London, to bear him the cup at the banquet.' The Pageant finished with the appearance of the Lady of the City Beautiful. (Various sources)

JULY 12TH

1894: This advertisement appeared in *Jackson's Oxford Journal* on this day:

OXFORD INCORPORATION

OFFICE OF PORTER

WANTED at the County Poor Law School an active SINGLE MAN to carry out the duties of Porter
Salary £12 a year, with board, lodging and washing. Information as to the duties may be had from Mr J.H. Bell, Superintendent of the School.
An applicant who could undertake the training of a Drum and Fide Band would be paid an additional salary.
Written applications stating age &c. with copies of testimonials of character and qualifications should be in the hands of the undersigned by Ten o'clock a.m. on Monday, 30th July, 1894

(*Jackson's Oxford Journal*)

JULY 13TH

2001: On this day the Oxford Preservation Trust outlined the measures to be taken to ensure that the Martyrs' Memorial would not become ruined. The memorial in Magdalen Street, to the north of St Mary Magdalen Church, commemorates the Protestant martyrs Latimer, Ridley and Cranmer, who were burned at the stake in Broad Street during the reign of Mary I. The monument, which was designed by the noted architect George Gilbert Scott, was erected in 1841. The trust had agreed to foot the bill for the restoration programme, which was expected to be about £120,000, of which £52 would be given by the City Council. Secretary of the trust, Debbie Dance, said that they had become involved in order that work could begin. This wasn't the first time the trust had been involved in a municipal restoration scheme; they had cooperated with the council before and raised more than £260,000 when Magdalen Bridge needed repairs in the 1980s. Mrs Dance described the memorial as being in a very sad state but said he looked forward to eventually seeing it restored to its former glory. For months its base had been fenced off and former Lord Mayor, Maureen Christian, had complained that it had become a dumping ground by builders carrying out roadworks. (Various sources)

JULY 14TH

1833: It is generally agreed that the world-famous Oxford Movement started on this day in the University Church of St Mary the Virgin, when John Keble, a Fellow of Oriel, preached the Assize Sermon. The sermon, the origins of which go back at least to the sixteenth century, marked the beginning of the Assizes when a high court judge would visit the town to deal with court cases. It survives in the annual Court Sermon preached at Christ Church. Keble's sermon, which was later published under the title 'National Apostasy', contained a criticism of the suppression of ten Irish sees – evidence of unjustified state intervention in religious matters. The question raised was whether the Church of England was to become a sort of government department or remain 'an ordinance of God'. The opinions of the best brains of the Senior Common Room at Oriel were divided into those who agreed with Keble, like the vicar of St Mary's, John Henry Newman (who would convert to Catholicism and later become a cardinal), and Edward Pusey, and those who did not, which included Thomas Arnold, the great educationalist, headmaster of Rugby School and father of the poet Matthew Arnold. (Various sources)

JULY 15TH

1830: On this day:

The funeral of our beloved Monarch [George IV] took place and was observed throughout this University and City with great solemnity. Sir Joseph Lock, Mayor, issued a handbill requesting a due observance of the day, and this was strictly complied with; all the shops were closed, as business was entirely suspended. The bells of the various chapels and parish churches tolled half-minute time from twelve till one and again in the evening from nine till ten. The variety of tones, from the tinkling of the chapel bell down to the deep thunder of the 'mighty Tom' [the great bell which hangs in Tom Tower, over the Fair gate at Christ Church] rendered the effect singularly solemn.

A few days earlier, a number of gentlemen had been elected to be delegates of the University and to present an 'Address of Condolence on the Death of the late King and Congratulations on the Accession of his present Majesty [William IV], to the King in person.' These included the Heads of House of Christ Church, Jesus, Balliol, Exeter, Wadham, Trinity, All Souls, Merton and University Colleges, Magdalen Hall, the University Registrar and holders of some of the leading professorships. (Mary Latimer's Diary, Oxfordshire Record Office)

July 16th

1887: On this evening:

The concert given in the Sheldonian Theatre by the children attending the Elementary Schools in this City, under the conductorship of Mr C.J. Moss, was well-attended and was throughout a great success. The programme consisted of the cantata 'The Queen's Jubilee' by Messrs J. Hatch and E. Hatton, the choruses in which were excellently rendered by some 500 children grouped in the ladies' gallery and semi-circle, the Vice-Chancellor's seat being reserved for Britannia and the front of the semi-circle for the infants attending St Barnabas's, whose drill was remarkably attractive. The argument of the cantata is as follows, Britannia, as the representative of the Queen, causes it to be proclaimed that her Majesty is unwilling that all the credit for the success of her reign should be awarded to her and that she has authorised Britannia to bestow public recognition on all who can claim to have contributed to the greatness of England during the past fifty years.

'The doors were so besieged' that the stewards had their work cut out to cope with the prospective audience; nevertheless the evening went off well and £50 was raised for the Orphans Benevolent Fund. (*Jackson's Oxford Journal*)

JULY 17TH

1888: On this day, Robert Upton was executed for the wilful murder of his wife, Emma. Such events are harrowing at the best of times, but this execution went horribly wrong. After the prisoner had dropped out of sight, 'then followed a sharp thud as the full extent of the rope was reached, and those looking on were horrified to hear a splashing noise proceeding from the pit … the scared look of the executioner was proof that something unusually horrible had happened.' The reporter from *Jackson's Oxford Journal* looked down and saw that Upton's head had been almost severed from his body. 'The walls of the pit were bespattered with blood which was liberally spurting from the culprit's throat and his clothes were quickly saturated and the gory stream ran from the toes of his boots on to the stone floor below', like a tap being turned on full. The executioner had miscalculated the length of rope to be used and as a consequence the drop was far too long. Instead of a clean break to the neck, 'the jugular vein, skin, gullet, windpipe and all the soft parts of the neck were torn through'. (*Jackson's Oxford Journal*)

JULY 18TH

2000: On this day permission for the construction of a controversial Islamic Centre was passed by just one vote. The opinions of the city councillors were so equally divided that the Lord Mayor, Maureen Christian, had to step in and use her vote to break the deadlock. The question was whether or not the planning committee should be asked to reconsider plans for the proposed complex in the Marston Road. The full council had been requested to decide on a possible revaluation following a flood of complaints. As she had been chair of the planning committee that had approved the proposal that April, Councillor Christian felt it right to uphold the decision. A further consideration was the fact that a planning appeal would prove expensive. Objections to the building of the centre included: the fact that its 108ft minaret would ruin the ancient Oxford skyline; its proximity to Magdalen College, which owned the land; and the disturbance caused by the sound of a muezzin's call to prayer. The project's supporters, who included the Prince of Wales, countered the last complaint by pointing out that it would only take place on Fridays and in any case, not everyone appreciated the sound of church bells. (*Oxford Mail*)

JULY 19TH

1821: This, the Coronation morning of George IV, 'was ushered in by the ringing of bells which was continued at intervals throughout the day'. Further 'appropriate demonstrations of loyalty and attachment to the throne' followed. Children from the city's charity schools were given an indigestible meal of meat and plum pudding, the joints being carved by leading tradesmen. Several barrels of beer were distributed in various parts of Oxford and the prisoners in both city and county gaols 'were regaled with a pound of meat and a quart of beer each man'. In the evening, 'a brilliant illumination took place, in which several very elegant transparencies and appropriate devices were exhibited'; the display outside the house of the Mayor, H. Parsons, Esq., was singled out for special praise. The fronts of Magdalen, Brasenose, Wadham, St John's, Pembroke and Trinity College, as well as the Town Hall and Butter Bench, were all 'tastefully decorated'. Later, as it was very calm, candles were placed out in the open, which added greatly to the atmosphere, and some fine sky rockets and a vast assortment of squibs lit up the summer sky, and the evening '(except in the instance of a few windows being broken by the mob) passed off quietly'. (*Jackson's Oxford Journal*)

JULY 20TH

2000: This was the day when it was announced in the *Oxford Mail* that Philip Pullman, one of the city's award-winning authors, was set to become a multi-millionaire as he signed a film deal with New Line. The company, who produced the blockbusting *The Lord of the Rings* trilogy, secured the rights to Mr Pullman's children's fantasy trilogy, *His Dark Materials*, which he began writing in 1995. He and Scholastic, his New York publishers, liked the way in which New Line had treated *The Fellowship of the Ring*, the first part of J.R.R. Tolkien's trilogy. New Line said that they planned to film *Northern Lights*, the first book in *His Dark Materials*, within three years of the contract being signed. Shortly before the signing, the third book in the trilogy, *The Amber Spyglass*, had been the first children's book to win the £30,000 first prize in the prestigious Whitbread Book of the Year competition. The managers of the national theatre were also negotiating the stage rights to all three novels. Philip Pullman, who lives in North Oxford, is a graduate of Exeter College where he read English, a course which he admits he did not particularly enjoy. (*Oxford Mail*)

JULY 21ST

2007: On this day Oxford was in the grip of the worst flooding that it had known for decades. People in West Oxford were forced to leave their houses and the damage from mud and water affected some homes for months. Especially hit were the train services in and out of the city. Following the previous day's torrential rain and floods, First Great Western was advising passengers not to travel unless it was essential, due to overcrowding on the limited services it was running between Oxford and London, and from Didcot to Swindon and Bristol. The company also stated that the Cotswold Line between Oxford and Worcester, via Charlbury and Kingham, would be closed for up to a week while Network Rail carried out repairs to the track in the Evenlode valley. Alternative road transport during the closure was not provided. FGW announced that an emergency timetable would continue the next day. Services on FGW, Chiltern Railways and Virgin CrossCountry via Banbury were not expected to resume for a day or two because the lines in the town were flooded, and no replacement buses were available because of flooding on roads in the Banbury area. (Various sources)

July 22nd

1861: On this day Newsome's Alhambra Circus opened in St Clement's. The main attraction was: 'A TRIBE OF REAL BEDOUIN ARABS from Morocco, 10 in number, the most wonderful Tumblers in the world, and executing the most difficult feats and positions to be imagined.' Their exploits were met with wonder:

It is impossible to describe the feats of these wonderful Artistes, their very movement is replete with daring dexterity, and while they astonish each spectator, they banish fear with their easy nonchalance. Never, since the first Equestrian performance was given, to the present day, have they been equalled and both the Profession and the Public have pronounced them the Ne Plus Ultra of Artists, who have created the greatest excitement at Her Majesty's Theatre, London.

They execute the following most wonderful scenes – Tourbillons Judicus and Somerset a Terra; Tiger leap and terrific Lion Leap; Saults Laitand or Moorish Vaulting; Jeu des Sabres or Sword Play; Scarf Leap; terrific Somersaults over Horses from a Solid Stone; Tour de Fusile; Eastern Rifle Practice; La Pyramide Humane; and a variety of other feats too numerous to mention.

Seating was in private front and side boxes, the pit, promenade and gallery, and prices ranged from a guinea for a box for six to 6d for children.

(*Jackson's Oxford Journal*)

JULY 23RD

2001: On this day in two men were being questioned by police in connection with an attempted burglary at the world-famous Ashmolean Museum. Around noon a few days previously they had tried to make off with exhibits from a glass case in the museum's Farrar Gallery. Using a hammer or axe, they had attempted to smash the case and snatch some very valuable seventeenth-century European gold boxes. Fortunately, the reinforced glass did not give way, and members of the museum staff were alerted by the noise the thieves were making and raised the alarm. Security at the Ashmolean had been improved following the theft of a priceless Cézanne. The would-be robbers ran out of the building and jumped into a stolen Subaru car but were eventually arrested after a high-speed car chase through south-west London some twenty hours later. That day, detectives from Oxford were going up to London to interview the thieves. Other exhibits stolen from the Ashmolean over the years include drawings by Old Masters, Greek and Roman antiquities, and works by Leonardo da Vinci, Turner, the Pre-Raphaelites and Picasso. In 1997 thieves made an attempt on the Anglo-Saxon Alfred Jewel, but they set off the alarm. (Various sources)

JULY 24TH

1663: On this day the body of William Laud, Archbishop of Canterbury, who had been beheaded in 1644, was brought to Oxford for reburial in St John's College chapel. After his execution, he had been put into a lead coffin and buried in the London Church of All Hallows, Barking, but at the college Fellows' request he was returned to Oxford. He had been Chancellor and President of St John's and it was only fit that he should be interred in the college. A good number of the Fellows went out to Wheatley to meet him, according to Anthony à Wood, 'laying in a horse litter on 4 wheels drawn by 4 horses'. About 10 p.m. the cortege returned via High Street and Catte Street to the rear of the college. After a speech by the Vice-President, they laid him 'inclosed in a wooden coffin, in a little vault at the upper end of the chancel between the founder's and archbishop Juxon's. The following day they hung up seven streamers'.

According to one of Oxford's numerous ghost stories, Laud and Charles I, both of whom were beheaded, play a game of bowls with their own heads in the college library, along a floor which no longer exists. (*Life and Times of Anthony à Wood*)

JULY 25TH

1856: On this evening between 2,000 and 3,000 people turned up to listen to a concert given by the band of the Oxfordshire County Militia in Christ Church Meadow. The musicians played from inside the University, which was considered an improvement on previous performances at that venue as everyone could see and hear them, as well as 'enjoy [an] uninterrupted promenade'. From the orderly behaviour and the enthusiastic applause it seemed that this type of entertainment, which was new to Oxford, was much appreciated. The river, too, was full of people in boats of all kinds, eager to hear how the music carried over the water. The band's repertoire included pieces by Bellini, Schubert, Verdi, and a 'Glasgow March' and 'Carnival Schottische', both composed by the bandmaster, M. Viesohn. And, of course, they finished with the National Anthem. The success and popularity of the militia band was proved by the large audience in attendance on the following night. Their popularity was further evidenced by the fact that they were hired to perform at a flower show in Wadham College Gardens, and to perform a benefit trip by river to Nuneham Park later in the same week. (*Jackson's Oxford Journal*)

JULY 26TH

2009: On this evening, three members of one of the country's most famous acting families took to the stage in a production called *For One Night Only* in support of Oxford Playhouse's 70th Anniversary Campaign. They were Prunella Scales, better known as Sybil Fawlty, who was joined by her husband, Timothy West (who has starred in *Brass*, *King Lear*, *Bleak House*, *Edward VII* and many more), and their BAFTA award-winning, film-star son, Samuel West, whose successes include *Howard's End*, *Rupert's Land* and *Iris*. It was by no means the first visit to Oxford for any of them; Timothy has performed in the city a few times, and Prunella has, on several occasions, provided the readings for carol concerts at the Sheldonian Theatre, while Samuel read English Literature at Lady Margaret Hall. Interviewed during rehearsals before the event, Timothy West said that they didn't often get the opportunity to work together as a family but that they were very much looking forward to doing so. The staff of the Playhouse replied that they were very much looking forward to having them there. All the proceeds raised from the evening's performance went towards funding new productions, learning activities and improved facilities at the theatre. (*Oxford Mail*)

July 27th

2000: On this day it was discovered that a postcard which had been posted on 11 May 1960 had finally been delivered. John Crabtree could hardly believe what he found when he looked at his post at his home in Walton Street. The card, which had no stamp, was addressed to a Mr P. Renshaw and had been written by the secretary at the Queen's College, Oxford – less than a mile away from John's home. It requested that Mr Renshaw complete a form and send it back as soon as possible. John Crabtree said that he thought it was rather funny. The post mark showed that the card had been right up to Sheffield. He described it as a record, even for the Royal Mail, and that he had lived in his present home since 1992 and had never heard of Mr Renshaw. A Royal Mail spokesman said:

> Any items without the correct postage will be dealt with locally; there is no special office in Sheffield for that. It is quite likely this has never been in the postal system until now. We refurbish offices regularly so it has not been sitting on a shelf for the last 40 years.

(*Oxford Mail*)

JULY 28TH

1887: On this day the highly acclaimed Golden Jubilee illuminations of the previous Tuesday were repeated, and a huge crowd of visitors came into the city to admire them. Oxford, it was felt by spectators, was in a position to put on a show to rival that of London. The city's range of buildings surpassed that of the capital, those in the High Street in particular being singled out for attention. Magdalen Tower was topped by 'Greek fire', and its 'little gem of a gateway [was] bright with the Royal letters and star'. All Souls, Queen's and University Colleges were also lit up and from there to Carfax there was 'not a house without a token of rejoicing', with St Mary the Virgin 'alone, standing majestic, unrelieved, against the summer sky'. One of the best things about the Jubilee was the way that the importance of the great occasion had been:

> ... impressed upon the imagination of the rising generation. The children of Oxford have been especially cared for. Every spectacle, even the commemoration of a fifty year reign, must be evanescent and ephemeral, but the best way to make its memory endure is to confide it to the happy recollection of the children.

(*Jackson's Oxford Journal*)

JULY 29TH

2008: On this day it was announced that the mound at Oxford Castle had been reopened to the public after undergoing repair work which had cost tens of thousands of pounds. The problem arose in February 2007 after a large part of the Norman structure, erected in the eleventh century, slipped several metres in the direction of New Road due to heavy rain. Since that time, contractors working for the County Council had made good the damage and made sure that it was safe for public access. Emily Hirons, manager of the castle visitor centre, said that it was fabulous to have the mound open again. A lot of work was needed but excavations carried out had brought to light numerous interesting finds and generated public interest. Most significant was the exposure of the foundations of a ten-sided stone tower which had once topped the mound and which had been hidden from view for some three centuries. Groups of eighty people were taken to see the progress of the excavations each weekend and it was surprising to see just how extensive the castle would have been in its heyday. (Various sources)

July 30th

2003: On this day, after nearly fourteen years, details were released of a movement to restore a historic fountain – the Victoria Fountain on The Plain. It was built in 1899 as a memorial to Queen Victoria's Diamond Jubilee at the expense of George Morrell, a member of the brewing family. An appeal launched in 1989 to put it back into proper working order came to nothing, due to an ongoing difference of opinion between the campaigners and the City Council. Morrell's Brewery had agreed to pay half the £8,500 restoration bill and St Hilda's College also offered support. The second attempt was organised by the original coordinator, Erica Steinhauer. In its heyday, it was a public drinking fountain with four jets of water round its edge and troughs for horses on the outside. It had been dry for about sixty years, but its position over a natural spring made reconnection possible. Although its brass lion's head had long disappeared and the wooden roof was rotting, cleaning the stonework and removing graffiti would go a long way to restoring it to its former glory. (*Oxford Mail*)

JULY 31ST

1659: On this day:

A terrible wind hapened in the afternoon, while all people were at divine service. Two or three stones and some rough cast stuff were blown from off the Tower of S. Martin alias Carfax; which falling on the leads of the church, a great alarm and out-cry was among the people in the churche. Some cryed 'murder!' – and at that time a trumpet or trumpets sounding neare the Crosse-inne dore, to call the soldiers together because of the present plott, they in the churche cryed out that the Daye of Judgement was at hand. Some said the Anabaptists and Quakers were come to cut their throats; while the preacher, Mr Georg. Philips, perceiving their errour was ready to burst with laughter in the pulpit to see such mistaken confusion, and several of the people that were in the gallerys hanging at the bottom of them and falling on the heads of people crowding on the floore to get out of the dores.

(*Life and Times of Anthony à Wood*)

AUGUST 1ST

1874: On this day an horrific accident happened to an assistant in the brewery at Magdalen College. That evening, the man, twenty-six-year-old James Comb of Princes Street, who had been employed there for two years, was busy moving a piece of equipment called a skoot in order to allow the sweet wort to run off into a 250-gallon vat. Suddenly he lost his footing, and slipped and fell backwards into the liquid, which was almost at boiling point. Fortunately Mr Wood, the college gardener, was not far away and was able to come to Mr Comb's assistance within a few seconds of his falling into the vat. Wood managed to pull him out and he was taken off in a cab to the Radcliffe Infirmary where the house surgeon treated him on arrival. It was found that he had been badly scalded on the arms, sides, chest, back, face and head, and only the lower parts of his body had escaped injury. When his clothes were taken off, some little bits of his flesh came away with them and he was said to be in a very critical condition. (*Jackson's Oxford Journal*)

AUGUST 2ND

1824: On this day, two poachers, thirty-eight-year-old William James and Henry Pittaway, aged twenty-five, who already had convictions for taking deer, were hanged at Oxford Castle for the murder of gamekeeper James Millin in Wychwood Forest. At 6.45 a.m. they were harangued by the prison chaplain, who used every means in his power to prepare them for what was to come. Then the Holy Sacrament was administered to them 'in a most solemn manner' before they ascended the scaffold at 9 a.m. in front of a large crowd of onlookers, who, it was noted, were remarkably quiet and orderly. William James was the first to have the rope and cap put on him, and while the same was being done to Henry Pittaway, he said in an unconcerned way, 'The rope is tight enough for me already but I suppose it will soon be tighter!' Still protesting their innocence of the murder, they were 'launched into eternity'. When they had hung the usual time, their corpses were delivered to Mr Whitworth, the surgeon of the gaol, by whom they were dissected and anatomised, as was the custom at that time. (*Jackson's Oxford Journal*)

August 3rd

1998: This day saw the outcome of an unsuccessful attempt which had been made to invoke Magna Carta by a cyclist who had been stopped by the police for riding without lights while accompanied by his pet spaniel, Buster Brakespear III. Two police cars were needed to stop the resolute cyclist, who then punched one of the policemen in the face. He informed the bewildered officers, 'I have a right of carriage under the Magna Carta.' There was a struggle which resulted in both men rolling around in nettles by the side of the road. The accused was at last arrested and taken to the police station in Reading, where an exhausted Buster Brakespear III curled up and fell asleep. Finally, the cyclist pleaded guilty on three counts: those of assaulting a police officer, careless cycling, and riding without lights. Oxford magistrates had recourse to another clause in the famous historical document – that of the right of every man to a fair trial – and promptly gaoled him for ninety days. As he was led away after being sentenced, he asked the magistrates to make sure that Buster Brakespear III was properly cared for while his master was unavoidably detained. (*Oxford Mail*)

AUGUST 4TH

1998: On this day it was questioned whether the closure of Harry Ramsden's Oxford restaurant was because the city was too posh for fish and chips. The *Oxford Mail*'s Chris Gray wrote:

> How out of tune it all seems in a sophisticated, cosmopolitan city like Oxford. Palates more used to balsamic vinegar are bluntly offered Sarsons. Drinkers of Earl Grey and lapsang get only Yorkshire tea. Folk who might agonise between demi-glace or chasseur sauce must settle for Bisto onion gravy. And lovers of a thick wedge of crusty wholemeal bread have only sliced white or brown, ready buttered. Without being snobby about it, what happens at Ramsden's is that the clock is turned back 40 years to an era that most of us over 40 will remember with no real pangs of regret – the days when food's only purpose was to fill you up.

But fellow *Oxford Mail* critic George Frew disagreed, 'The cod was a poem, the likes of which I have not tasted since the summers were longer and the policemen all looked older. I left this cathedral of fish and chips whistling a hymn of praise.' In the end, the restaurant's position was blamed. (*Oxford Mail*)

AUGUST 5TH

2000: On this day, the less attractive side of summer in Oxford was shown. This was the inconvenience caused by some 18,000 students, from more than forty language schools, who descend on the city every summer. This invasion provoked numerous complaints from bus users. Passengers at Headington, for example, said that they were being left standing at bus stops when they tried to get to work in the morning as the buses were already packed. This was echoed by travellers all over the city who added that even if they managed to get onto a bus, the journey was uncomfortable due to overcrowding and on many occasions older people were forced to stand. Regular users argued that the language schools should charter their own buses or at least stagger the times of classes. In an attempt to improve matters, an extra service had been introduced and members of the administrative staff at the bus companies were being employed as drivers. Although it was often said that foreign students contribute millions to the local economy, this was little consolation to those who paid out for expensive season tickets, only to watch as students sailed past and they were left behind. (*Oxford Mail*)

AUGUST 6TH

2002: On this day Vicky Jewson, a sixteen-year-old pupil at Wychwood School in North Oxford, had nearly finished ten days of filming for her 30-minute feature *Lillys White* which she was making in the grounds of her home in Hamels Lane, Boars Hill. She said that working on the film, which has a cast of teenagers from St Clare's and d'Overbroeck's colleges, had been an intense experience and had taken six months to plan. Vicky wrote the film script and made some of the storyboards for it, while her fourteen-year-old sister Olivia was in charge of researching and locating the costumes. A bedroom in the family home had been turned into a room from the 1940s with the help of props. The film tells the story of two couples and how they managed to cope when the men went off to war, she explained, and this made it 'quite draining and emotional'. Once the editing was done, Vicky hoped to hold a black-tie premiere in an Oxford cinema in September. After her A-levels, she intended to do a course in film studies. She went on to make *Lady Godiva*, which was released in 2008. (*Oxford Mail*)

AUGUST 7TH

1875: This was the day that the men employed at the Clarendon Press had their annual 'wayzgoose', or works outing, to London. Their excursion train left Oxford just after 6 a.m. and reached the capital three hours later, it being a stopping service. As it was the weekend, some of the men stayed in London, and those who came home the same day arrived back very late. The younger employees, who were not considered old enough to go to London, had their own entertainment held that same afternoon in St Edward's School cricket field in Summertown. Under the supervision of Mr E.P. Hall, the manager of the Bible Side, the boys marched there from Jericho behind the Press band and enjoyed all sorts of games and other amusements for several hours. They made short work of the refreshments provided for them by Mr A. Parker, the landlord of the Clarendon Arms in Walton Street, which had been specifically built two years previously to 'supply the Press with good wholesome beer'. On going back to the Press, an excellent tea awaited them in the schoolroom, after which they were sent off home, after a really lovely day. (*Jackson's Oxford Journal*)

AUGUST 8TH

2000: On this day, England and Arsenal star Martin Keown expressed his shock and disgust at learning that vandals had carried out a series of attacks on the grave of a fan, Nigel Jennings. The footballer launched a blistering attack on the hooligans who had desecrated the grave of the twenty-two-year-old who had died of leukaemia. Martin had visited Nigel at his home in Rose Hill when he was seriously ill in hospital and Arsenal FC sent him a signed shirt as a present when his own had been stolen while he was in hospital. The vandals destroyed floral arrangements on the grave in Iffley Cemetery, left a footstep on the soil of the grave while it was still fresh and went off with vases and pots. Vases and wreaths on Nigel's grandparents' graves were also violated. Wheatley resident Martin called the attacks sickening and he was appalled and sorry for Nigel's family. He said that graveyards were places where people could come to grieve and not be exposed to this sort of behaviour. He thought that the culprits of these mindless attacks sounded like youngsters who didn't realise what effect their actions would have on those concerned. (*Oxford Mail*)

AUGUST 9TH

1986: Early this morning in 1986, on the 41st anniversary of the dropping of the atom bomb, Headington's most (in)famous landmark arrived on the scene. It looked as if a light aircraft had crash-landed on the roof of a terraced house. In reality, it was the body of a 25ft-long fibreglass shark positioned through the roof of No. 2 New High Street, which dates from the 1860s. This creation, which weighs 4cwt and is called 'Untitled 1986', is the work of the sculptor John Buckley. The owner of both house and shark is American Bill Heine, the owner of two local cinemas. The City Council, supported by many (but by no means all) of the local residents, tried to force Heine to remove the shark, on both safety and aesthetic grounds. On inspection it was declared safe, at which the council offered to rehouse the fish at a swimming pool or other suitable venue.

In 1990, Heine was refused retrospective planning permission so he successfully appealed to the Secretary of State for the Environment, Michael Heseltine. For a time scores of visitors were attracted to the sight which, for a while, rivalled an Oxford college for its photographic potential. (Various sources)

AUGUST 10TH

2008: This was the day that Oxford's forty-first Blue Plaque was unveiled. It commemorates William Buckland (1784–1856), a Fellow of Corpus Christi College and Canon of Christ Church Cathedral. The plaque is at his country home, the Old Rectory at Islip. Buckland came to the public's notice in 1824 with his study of the fossilised Great Lizard of Stonesfield in Yorkshire, later given the title Megalosaurus. Principally a geologist, Buckland was interested in all branches of science and transformed its teaching at Oxford, earning him the Royal Society's most prestigious award, the Copley Medal. His collections survive and are housed in the University Museum of Natural History; its director, Professor Jim Kennedy, said that they were delighted to be associated with the Blue Plaque. Brilliant scholar that he was, Buckland was also known for his showmanship and eccentric behaviour, in particular the fact that he was eager to eat anything. He is supposed to have remarked that the only thing that tasted worse than mole was bluebottles, and is credited with gobbling down the heart of a French king while dining at Nuneham Courtenay. His pet bear, Tiglath Pileser, used to roam happily round Islip searching for sweets. (Various sources)

August 11th

1998: On this very hot day, protestors against the plans to widen Park End Street climbed out onto the roof of the Sheldonian Theatre in order to publicise their opposition. The five protestors, who had paid their entrance fee and come into the Wren building like ordinary visitors, hung two banners round its parapet. One called 'Dave', who handed out leaflets to passers-by in Broad Street, said that it had been very easy to get onto the roof by climbing out of a cupola window. The Sheldonian was chosen because of its high profile. The protestors were occupying the disused Grade II-listed London, Midland and Scottish (LMS) railway building in Park End Street because they objected to it being moved to a railway centre in Quainton, Buckinghamshire so that the road could be widened. Members of staff at the Sheldonian were unaware of the trespassers' activities until informed by tourists in the cupola. After several hours they left the roof of their own accord due to the heat and lack of food and drink. Not long afterwards, the three-month occupation of the LMS building came to a close when the University obtained a possession order and evicted the squatters. (Various sources)

AUGUST 12TH

2002: On this day, the staff of an Oxford post office chased a man after he stole £700 worth of phone cards. At about 6.15 p.m. he had stretched over the counter at the office in Courtland Road, Rose Hill, and snatched the cards which were in a container fixed to the desk. Then he fled from the shop, with three of the employees in hot pursuit. He jumped into a red F-registration Volkswagen in which three men were waiting for him. The manager of the post office, Bharat Dalal, said that the car drove off along the wrong side of the road and nearly hit a Royal Mail van as it sped away towards the A34. He stated that none of the staff were physically hurt but such an incident taking place was unnerving. The thief was described as black, clean-shaven, with short hair and was 6ft 3in in height, and wearing a cap. A spokesman from Thames Valley Police said that it would have been a busy time of day, but they did have a good description of the thief. He appealed for any witnesses to the robbery to come forward. (*Oxford Mail*)

AUGUST 13TH

1998: On this day the Oxford University Press published its New Oxford Dictionary of English, the first to be compiled from scratch for more than seventy years. It had been produced over six years at the press' offices in Great Clarendon Street. This epic task meant redefining every word in the English language and giving its current meaning. In excess of 2,000 new words were included. There are also substitutes for old-established words considered 'sexist and patronising' so that 'profoundly deaf' should be used in place of 'deaf mute', 'disabled person' instead of 'cripple' and 'learning difficulties' instead of 'mentally handicapped'. The use of black and white or 'person of colour' were, however, still acceptable. The company's marketing director, David Swarbrick, told the *Oxford Mail*: 'We included this because it was the kind of information that people wanted to know. We get many inquiries about it and it's one of the most complicated areas of usage. What we try to do is analyse current usage as it is today.' Words and definitions had been compiled from novels, reference books, magazines, newspapers and transcripts of the spoken language. The new edition contains some 350,000 words but fewer meanings for individual words are given than in earlier dictionaries. (*Oxford Mail*)

AUGUST 14TH

2000: On this day it came to light that those living in Rose Hill were facing the same issue which had arisen when the notorious Cutteslowe Walls had divided private from local authority housing in North Oxford from 1934–59. Those living on the estate complained that they were being refused access to the adjacent more up-market Iffley because the University had locked them out. People couldn't get to Iffley Church, visit the churchyard, go shopping or stroll by the river. For years they had walked to Iffley village by going through a gate at Court Place Gardens, a block of student accommodation, but this had been locked, adding about 15 minutes to the journey. This reminded those whose way was barred of the Cutteslowe Walls, so the name Brandenburg Gate was suggested. Residents had been campaigning for three years to have the gate opened for them, and now intended to apply for it to be designated as a public right of way. It was claimed that the University had not submitted detailed plans for Rose Hill residents to object to when it had sought planning permission for the block. Nobody from the University was available to comment. (*Oxford Mail*)

August 15th

1872: On this day the foundation stone was laid for a new church in New Inn Hall Street by the Bishop of Oxford. It was a new building for the ancient parish of St Peter-le-Bailey, whose Georgian church was about to be demolished, and was paid for mainly by subscription. The new building, put up some 200 yards away, adjoining New Inn Hall itself, was to have a nave, a chancel, two aisles, a square tower and an octagonal turret; it was to be built in the Decorated style. It was designed by architect Basil Champneys and built by a local firm, Honour & Castle. As well as stonework from the older church, as much furniture and fittings as possible was transferred to the new one. After 'some suitable prayers and a psalm' were read, 'the Bishop proceeded to lay the foundation-stone with a silver trowel and handsomely-polished mallet with which he had been furnished'. After a further prayer the choir sang the hymn beginning 'This stone to Thee in faith we lay'. Following the benediction, a collection in aid of the building fund was made, which raised a total of £29 9s 4½d. 'The proceedings then terminated.' (*Jackson's Oxford Journal*)

AUGUST 16TH

2001: By this day in 2001, businesses in the Oxford area were experiencing a critical shortage of workers as the BMW car factory enlarged their workforce in order to cope with the worldwide demand for the new Mini. The Cowley factory was engaging 1,800 temporary staff in order to construct 30,000 cars by the end of that year and 100,000 the following one. Among the positions to be filled were production supervisors, electrical engineers, panel beaters, welders and paint sprayers. By this time some 600 vacancies were still to be filled. This impacted on other firms which were already experiencing a staff shortage because the high cost of living in Oxfordshire meant that many people could not afford to settle there. Particularly vulnerable were the Oxford Bus Company, Stagecoach buses and local taxi companies, all of which were having difficulty recruiting new drivers and keeping existing ones because the pay offered at BMW was so much better. Despite the fact that bus drivers in Oxford were being paid some of the country's highest wage rates (for bus drivers), companies had been forced to bring in people from Wales, Scotland and even France. Managers and engineers were volunteering to drive in an attempt to improve the situation and avoid turning away business. (*Oxford Mail*)

AUGUST 17TH

1892: On this day, the Mayor and several of his colleagues on the City Council, took part in the ancient ceremony of 'walking the franchise', a version of beating the bounds or boundaries. As most of Oxford's boundaries are on, or near, water, it was generally agreed by spectators that 'the spectacle of a Mayor and his officials getting a good ducking in the river is worth walking a mile or two to see'. An even better joke was watching them wring the water and scrape the mud from their robes, but when the mace, 'the emblem of authority and dignity', had to be fished up from the riverbed, the ceremony became ridiculous. At Wolvercote, the vicar, together with several parishioners, 'endeavoured to prevent the passage of the beaters, and a conflict at one time seemed likely'. As the weather was fine, 'a very enjoyable day was spent by those who did not take an involuntary bath or get scarified by barbed wire'. However, all was not joy as 'a sad event happened in the drowning of a man, unconnected with the civic party, who by some means fell from a punt as the party was passing Marston Ferry'. (*Jackson's Oxford Journal*)

AUGUST 18TH

2001: On this day it was reported that Oxford United had seating problems despite the fact they had just moved into their brand new state-of-the-art Kassam Stadium. Officials had to remedy the fact that more than 100 seats had restricted views of the pitch, and worse still, that some supporters who turned up found that their seats didn't exist. The stadium, which cost £15 million, was supposed to have a 100 per cent unobstructed view from each of its 125,000 seats, but this was obviously not the case. Thick metal safety barriers over the stairway entrances in the South Stand meant that dozens had restricted views of what was happening on the pitch. United's secretary, Mick Brown, said that the club was very disappointed by this defect and that it had never crossed their minds even after they had studied all the plans very carefully. The fault meant that not all fans could be moved to better seats, and although season tickets holders were relocated whenever possible, sometimes they were not happy with their new seats. It had proved necessary to check out if seats actually did exist before money for them changed hands. The situation was one which could not be allowed to continue. (*Oxford Mail*)

AUGUST 19TH

2000: On this day one of Oxford's oldest colleges, Hertford College in Catte Street, which was founded as Hart Hall by Elias de Hertford in the late thirteenth century, achieved a very modern first. Hertford had just installed telephone and data points in all student rooms, becoming the first of the Oxford colleges to provide this level of access to the Internet. Greg Jennings, the college's IT manager, said that previously they had installed data points in student rooms on an 'on demand' basis. During the 1998/9 academic year, however, during the first week of term alone, forty-seven students requested that an Internet access point be installed in their room, and the previous year 30 per cent of Oxford undergraduates owned their own computers. At Hertford at 40 per cent, the number was above the University average. As an ever-increasing amount of teaching and research material was being made available on-line, with the Internet a key research tool, Mr Jennings thought that it was extremely important that students could access it from their rooms. Leading-edge cabling was installed throughout the college site by Molex Premise Networks, with 290 data points and 230 telephone points. (*Oxford Mail*)

AUGUST 20TH

2004: On this day, new figures showed a rise of 17 per cent in people using the River Thames that year compared with the previous year. Boat-hire businesses reported a booming trade and the Environment Agency stated that boat licence figures showed 1,273 motorised boats on the river in the first six months of the year, an increase of 189. According to numbers submitted by lock-keepers, the number of small crafts, such as rowing boats and canoes, increased by 4 per cent from 4,028 to 4,202. A spokesperson from the Environment Agency, which is responsible for the Thames in Oxfordshire, said that it was expecting the increase to continue. It had therefore upgraded its website in order to suggest and give particulars of days out and places to visit along the Thames, as the river seemed to be where everyone wanted to be. She added, 'Outside London, the rural river has been buzzing with a mini boating renaissance.' The reason for this popularity was difficult to explain but it was expected to continue and even increase. An Oxford institution since 1858, Salter's Steamers, based at Folly Bridge, agreed that both private hire and scheduled trips to Iffley Lock and Abingdon had increased. (*Oxford Mail*)

AUGUST 21ST

1998: On this day a story unfolded which was like something from a science fiction film. Early one morning, Pete Dalton of Blackbird Leys Road got up to go to the toilet and was greeted by the sound of buzzing when he opened the bedroom door. He saw wasps swarming round the loft hatch. Pete had a phobia of wasps because he had been badly stung as a baby. He shut the bedroom door and had to work out what he could do. He decided that to escape the wasps he could either try to get downstairs or go out of the bedroom window, but as it was high up he didn't fancy doing this. He didn't fancy going down past the wasps either. Fortunately he then heard a neighbour letting her dogs out, and shouted to her for help; she rang the emergency services. The firemen arrived with a ladder and Pete was able to climb out of the bedroom window. He said that he felt a bit silly but they assured him that this was the sensible thing to do to get away from the swarm of scary wasps. After he had made his getaway, council environmental health officers came to his house and removed the invaders. (*Oxford Mail*)

AUGUST 22ND

1998: The lives of families in streets off the Cowley Road were being made a misery by a plague of giant rats. Residents had virtually become prisoners in their own homes and were scared that the invaders might attack small children or pets. One resident said that they were at their wits' end with worry and that the area was in chaos. The rats were described as the biggest they had ever seen. Where they had come from was a mystery, but one lady said that she had spotted them emerging from drains in the road. 'A whole gang of them' came out at night and walked along the Cowley Road. Another said that they had contacted the environmental health department, who had visited a week previously, but nothing had happened since. A city councillor agreed that rats were a growing problem and said the council would have to investigate. He said that Thames Water might be expected to pay part of the costs involved in dealing with the infestation if the rats were in fact coming from the sewers. However, a spokesperson for Thames Water stated that this was very unlikely as modern sewers were not attractive breeding places for rodents. (*Oxford Mail*)

AUGUST 23RD

1873: On this day the results of that year's Oxford Local Examinations were announced. It came as a surprise that the candidate who headed the list in the first division obtained first classes in English, Music and Languages (Latin, Greek, French and German). A greater surprise was that this exceptionally gifted person was female. Miss Annie Rogers, the first girl to appear in the first-class list, was the daughter of the Tooke Professor of Political Economy at King's College, London. However, this success was not without its problems, as certain college Exhibitions (a sort of scholarship) were offered by Balliol and Worcester Colleges to successful candidates in the Oxford Local Examinations. The question was raised concerning admission of women to University residence, examinations and degrees. As the candidates were listed only by their initials and not by their full names, it was not at first apparent that Annie Rogers was in fact a girl, was she was awarded an Exhibition on the strength of her results, only to have it abruptly withdrawn when her gender was realised. Eventually she became a Fellow of St Hugh's College, and a pioneer of women's higher education. (*Jackson's Oxford Journal*)

AUGUST 24TH

1753: John Billingsgate, condemned to have his tongue cut out for his foul mouth, had his sentence carried out on this day. *Jackson's Oxford Journal* relates how:

> He behav'd thro' the whole Affair with great Decency and did not swear above a Dozen Times from his House to the Foot of the Scaffold; when he came upon it, he told the Crowd he would make the last use of his Tongue in confessing the many Sins it had been guilty of. As he was beginning to rave, the Executioner told him his Time was elapsed and immediately performed his Business. Upon taking out the Tongue it blistered the hand that held it; and at several yards distance toasted Cheese like a Salamander Great Quantities of Water were then thrown upon it, but it was so much inflamed that it was found impossible to quench it – Some Dogs that came within its Influence were seized with a sudden Fit of Barking and Snarling, but what was odd was, at the same Time they lost the power of Biting. The Tongue was at last purchased by a famous Logician who touches the Lips of those Pupils with it who want the genuine Spirit of Altercation.

(*Jackson's Oxford Journal*)

AUGUST 25TH

1998: On this day, a German couple's dream honeymoon turned into a nightmare when a thief made off with their caravan, which had a sticker with a heart reading 'Just Married' in one of the windows. Their troubles began when the newly-weds stopped off at the newly opened M40 services between Wheatley and Oxford. While they were inside, a dark-blue car drew up and parked next to their VW Golf which was towing the blue-and-white caravan. The cheeky thief hitched his own VW Passat car to their caravan and when the bride attempted to stop him escaping, he sprayed gas into her face. In the meantime, the German man climbed onto the tow-bar but was carried off as the thief drove away with their honeymoon home. When the driver was forced to slow down on the A418, the man managed to jump clear, only to have his legs injured when he was knocked over as the thief accelerated away once more. Although the Golf was later found abandoned in Oxford behind a row of shops in Blackbird Leys Road, Blackbird Leys, the police had not been able to find the caravan by the time the crime was reported in the *Oxford Mail*. (*Oxford Mail*)

AUGUST 26TH

1856: On this day, during restoration work at Christ Church Cathedral, a stone coffin was discovered between the second and third columns on the north side of the choir, almost level with the ground, and probably had at one time formed part of the paving. Its lid was decorated with rich carving which included a long cross and other decoration. When the lid was removed, it was estimated that the coffin dated from the twelfth or thirteenth century although all that was left of the contents had decomposed, being only a piece of a shoe, the remains of burial clothes, one bone, but no skull. Also in the coffin were a pewter chalice and paten, which gave rise to the belief that the deceased was a high-ranking churchman whose status allowed him to be buried in such a prominent position in the cathedral. The coffin had been made from a single block of stone with a small circular cavity for the head. This was the second stone coffin which had been found, the first one being in a corresponding position on the south side of the choir, which had been left *in situ*. The identity of neither occupant is known. (*Jackson's Oxford Journal*)

August 27th

1998: The wait for the result of any examination is always very stressful, especially for A-level grades, which can make the difference of a lifetime. In 1998, four students from Magdalen College School discovered just how stressful it could be when they were marked down after a mistake by an examination board meant that their grades were lower than they merited. This happened in the German A-levels; one pupil dropped two grades and another was turned down by his first choice of university because of his unexpectedly poor results. Fortunately, it was later discovered that the board, the Oxford and Cambridge Examinations and Assessment Council, had failed to add the marks given for the oral part of the examination to the students' overall totals. In all, up to 200 pupils throughout the country were affected. The Master of Magdalen College School, Andrew Halls, commented that the boys were upset, one especially so because he had been told he should have obtained an A and got a B instead. Mr Halls contacted Cambridge, who finally admitted the miscalculation, and the boys were later given their correct grades and were able to make plans for their futures. (*Oxford Mail*)

AUGUST 28TH

2009: On this evening the citizens of Oxford were given the chance to hear how well-loved comedian Spike Milligan had assisted in the overthrow of Adolph Hitler and his regime. Despite the fact that at that date the former Goon had been dead more than seven years, the performance was more or less in his own words as *Adolph Hitler: My Part in his Downfall* had been written by Spike himself and adapted for the stage by Ben Power and Tim Carroll. As Spike explains, it all started when, 'A man called Chamberlain, who did Prime Minister impressions, spoke on the wireless; he said, "As from eleven o'clock we are at war with Germany". (I loved the "we"). "War?" said Mother. "It must be something we said," said Father.' To quote the Oxford Playhouse's publicity, 'Spike Milligan's celebrated war memoirs are brought to anarchic life in this hilarious new stage adaptation. This epic Everyman's odyssey through the Second World War, with a cast of extraordinary characters, charts Gunner Milligan's progress from joining the Royal Artillery through the North African and Italian campaigns. And with Spike's sense of lunacy, anything can happen along the way!' They also issued a warning: 'Contains barrack room humour.' (*Oxford Mail*)

August 29th

1636: On this day the King, Charles I, Queen Henrietta Maria, Prince Rupert and many of the nobility came to Oxford from Woodstock, where they had been staying at the old royal manor house which was later held by Parliamentary troops and eventually demolished to make way for Blenheim Palace. Four-year-old Anthony à Wood, who was carried by a servant, went along with his father and mother to the house of a Canon of Christ Church. In the garden was a mound from where they could get a good view into St Aldates, then called Fish Street, and they saw the King and Queen and their entourage come down St Aldates and enter the great quadrangle at Christ Church. This was the first time that the young Anthony had seen royalty and their 'glorious traine' and it made so great an impression on him that he used often to talk about it when he grew up. Members of the royal family returned to Oxford on several occasions during Wood's lifetime, notably during the Civil War and when there was plague in London, and over the years he would lose this sense of wonder and develop quite a jaundiced view of courtiers. (*Life and Times of Anthony à Wood*)

AUGUST 30TH

1871: On this day *Jackson's Oxford Journal* carried an account of a suicide which was later reported in the prestigious *Manchester Times* of 4 September. A junior member of the University, Mr Francis John Cheshire Walker, a commoner of Balliol College, was found dead in his room on Monday morning. It appeared that he had shot himself through the heart with a revolver and there had been no accident or foul play involved. Despite the fact that suicides were by no means uncommon in both the town and the University, as can be seen by looking through the newspapers of the time, this one caused a great deal of excitement in the college and beyond, probably because no explanation or cause for self-destruction could be suggested. Francis Walker was known to have been in Lord Elgin's rooms up till midnight on the night he died. This Lord Elgin was Victor Alexander Bruce, 9th Earl of Elgin, 13th Earl of Kincardine, who was to serve as Viceroy of India from 1894 to 1899. An inquest was held on the body of Francis Walker during the course of that day and a verdict of 'temporary insanity' was returned. (*Jackson's Oxford Journal*)

AUGUST 31ST

1556: This is the day on which Queen Elizabeth I arrived in Oxford for an eagerly awaited visit. The Chancellor and the Doctors, in their robes, went out to welcome her, and at the East Gate she was received by the Mayor and aldermen who gave her a gilt cup and £40 in gold. The Queen impressed the academics by replying to an address in Greek in the same language. She heard a Te Deum in the University Church before settling into her lodgings at Christ Church. The following morning, however, she was not well enough to attend the morning service, although she did so in the afternoon. In the evening a Latin play was staged and the following days were spent listening to disputes, attending various forms of lighter entertainment, and visiting several colleges where she spent time chatting with the students. One of the Queen's favourite events was a performance of the play *Palamon and Arcite*, a tragicomedy specially written for the visit by Richard Edwards, and acted by members of the University. She also praised *Prague*, a morality play written by Dr James Calfhill, a Canon of Christ Church. (Various sources)

September 1st

1644: On this Sunday, about 150 Parliamentarian troops arrived in Wolvercote and rushed into the church, pistols drawn, while the preacher was in the middle of his sermon. They would have dragged him off by force, had not a gentleman in the congregation stood up to them, despite the fact that only two other men were wearing swords. Several parishioners joined him, locking the door against back-up from the soldiers outside, and one of them, armed only with a pair of white gloves, succeeded in bringing two of the soldiers to their knees begging for mercy; the only time, says the reporter, that they had ever knelt in a church. At last the rebels were overpowered and fled, taking with them the Duke of York's dwarf, who 'had his strength been equal to his courage, had been much too strong for any one of them'. They then ran across the field to Lord Lovelace's mansion at Water Eaton, where they expected to take him unawares and kidnap him. As he was absent, they bundled his wife into a coach and drove her the 7 miles to Middleton Stoney, where they turned her out and left her stranded. (*Life and Times of Anthony à Wood*)

September 2nd

1998: A half-clothed man, suspected of shoplifting, was chased through central Oxford on this day. The man was pursued along Market Street, into Turl Street, then Broad Street and into New College Lane, where he was captured. A witness told the *Oxford Mail* that 'Stuff was strewn all over the road – including a frozen chicken and various clothes, jeans and that sort of thing.' He described the chase as 'quite dramatic', and said: 'At first I wondered what the clothes and frozen chicken were doing on the road. All the tourists were looking at it. The butcher came and got the chicken back out of the road. I didn't know what was going on until I got round the corner and neither did the tourists. Some tourists had gone to pick up the chicken but had been stopped by the butcher. At last the would-be shoplifter was pinned down by two men thought to be store-detectives, in New College Lane. The runaway did not struggle much but was lying face-down with a man sitting on him.' A spokesman for Oxford police stated that an alleged shoplifter was being questioned at the police station in St Aldates. (*Oxford Mail*)

September 3rd

2002: A man who once worked as a cleaner at an Oxford college was sentenced to two years in prison for theft on this day. The forty-two-year-old man, said to be of no fixed address, had stolen a ring which once belonged to Oscar Wilde and two medals for rowing, worth a total of £37,000 from Magdalen College when he was employed there. He had already admitted one count of burglary at a previous court hearing. Oxford Crown Court was told that the items which had been stolen were irreplaceable and could not be recovered as the accused had sold them to a scrap dealer for only £150. The prosecution described how the man had used his knowledge of the premises to gain access through a skylight in the early hours of 2 May. After entering the college bar and drinking whisky, he moved on to the Old Library where he smashed a display cabinet and helped himself to an 18-carat gold friendship ring given by Wilde and his friend Reginald Harding to William Ward. Forensic experts found traces of blood belonging to the accused at the scene. The defence claimed that his intention had been to find evidence that his wife, the college's head gardener, was having an affair. (*Oxford Mail*)

SEPTEMBER 4TH

1885: On this day, *Jackson's Oxford Journal* contained this advertisement:

Cholera Safeguards – the Sanitary Importance of Washing at Home. This can be done with ease and economy and the clothes made beautiful, sweet and wholesome, lily-white and fresh as sea breezes by using Hudson's Extract of Soap, avoiding all risk of contagion with infected clothes at Laundries, or where the washing is put out. No rotting or fraying of the clothes by bleaching chemicals. No hard rubbing, scrubbing, brushing or straining. The Dirt slips away and wear and tear, labour and fuel are saved. Hudson's Extract of Soap is a pure, Dry Soap in dry powder, rapidly soluble, lathers freely, softens water. A perfect Hard-water Soap, a Cold-water Soap, Soft-water Soap, a Hot-water Soap Unrivalled as a purifying agent Sold everywhere in packet, 1d and upwards.

(Jackson's Oxford Journal)

SEPTEMBER 5TH

1666: Anthony à Wood's impression of the Great Fire of London:

The Great Fire of London broke out on 2 September and caused clouds of smoke to be blown through a gap in the Chiltern Hills as far as Oxford. The sunshine was darkened and at night the moon was covered by clouds of smoke and took on a reddish appearance. Wood writes of the citizens that 'every one being soe suspicious that noe sorry fellow or woman could pass but they examined him, noe gun or squib could goe off but they thought it was the fatal blow. On this fast day, three days afterwards, a butcher was driving some oxen over the cross-roads at Carfax. As he passed under the window of St Martin's church, he called out to the beasts 'Hi-up! Hi-up!' The members of the congregation were so on edge that some of them heard the cry as 'Fire! Fire!' and ran out of the church, closely followed by the rest of the worshippers 'with the semblance of death in their faces', some saying that [they] could smell smoke, others swore that it was pitch, and none of them could be persuaded that they had made such a mistake for a very long time afterwards.

(*Life and Times of Anthony à Wood*)

September 6th

2007: On this day, the University of Oxford was to follow the example set by Paris and introduce a bicycle loan project in order to lessen the city's worsening pollution and traffic jams. The pilot scheme was to be introduced that winter for University employees, who would be offered a free 'pick up and pedal' bicycle service. Oxford Brookes University was expected to take part in the trial also. It would work by setting up cycle stations in Headington and the city centre, where academics and other staff would be able to collect and drop off bikes. It was hoped that the scheme would be extended, first to include students and then to all city residents, with up to 2,000 bikes available for hire and state-of-the-art stations positioned all over the city to make up what would amount to a new type of public transport system. Oxford University had already been in discussion with the City Council and the bus companies regarding the viability of a city-wide scheme; it hoped to put bike-hire points at the City Park-and-Ride. Ten years before, a similar street-based cycle loan project in Cambridge had ended in tears after hundreds of bikes were stolen. (*Oxford Mail*)

September 7th

2005: It was reported on this day that an Oxford psychologist had come up with a new idea for reducing the number of road accidents. Dr Charles Spence of Somerville College had carried out experiments which showed that traffic accidents could be reduced significantly if the driver was warned of any possible dangers by a vibrating seat or steering wheel. This would involve the use of sensors which would show if a car is too close to another vehicle. Dr Spence, a lecturer in Experimental Psychology, said, 'It automatically grabs your attention; if something vibrates on your belly you know it's out there in front. If it's the back, you know it's behind you.' He explained that studies had been carried out in the lab and with simulators, with information about looking in front and perhaps braking when the car in front brakes, or accelerating when the one behind comes too close. Tests showed that up to 15 per cent of accidents which involved a car hitting the one in front could be avoided by 'feely' cars. Ideally, a combination of sound and touch warnings would be used. Citröen had already put Dr Spence's suggestions into practice in its C4 model, which has a vibrating seat cushion to wake up drivers wandering across motorway lanes. (*Oxford Mail*)

SEPTEMBER 8TH

1874: This was one of the two days of the annual St Giles's Fair. This year the main attraction was Edmonds's (formerly Wombwell's) Menagerie which filled up the far end of the fair, by St Giles' Church. Among the smaller attractions were a collection of waxworks, models moved by water power, marionettes, peep shows, roundabouts, flying horses and swings. There was a range of curiosity and freak shows, with two fat women and what was claimed to be the champion bulldog of England. Play-goers were catered for by excerpts from Shakespeare tragedies which were rattled through in 20 minutes, murders, music and the odd dance or two. There was only one cheap-jack, who was comparatively quiet as he did not have to shout down any opposition. The stalls included the usual one with Bibles and related literature, and the two largest displays belonged to Mr Harris's fancy goods and Mr Arnatt's confectionary. Fruit sellers moved among the crowds and the Punch and Judy show was as popular as ever with young and old alike. One less pleasant aspect was the number of novelty squirting devices which, when pressed, shot streams of liquid onto people's necks, eyes and ears. (*Jackson's Oxford Journal*)

SEPTEMBER 9TH

1850: The following commentary was written about the successful St Giles's Fair of 1850:

Our annual pleasure fair took place on Monday and Tuesday last and in consequence of the fineness of the weather and the harvest being in a great measure completed, the influx of holiday folks into Oxford was unusually large; the appearance of St Giles' on the Sunday previous, gave signs of a larger number than usual of exhibitions and stalls and the approaches to this city, especially on the Summer Town roads, were crowded with caravans and vehicles of various descriptions. No sooner had the clock struck twelve that night, than the whole poured into St Giles' and the proprietors of the various exhibitions and stalls took possession of the spots they had previously selected and commenced operations. Owing to the excellent arrangements made by both the City and University authorities, and the large number of police supplied by both bodies, there was an entire absence of that disorder, rioting and confusion which has usually characterised the commencement of the fair. We understand that in future no exhibition, vehicle or stall will be allowed to take up its position in St Giles' before four o'clock on Monday morning, so the confusion arising from so many pouring in on Sunday night as at present will be obviated to the great comfort of the inhabitants in that part of the town.

(Jackson's Oxford Journal)

SEPTEMBER 10TH

1822: At this St Giles's Fair, one of the highlights was the:

MECHANICAL THEATRE
During St Giles's Fair, Oxford
MR SEWARD respectfully informs the Ladies and Gentlemen
of Oxford and its vicinity that on MONDAY and TUESDAY
NEXT he intends exhibiting his wonderful
AUTOMATON and MECHANICAL FIGURES

From New Sadler's Wells, Cheltenham, Bath, Bristol &c
A commodious Theatre will be fitted up opposite the Lamb Inn,
St Giles', where every attention will be paid to the comfort and
convenience of those who will honour him with their company.
The Performance will consist of the astonishing AUTOMATON
ROPE-DANCING FIGURE actuated by Clock-work Machinery
contained in the trunk of the body, and the sole invention of
Mr Seward; a most eccentric ITALIAN SCARAMOUCH; a
wonderful LITTLE POLANDER, who exhibits various feats with
a Spontoon; also a most correct likeness of MOTHER SHIPTON
who will, very naturally, take a candle, light her pipe, and smoke it,
to the utter astonishment of her beholders. Another truly wonderful
Figure will be shown, called the ENCHANTED TURK who will,
without any assistance, metamorphose himself into six different
Figures, namely the arms will become figures, the legs the same, the
head also, and lastly the body will transform itself into a dwarf; this
Figure alone is well worthy of the notice of the curious.
Admission – Front Seats 2s – Second seats 1s – Gallery 6d.
(*Jackson's Oxford Journal*)

SEPTEMBER 11TH

2004: On this day it was revealed that the delinquents who had been pushing over gravestones in the churchyard at St Lawrence's parish church, South Hinksey, were none other than officers from the Vale of White Horse District Council. Relatives of those whose graves had received this treatment branded them vandals. About forty-five stones were knocked over during a visit as the council officers said that they were in a dangerous condition and likely to fall over if pushed. Visitors to the graves were shocked and distressed to discover that their loved ones' memorials were lying flat on the ground. One lady whose eyesight was bad following an eye operation said that she had not seen the signs which the council had displayed in the churchyard informing the public that safety checks were to be made on the gravestones. As there had been cases of people injured and even killed by stones falling on them, the council had to carry out checks. The lady tended eleven graves of family members, including her parents and grandparents, and making enquiries the lady learnt that it would cost £150 plus VAT per stone to have them put back up safely. (*Oxford Mail*)

SEPTEMBER 12TH

2005: On this day, Jeremy Clarkson, the controversial presenter of BBC *Top Gear*, arrived in Oxford to receive an honorary doctorate from Oxford Brookes University. The decision to award Clarkson the degree had been greeted with considerable opposition mainly because of the presenter's irresponsible attitude towards environmental issues. A petition of some 2,700 signatures against the award had been collected. Clarkson was met by a peaceful demonstration of about twenty protestors who were registering their objections in person. After the ceremony was over, however, and a photocall was in progress, one campaigner launched a banana meringue pie in the face of the newly made doctor. Dee Lock, one of the student activists involved, said that, 'The problem with Mr Clarkson is that he's a bit of a joke and a bit of a buffoon. The problem with awarding his honorary degree is that Brookes is proud of its environmental and inclusivity programmes and Clarkson is the antithesis to this.' She described the demonstration as good-natured and said of the missile: 'It was all organic and free range and fair trade I'm told.' Prior to the appearance of the pie, a spokeswoman for Oxford Brookes University stated that 'Mr Clarkson seemed very relaxed.' (Various sources)

SEPTEMBER 13TH

2004: This was the day that Oxford's new university, Oxford Brookes in Headington, received praise from the oldest university in the English-speaking world. The Vice-Chancellor of the University of Oxford, Professor Sir Colin Lucas, paid tribute to the 'warm collaboration' between the two academic institutions on the occasion of his being awarded an honorary degree of Doctor of the University (Hon D Univ) by Oxford Brookes. Sir Colin, who had been Vice-Chancellor since 1997, said, 'To receive this award is a double pleasure for me because it is a degree offered to me by Oxford Brookes, my own sister university.' He went on to say that Oxford now had two excellent universities, each with its individual policies. Dr David Langford, Dean of the Westminster Institute of Education at Oxford Brookes University, said of Sir Colin: 'As leader of one of the world's oldest and most distinguished universities he has held out a firm and unwavering hand of friendship to Oxford Brookes University,' a sentiment echoed by Brookes's own Vice-Chancellor, Professor Graham Upton, who pointed out that other new universities had experienced less cordial relationships with their longer-established neighbours. One of Sir Colin's fellow honorands was naturalist, writer and broadcaster David Bellamy. (*Oxford Mail*)

September 14th

1727: Stephen Fletcher died on this day. His life was described by Thomas Hearne in his diary.:

On Thursday last St Mary's Great Bell rang out in the evening as did some other bells for Mr Stephen Fletcher of the said Parish of St Marie's in Oxford, Bookseller, who died ... of a violent feaver aged forty-seven, being born anno 1680. He had lived for some time at London, coming down however sometimes to Oxford where his wife and five children lived in his shop ... He was born in Salisbury, was 'prenticed to old Mr Oxland of St Peter's in the East Oxford as a bookbinder (Mr Oxland being both a bookbinder and bookseller) but being out of his time, he never followed the binding trade but wholly betook himself to bookselling, and marrying a good natured young woman, he first lived by the Turl Gate in Oxford and afterwards removed to St Marie's parish. He was a very proud, confident ill-natured, impudent Fellow, peevish and froward to his wife (whom he used to beat), a great sot and a whoring prostituted wretch and of no credit, tho' he always made a great Stir and Bustle.

(Thomas Hearne, *Remarks and Collections*)

September 15th

1998: On this day a few alternatives to the usual fast-food options were suggested by leading Oxford University academic George McGavin. Dr McGavin claims that worm burgers, for example, are healthier for us than those served in fast-food restaurants. The Zoology lecturer had had considerable experience of edible oddities, one of his favourite ways of serving creepy-crawlies being to fry them in olive oil and then wash them down with a glass or two of chilled Chardonnay. He told the *Oxford Mail*:'Before you say "Ugh", think about it. Earthworms are 80 per cent meat and there are plenty of them around. Weight for weight, the nutritional value of insects, and earthworms come to that, is certainly higher than your average fast-food burger.' He added, 'Tastes shouldn't be taken too seriously, as they can always be improved if you use the right ingredients. What would a prawn taste like if we didn't smother it with ginger and garlic? It's all a matter of getting the recipe right.' Dr McGavin said that he first started to eat bugs in Papua New Guinea and continued eating them for years without any adverse effects. His all-time favourite is a 2in-long African beetle. (*Oxford Mail*)

SEPTEMBER 16TH

2002: On this day, a shopkeeper in Oxford chased after an armed robber clutching a bicycle pump because she was so angry that he was trying to relieve her of her hard-earned takings. He was armed with a penknife and wearing a balaclava. Thirty-nine-year-old Lorraine Walls, who was alone, had hoped that she would find a Stanley knife hidden away under the counter, but grabbed the pump instead and shook it at the masked raider. The would-be thief was sentenced to two years of community rehabilitation at Oxford Crown Court after pleading guilty to a charge of attempted robbery. After the trial Mrs Walls, who ran Donnington Bridge Stores with her husband, said that anger had made her brave. She had to stand in the shop all day and work really long hours and thought why should he just walk in and be given the money for doing nothing? She had been expecting to find a knife under the counter but could find only the bicycle pump so used that instead, waved it at the thief, and shouted, 'Get out!' After he had run away, she began to shake all over. The thief was later arrested by police on the towpath. (*Oxford Mail*)

SEPTEMBER 17TH

2008: On this evening a potential future member of the royal family was said by fund-raisers at the newly opened Oxford Children's Hospital to be helping them to raise £50,000. Prince William's girlfriend, Kate Middleton (now in fact his wife, the Duchess of Cambridge), was going to join with Holly, the daughter of Kidlington tycoon Sir Richard Branson, and National Hunt jockey Sam Waley-Cohen, to organise a roller disco held at the Renaissance Rooms in Vauxhall, South London. The cash raised was to be used towards Tom's Ward, a general surgical ward which cared for tiny babies to older children suffering from a variety of medical conditions, and named after Sam Waley-Cohen's brother Tom, who lost a battle with cancer in 2004. Tom, from Edge Hill, near Banbury, died from a rare type of bone cancer when he was only nineteen and his family had been involved in fund-raising for the Oxford hospital ever since. Alice Gosling, director of fund-raising for Oxford Radcliffe Hospitals, said that it was great that Kate Middleton and Holly Branson and their friends had organised the event in order to raise money for Tom's Ward. (*Oxford Mail*)

SEPTEMBER 18TH

2006: A man who was gaoled for life in 1978 for setting fire to an Oxford church, but after public protest was allowed out on licence, completed a cycle ride from Land's End to John O'Groats on this day in 2006. Fifty-five-year-old David Blagdon, who did the ride to raise money for the Oxford Transplant Campaign, took three weeks to get from one end of Britain to the other. He had three punctures over the 900-plus miles, and dropped from 11 stone to 9. He was nearly knocked off his bike while riding through a tunnel in Birmingham and it took him four hours to cross the Pennines, which were hard work as he had to get off to push. He spent the night in campsites along the route and for the last part of the trip went by ferry from Inverness. One of the most tiring parts was the Bank Holiday train journey down to Penzance from Oxford, when he had to stand for five hours. Despite his aches and pains he said that he had had a great trip, met some great people and had a few adventures along the way. He hoped to raise more than £1,000 for the charity. (*Oxford Mail*)

SEPTEMBER 19TH

1663: From the diary of Anthony à Wood:

Being then Saturday, open proclamation was made in Oxford market by the Mayor's appointment that Wednesday following, on which the King had appointed to see Oxon, the corne carts and other sellers of wares that cumbered the street should stand in Bocardo and new Yn hall lane, and that the butchers also should stand in the old Bocherew [Butchers' Row] but within a few hours after, the vice-chancellor sent the University bellman to contradict the Mayor's command and proclaimed that the market should be on Tuesday in the usuall places where it was kept.

About 6 p.m. that evening the King and Queen arrived and were greeted by the University dignitaries and, after a speech by the vice-chancellor, the King was presented with 'a larg fair Bible covered with black plush and bossed and clasped with silver double-quilt' and the Queen and the Duke and Duchess of York were all given rich gloves. Then came the turn of the city fathers; the Mayor surrendered his mace to the King, who promptly returned it to the Mayor. A rich embroidered purse containing £300 in gold was then pocketed by the monarch and the Queen received more rich gloves. (*Life and Times of Anthony à Wood*)

SEPTEMBER 20TH

2001: On this day two members of staff at Ruskin College in Walton Street were told by the college's general secretary to remove the Union Flags that they had placed on their desks in the wake of the previous week's atrocities in the United States. One member of staff, who did not want to be named, said that the two colleagues who had put flags on display had done so in order to demonstrate their patriotism and their solidarity with the United States but they had been told to remove them. This was felt to be wrong by many who thought they should be allowed to display the flags. Defending his order, the college secretary replied that the college as a whole was outraged by what had taken place in the United States and great sympathy was felt for those who had suffered. However, the fact that they had students from all over the world as well as some from ethnic minorities at Ruskin led the authorities to feel that it was important not to highlight differences among them, and that the flags suggested dividing rather than uniting people. (*Oxford Mail*)

SEPTEMBER 21ST

2009: On this evening, Michael Palin paid another visit to Oxford for his programme titled *The First Forty Five Years* at the Oxford Playhouse. The world traveller and former Python had come up to Brasenose College in 1962 to read for a BA in Modern History. He had then met fellow Python Terry Jones who was at Oxford at the same time, reading English at St Edmund Hall. The Oxford Revue at the 1964 Edinburgh Festival gave Michael Palin his first experience of writing and performing comedy. The Playhouse performance was staged to complement the appearance of his second volume of diaries, *Halfway to Hollywood: Diaries 1980–1988* in which he looks back over his life to date. The Playhouse billing stated that the performance would include 'some bad language' but 'No gratuitous violence, and nudity unlikely'. Premium tickets, which included a top-price seat and post-show drinks with Michael Palin, cost £29. The family's connection with Oxford went back to the 1860s, when his great-grandfather, Edward Palin, was a senior member of St John's College, and it is his experiences which formed the basis of the film *American Friends*, which Michael directed and starred in. (Various sources)

SEPTEMBER 22ND

2008: On this day, it was suggested by its founder that a food bank which provided meals for families on the breadline might have to expand because of demands made on it by the credit crunch. The Community Emergency Foodbank had been giving out parcels of food to more than 200 people since its creation that April. Three days' food was given to families who had been referred to the bank by community groups, the social services and doctors. Those people referred were given a voucher to hand in to the volunteers at the food bank at St Francis's Church in Hollow Way on the borders of Cowley and Headington. At that time, the service was available for two hours on Tuesdays and Thursdays. The founder, Jane Benyon, said that they had had a good response concerning what they had done to help people get through a difficult time but, with the crunch biting, it would soon be necessary to open on more days to cope with the increase in applicants. These people came from a really wide range of backgrounds and donations were received from various local churches. She added that the relief given out was limited and short-term. (*Oxford Mail*)

September 23rd

1998: On this day leading Brazilian minister Roberto Garcia dropped his wallet in one of Oxford's busiest streets. As it contained nearly $3,000 and gold credit cards, the finance director of Brazil's Ministry of Agriculture thought he had no hope of ever seeing it again. However, Senhor Garcia had underestimated the honesty of the citizens of Oxford, or at least two of the younger generation. Seventeen-year-olds Joanna Martin and Kirsty Wall from Wychwood School found the wallet and took it straight to the nearest police station. So impressed was Senhor Garcia that he went up to the school in the Banbury Road to thank the schoolgirls in person. He also issued a standing invitation for them to visit him at his home when he returned to Brazil. He said he would send them a present as a token of his gratitude. Senhor Garcia had only been in the city for a day on a visit to his solicitor, but he returned specially with an interpreter to thank the girls. He called them beautiful people and said that he had his own private jet and would take them to Brazil. Joanna said that they intended to take him up on his offer. (*Oxford Mail*)

September 24th

2002: Unusually, the brickbats that came Oxford United's way on this day concerned the catering rather than the team's performance on the pitch. The complaints were due to the fact that the east stand at the Kassam Stadium, which is sponsored by the *Oxford Mail*, ran out of pies after hungry fans had queued for between 20 and 25 minutes. The pie statistics are as follows: a total of 720 of them are made available to fans at each game held in the 12,500-capacity stadium and, of these, 240 are sold from kiosks in the *Oxford Mail* stand. The twelve machines for keeping the pies warm at the Kassam each hold sixty pies; the hitch on this occasion was that, according to the club, it does not have sufficient electricity or space to provide any more. A spokesman from the fanzine *Rage On* commented that if the club was running out of pies, there was evidently a catering problem and the obvious answer was to get more warming machines. However, he personally went to watch the game and thought that money was better spent on the team than on pies, and it was an improvement on the Manor Ground. (*Oxford Mail*)

September 25th

1665: On this day, Charles II came to Oxford from Salisbury to avoid the plague which was raging in London, and took up his lodgings in Christ Church, the traditional place for members of the royal family to stay while in the city. His father, Charles I, had resided there during the Civil War while the court was at Oxford, and his mother, Queen Henrietta Maria, had her own lodgings along the road in Merton College. The door which was made in a wall at Corpus Christi College (between Christ Church and Merton) to allow the royal couple to meet, can still be seen. The King was accompanied from Salisbury by his illegitimate son, the Duke of Monmouth; his brother, the Duke of York, the future James II, came from Warwick to join them the same day. Other members of the court came from London to escape the Great Plague, among them the Spanish ambassador who lodged at New College and the French ambassador who was at Magdalen. The next day, the Queen, Catherine of Braganza, following in the footsteps of her mother-in-law, took up residence in Merton. The court remained in Oxford until January. (*Life and Times of Anthony à Wood*)

SEPTEMBER 26TH

1998: This was a particularly joyous day for a family which was celebrating the birth of two sets of twins (one set identical), of which one was a girl and three were boys. They were born in the maternity unit at the world-famous John Radcliffe Hospital in Headington. The quads' mother Min Smy and her husband Nicholas, both of whom were in their thirties, came from Begbroke and were said to be over the moon at the arrival of the quads, who were their first children. In an interview, their Uncle Richard, Mr Smy's brother, said that the whole family was delighted at the news. The boys' names – Victor George, William Joseph and Jamie Cammeron – and the girl's, Rosie Jacqueline, had already been chosen before the birth. The quads' grandfather had died from a stroke only six weeks previously and so their arrival was seen as a new breath of life for the Smy family and had rejuvenated them. Richard Smy said, 'The whole family has rallied round to get bits and pieces for the babies. Our great-grandmother, who is ninety-two, has even knitted blankets for the babies' beds.' (*Oxford Mail*)

SEPTEMBER 27TH

2006: It was reported on this day that a patient recovering from a combined kidney and pancreas transplant had discovered an unexpected talent for baking. Eighteen months before, Michael Rowland could hardly walk more than a few yards before he became exhausted and had to inject himself with four shots of insulin. He also had to swallow ten pills and use a dialysis machine every five hours simply to keep himself alive. After the transplant, which took place in the Oxford Transplant Centre in Headington, he literally had a new lease of life. One bonus was that he could now eat a wide range of foods that were denied to him before the operation and this resulted in his interest in making cakes and, as he put it, 'I've gone from can't cook, won't cook, to someone who's in the kitchen whenever I get a chance.' He progressed from cookies to fruit cakes and then Christmas and birthday cakes. This interest in cake-making became evident soon after he got home from the John Radcliffe Hospital after his nine-hour operation. He was not able to explain his new-found abilities but it had crossed his mind that the anonymous donor of his new organs might have been a chef. (*Oxford Mail*)

September 28th

1998: A group of musicians and dancers made the streets of central Oxford resound on this day as they demonstrated against increased traffic in the city. Members of Reclaim the Streets met at Carfax, where they played drums and home-made banjos for an hour before moving off down Cornmarket (accompanied by an escort of mounted police) and finishing up in Magdalen Street. The fifty or so protestors who remained were watched by 140 policemen as they danced, juggled, played football and held an impromptu street party. Most passers-by smiled at their antics, although one elderly gent brandished an umbrella and mumbled 'riff raff' at anyone obstructing the pavement. The expected street party had officially been cancelled but some sympathisers turned up to point out that there are too many cars on the streets, making it dangerous and smelly for cyclists and pedestrians. Many people were loud in their criticism of the City Council, which they claimed was refusing to listen to the views of residents and had instead insisted upon a traffic scheme which was proving very unpopular with shoppers and tradespeople alike. But for a few hours, what with children, dogs, dancers, performers and onlookers, Magdalen Street East was indeed reclaimed. (*Oxford Mail*)

SEPTEMBER 29TH

1900: On this day, one resident wrote:

For the first time in 1900 I was this week piloted through the streets of Oxford in a motor-car and was much impressed with its comparative smoothness of motion on cobbled roads, even though the tyres were solid, and especially also by the almost instantaneous action of the powerful brake. Motor-cars have increased in number everywhere and I venture to predict that in two or three years' time they will be so numerous that speed regulations will have to be made by the City Council. These horseless carriages can run with ease at twenty miles an hour but I think my readers will agree that eight miles an hour in a town ought to be the maximum rate of speed. The streets are for the infirm and aged as well as the young and strong, for the little children with their hoops – and a great nuisance they are sometimes – as well [as] grownups with their hoops in the form of cycles and other wheels. A restriction to eight miles an hour would be no hardship, and I would impose this limit on motors, cycles, carts and carriers impartially.

(Written by 'M.A. Oxon' in *Jackson's Oxford Journal*)

September 30th

1885: An insight into ladies' fashion was published on this day:

ELASTIC STOCKING WITHOUT LACING at a Reduction in Price of One-fourth. To Sufferers from Varicose veins, Weak Ankles, &c. these Stockings are confidently recommended having received the patronage of the most eminent Surgeons of the day. They are manufactured on a new and entirely improved principle, possessing advantages over every other Stocking hitherto introduced. They are light, durable and admit of a free escape of perspiration, never lose their elasticity, will wash well and are drawn on as an ordinary stocking. As there are other Elastic Stockings advertised, the public are respectfully requested to observe that the only Agents for Oxford and its District are Cousins, Thomas and Co, Dispensing Chemists, 20 Magdalen Street, where a Stock of the above in Stockings, Socks, Knee-caps, Leggings etc are always on hand. P.S. Water-beds, Pillows and Air Cushions always in Stock for immediate use.

(*Jackson's Oxford Journal*)

OCTOBER 1st

1555: We know what the Oxford Martyrs – Nicholas Ridley, Hugh Latimer and Thomas Cranmers – had for dinner on this day in 1555 and how much it cost. The three Protestant leaders were incarcerated in the old Bocardo Prison over the North Gate of the city, prior to being burnt at the stake in Broad Street. Although they were confined to separate cells, they were sometimes permitted to eat together, the average cost of each meal being between 3 and 4s, seldom more. On this occasion they had bread and ale (2*d*), oysters (1*d*), butter (2*d*), eggs (2*d*), ling – a type of fish – (7*d*), fresh salmon (10*d*), wine (3*d*) and cheese and pears (2*d*). From the accounts kept it appears that they ate both dinner and supper, that they finished the meal with pears and cheese, and that they had wine with it. The cost of other items on their menu were a goose costing 14*d*, a pig 12*d* or 13*d*, a rabbit 6*d*, a woodcock 3*d* or 5*d*, a couple of chickens 6*d*, three plovers 10*d*, half a dozen larks 3*d*, a breast of veal 11*d*, a shoulder of mutton 10*d*, and roast beef 12*d*. (*Jackson's Oxford Journal*)

OCTOBER 2ND

1972: On this day, a set of new Emperors' heads costing almost £27,000 appeared in Broad Street. The thirteen bearded classical heads which decorate the railings on the north side of the street, between the Museum of the History of Science and the Clarendon Building, are variously known as the 'Emperors', the 'Philosophers' and sometimes even as the 'Apostles'. The originals were so decayed that they had to be replaced in 1868, but the replacements met the same fate after only another 100 years. They suffered so badly from being daubed with paint by generations of undergraduates – the subsequent paint removal leading to 'very rapid deterioration' – that by the 1960s they had become unsafe. Because of their architectural importance, the Royal Fine Arts Commission advised conservation rather than replacement. Three heads were removed in October 1968 for experimentation by the Ministry of Public Works, which advised that they were beyond conserving, so the new heads were commissioned. Sculptor Michael Black's 'signature' can be found at the back of one of the new Emperor's heads: a blackbird nestling in his mass of curls. In 1980, however, the new set was also daubed with paint. (Various sources)

OCTOBER 3RD

1864: On this day, this advertisement for the exciting advancements in hair care was published:

HAIR BRUSHING BY MECHANICAL POWER
SPIERS AND SON
102 AND 103, HIGH STREET, OXFORD
RESPECTFULLY beg leave to announce that they have
adopted, in their Hair Cutting Rooms, the use of
CAMP'S PATENT ROTARY HAIR BRUSHING
APPARATUS

This admirable invention has now stood the test of upwards of two years' experience and is considered to be the only perfect mode of brushing the hair. Independently of the ease, the quietness, the regularity and the certainty by which the hair is cleaned and softened, the system is highly recommended by the medical profession for its healthy and refreshing action upon the skin of the head, gently exciting the circulation, and, by its frequent use, promoting the growth of the hair, checking the change of colour and preventing baldness.

Besides their usual terms of subscription for hair cutting (5s per annum), they have now adopted a scale of charge for frequent or daily hair brushing and for head-washing for which latter purpose they have now greatly improved facilities. The extensive nature of their premises admits of their rooms being used as a TOILET CLUB, a convenience which they believe has long been desired by many of their customers.

(*Jackson's Oxford Journal*)

OCTOBER 4TH

2001: On this day, it was reported that a national newspaper had implied that William Straw, son of the Foreign Secretary, might be about to involve himself in more controversy. Will Straw first came to the notice of the public in 1998 when he received a caution from the police for selling cannabis. Despite this, he did sufficiently well in his A-level exams to gain a place at New College. Earlier in 2001 he had led a strike against college rents and was later fined £55 by the Proctors for taking part in a sit-in in the Divinity School over fee increases. The forthright President of the New College Junior Common Room was considering running against any candidate which the Labour Party put forward for the presidency of the Oxford University Student Union (not to be confused with the prestigious Oxford Union Society). A decision to stand as an independent candidate rather than a Labour one was certain to cause more embarrassment for his long-suffering father. When asked, Will, who was about to start his third year reading PPE, declined to confirm or deny the rumour until nominations for the presidency closed on 1 November. (Various sources)

OCTOBER 5TH

1872: On this day, it was reported by *Jackson's Oxford Journal* that the 'melancholy death by drowning' of a University waterman took place on the Isis near Iffley Lock. George Bossom, his brother-in-law and a nine-year-old nephew set out in a dinghy one morning to go fishing and to shoot moorhens. They went up the river as far as Abingdon then returned home in the evening, and when they had got just past Iffley Lock, the two men stood up in the boat in order to change places. Unfortunately, the boat capsized and all three were thrown into the water. Bossom attempted to rescue his companions, but despite being a good swimmer, he was drowned while doing do – it is assumed because of an attack of cramp. His body was recovered from the river as soon as possible and an inquest held on it. His brother-in-law and nephew were hauled to safety by the lock-keeper at Iffley. George Bossom left a widow and three children, with a fourth expected any day. A subscription fund for their assistance was set up and advertised in the local press, with contributions requested from both Town and Gown. (*Jackson's Oxford Journal*)

OCTOBER 6TH

1999: On this day, Andrew Luce from Harcourt Hill, a Didcot to London rail commuter, related how he would normally have been in the first-class carriage that was involved in the tragic Paddington train crash which had taken place the previous day. As luck would have it, though, on the day that it happened, he discovered that he had lost his season ticket and had to fill in forms at the station while the train left without him. Instead, he caught the 7.37 to Paddington which was delayed outside London because of the crash. As it was, when he got to Reading it was chaotic, with nobody knowing what was going on or how long the delay would last, so he turned round and came back to Oxford.

He told the *Oxford Mail* that he was feeling really strange, as any other day he would have been right in the middle of the disaster. Malcolm Nisbet had a similar escape when the interview which he was due to attend in London was cancelled the night before, much to his annoyance at the time. He admitted that he was 'a bit miffed' but the interviewer might have saved his life. (*Oxford Mail*)

OCTOBER 7TH

2003: On this day, parties were held by parishioners on the retirement of a clergyman who held the joint living of three parishes in West Oxford. The Revd Robert Sweeney had been the incumbent of St Frideswide's in Botley Road, St Thomas the Martyr in Becket Street, and St Margaret's at Binsey, for twenty-four years. Father Sweeney had read Classics at Christ Church before studying Theology at Cuddesdon College and was ordained in 1965. He went on to become a curate, firstly in Cheltenham and then Gloucester. He was then a school chaplain before having his own parish in his native Gloucestershire; he returned to Oxford in 1979. On his retirement, Father Sweeney stayed on for a few weeks at St Frideswide's vicarage before going back to Cheltenham. His parishioners there presented him with a cheque towards a visit to Germany, and those at St Thomas's gave a specially made oak bookcase for his new home, where he looked forward to reading and listening to opera and choral music. Father Sweeney said that lots of restoration work had been done at all three churches during his time, including replacement of much of the roof and floor at St Frideswide's and a new ten-bell peal at St Thomas'. (*Oxford Mail*)

OCTOBER 8TH

1874: Oxford students have always known how to look after themselves, as this advertisement for Turkish baths from 1874 shows:

University Turkish and Warm water Baths, 54 Corn Market Street, Oxford. The Turkish Baths are constructed on the most approved principles to insure perfect ventilation; the temperature of the Sudatorium is not raised to a great extent; the Frigidarium is handsomely fitted with dressing-stalls, and has attached to it a room for smoking the whole replete with every comfort. The baths are open for gentlemen daily, ladies Tuesdays and Fridays from 9 a.m. to 2 p.m. Private baths must be ordered before. Mercurial, Sulphur and Iodine Vapour Baths [are] always ready, under the management of experienced attendants. Charles Dolling, Proprietor.

The premises were previously a wine merchant's and are now Barclays Bank. (*Jackson's Oxford Journal*)

OCTOBER 9TH

1953: On this day, the tenth-century church of St Michael at the North Gate, which is known for its Saxon tower, faced total destruction. The fire was started deliberately in the organ by an arsonist, who was probably attracted by the church's central and prominent position in Cornmarket Street. The flames quickly spread throughout the building and the interior was gutted. Despite its decrepit condition, that December the church defiantly displayed a lighted Christmas tree outside its door. Repair work to the inside continued well into 1954, and one of the sights that spring was that of a member of the Oxford Fire Brigade perched at the end of a very long ladder, busily restoring the hands of the newly illuminated clock face. Fortunately the church survived and is now a visitor attraction because of its small museum and the views which can be enjoyed from the top of its tower. When All Saints Church in the High Street was deconsecrated and turned into the library of Lincoln College in 1971, St Michael's, now the United Benefice of St Michael, with All Saints and St Martin's, became the City Church – a title which it proudly holds to this day. (*Oxford Mail*)

OCTOBER 10TH

2007: On this day great-grandmother Dorothy Gibson, of Cuddesdon Way, Blackbird Leys, was holding an exhibition of oils and watercolours in the Stables Gallery in Green College, Woodstock Road, Oxford, as she had done for the previous twenty-one years. That year she had painted more than thirty new pictures to go on display and these included the city's buildings, estuary views and a set of abstracts. All this was unusual enough, but it was even more so because the artist was in her 100th year. Mrs Gibson did not take up painting until she was sixty-one and found it gave her great pleasure and took her mind off any anxieties. She had travelled abroad on painting holidays. She said that the artist whose work she preferred was the French Impressionist Paul Cézanne, but William Turner was another favourite. There were three more paintings of Green College still in progress at Mrs Gibson's home. Her work usually sold for between £40 and £100 and she used to put the money towards paying for the taxi which brought her to and from the gallery. Her other interests included computing, which she started at the age of ninety, and the Blackbird Leys Choir. (*Oxford Mail*)

OCTOBER 11TH

2003: On this day it was reported that the ever-increasing demand worldwide for the new Mini had led to the creation of scores more permanent jobs at the plant in Cowley. A further forty-two workers who had been employed at the car factory on a temporary basis had been given full-time contracts, bringing the number of full-time jobs created since the car was launched some two years before to 800. Management at the Mini plant had to admit that they were still faced with the problem of not being in a position to manufacture a sufficient number of cars to meet the demand in main markets such as the United States. Mini sales reached another record that September when 18,650 models were sold worldwide – more than 11 per cent higher than in the same month the year before – and up to that point 137,130 Minis had been sold in 2003 – an increase of more than 33 per cent. The Cowley plant was working flat out seven days a week and still waiting lists were growing. In the UK, for example, customers could expect to wait up to six months for a top Cooper S car, and three months for other models was usual. (*Oxford Mail*)

OCTOBER 12TH

2005: It was reported on this day that a prestigious national award was won by Oxford's only bangers-and-mash restaurant. Coming ahead of more than 150 rivals, the Big Bang in Walton Street took first place in *Restaurant* magazine's Best Dishes Award 2005 in the Sausage and Mash category. The judges were impressed with the restaurant's winning dish, Oxford sausages served with mashed swede and a rich wine jus, because they felt that it showed a 'keen respect for sausage heritage'. Recipes for the traditional Oxford Sausage, which is made from pork, veal and sage, are among the first recorded in the United Kingdom. The meat for the Big Bang version, which did not include veal, was supplied by butchers in Oxford's Covered Market. The proprietor of the Big Bang, Max Mason, who had been a naval lieutenant, was delighted when he heard of *Restaurant* magazine's decision and said that the winning dish was very popular with diners and that the main reason it won was because the ingredients were local, coming from within 20 miles of Oxford. He added that his lovely trophy would be displayed in a place of honour in the Big Bang restaurant and that he was planning another restaurant in Cambridge. (*Oxford Mail*)

OCTOBER 13TH

1998: On this day Oxford Crown Court heard how a drunken sixty-eight-year-old from Cowley left the Mitre in the High Street after drinking eight pints of beer and went to demand cash from female cashiers at three banks, telling them that he had a gun. One of them told the jury that she had smelt alcohol on the would-be robber's breath when he came into Lloyds in Carfax at about 1.45. She said that he didn't look like a robber; he was very quiet and his speech was a little slurred. He told her he had a gun in his pocket, but she didn't take this seriously. He then informed another staff member that he'd committed a robbery and was escorted off the premises, but the police were not informed. He then went straight into next-door Barclays, queue-jumped, and made similar demands of the cashier there. She believed him and pressed the alarm while a customer grabbed him and took him outside. The next stop was the foreign till at the NatWest, where the cashier lay on the floor and set off the alarm. When the police arrived the pensioner claimed it was a prank. (*Oxford Mail*)

OCTOBER 14TH

2002: This day saw the end of a two-year-long search for a bilingual minister to take charge of a congregation, all of whom are Punjabi. The United Asian Baptist Church in Wytham Street in South Oxford placed an advertisement in an Indian magazine after being unable to find a suitable person in Britain. The new minister, the Revd Aroon Kumar Dass, came to Oxford from the Punjab with his wife and three children and was greeted with a packed church at his inaugural service. The increasing number of Punjabi Christians in the city had helped the church flourish since it started in the 1970s with just seven people who worshipped together in a house in Wytham Street. Initially, the families went next door to the South Oxford Baptist Church, but then decided to hold services in their own language in order to preserve their cultural identity. The Revd Anthony Clarke, minister of South Oxford Baptist Church, said that this arrangement had served to encourage cooperation between various ethnic groups, as well as expressing different aspects of Christianity. The Punjabi Church, which has more than 100 members, enjoys hymns in Punjabi, Urdu, Hindi and English, accompanied by traditional Indian music. (*Oxford Mail*)

OCTOBER 15TH

1998: This was a very special day for Mrs Kate Wren who, as the oldest resident of Oseney Court home for the elderly, was something of a celebrity. Surrounded by family, friends and staff, she was celebrating her 103rd birthday, and in the place of honour on the party table was a cake with her age written on it. Kate, the former landlady of the Greyhound pub in Worcester Street, had a sherry every evening at Oseney Court, and like many people who live to a great age, she put it down, in part, to a regular tipple. The Greyhound was demolished in 1987 during the redevelopment of Gloucester Green, and the following year Kate moved into Oseney Court. On this day she received cards from the staff and other residents of the home, as well as from Hugo Brunner, the Lord Lieutenant of Oxfordshire. In addition, flowers and a message of congratulation arrived for her from Oxfordshire County Council. The manager of Oseney Court said that she could just imagine the birthday girl as a pub landlady and described her as quite a character, with strength of mind and a good sense of humour. (*Oxford Mail*)

OCTOBER 16TH

1900: On this day, one of Oxford's most distinguished Victorians, Sir Henry Acland, who had been born the year of the Battle of Waterloo, died. He was a former Regius Professor of Medicine and a prominent figure during the cholera epidemics in the city, when he provided not only medical assistance but also wholesome food for those less able to afford it. When it was known that his health was declining rapidly, anxious enquiries were received from the Prince and Princess of Wales. He is remembered in 'Notes by an Oxford Lady', whose subject matter is normally much more frivolous:

In spite of his advanced age, Sir Henry Acland has been a familiar figure in our streets and at many public functions until quite recently. He went to the afternoon performance of Barnum and Bailey's circus the last time it was here. Several times during the summer I saw him in his chair or carriage watching the cricket in the Parks and he was at the Commemoration flowers show in the gardens of Wadham College. I am told that so recently as August he inspected the exhibition of the famous Wallace collection in London. By his death, another link with the past is removed.

(Various sources)

OCTOBER 17TH

1868: On this day, it was announced that the new heads outside the Sheldonian Theatre in Broad Street were about to be finished. Indeed, eight of them were completed and the remaining five were 'in the hands of the sculptor. The paint with which someone had so disgracefully smeared them the night before last Commemoration-day has been entirely removed'. The heads referred to are the bearded classical busts of the famous 'Emperors', which are also occasionally referred to as the Philosophers, although nobody knows who, if anyone, they represent. Set on pillars along a wall and metal fence, they act as 'herms' or 'terms', which mark the boundary of the site bordered by the Museum of the History of Science, the Clarendon Building, the Bodleian Library and the Sheldonian itself. The original sculptures, which date from the 1660s, were so badly decayed by the 1860s that they had to be replaced and it is this set which features prominently in Max Beerbohm's novel *Zuleika Dobson*. However, these heads suffered the same fate as their predecessors and a third set, based on a study of the seventeenth-century heads and carved by sculptor Michael Black, was erected in 1972. (*Jackson's Oxford Journal*)

OCTOBER 18TH

1770: The world-famous Radcliffe Infirmary was opened on this St Luke's Day, he being the patron saint of physicians. Shortly afterwards, on 30 November 1770, the Bishop of Oxford consecrated the Radcliffe Infirmary's burial ground (long since buried itself), and the congregation prayed that it might be the 'only useless part of the Establishment'. The hospital stood on a five-acre site in what were then the open fields of St Giles' parish, which was at that period well away from the city, and had its own three-acre garden. When it opened there were only two wards, male and female, but such was the demand by patients that another was opened by the end of the year and three more in October 1771. Such heavy use might seem surprising given the fact that many conditions were barred by the rules. Patients suffering from smallpox (or any infectious disease), epilepsy, ulcers, inoperable cancers, tuberculosis or dropsy were not admitted; neither were pregnant women, children under seven (except for major operations) or the mentally ill. The Infirmary was closed in 2007, having been superseded by the new John Radcliffe Hospital in Headington, and its site was redeveloped by the University. (Various sources)

OCTOBER 19TH

1835: On this day Queen Adelaide, consort of King William IV, visited the city and stayed at the Angel Hotel in the High Street. Her choice of lodgings was wrongly seen by some as a snub to Christ Church, the usual place for royalty to stay. The Queen's stay was a long one in comparison with other royal visits, which were usually flying ones. A grand reception was held for her in the Sheldonian Theatre where the Chancellor, the recently installed Duke of Wellington who had come to Oxford specially, read an address of welcome to which her Majesty replied. Four of her entourage were given the degree of honorary Doctor of Civil Law. During the ceremony, the Duke 'sharply reprimanded the great Dean Gaisford for the inhospitality that caused Her Majesty to put up at the Angel Inn'. Queen Adelaide went on to the Town Hall and later entertained the Duke to a splendid dinner at the Angel. The next day she strolled in Christ Church Meadow, afterwards arriving at the Queen's College, of which she was patron, where she lunched. Her portrait by David Wilkie, which the Duke requested after the visit, hangs in the Examination Schools. (*Jackson's Oxford Journal*)

OCTOBER 20TH

1900: Avant-garde fashion will always have its detractors, as evidenced here in this piece:

She looked very trim but her well-cut skirt struck me as a little too short for walking purposes in this day of lengthy garments. As I was meditating on the subject, she suddenly mounted [her bicycle] in a fashion which startled me, and I saw the garment I had taken to be an ordinary skirt was a divided one, and the cycle was of the masculine type with a cross-bar. Please don't be shocked; there was nothing the least shocking in the spectacle … This type of skirt would appear to meet the chief cycling difficulty as regards women who go on tours and do much riding since greater rigidity with less weight of metal can be produced in the cross-bar machine. Of course it does not touch the question of the danger of the skirt itself becoming entangled in pedals or cogs, except, to a limited extent, from its shortness. Still, I don't imagine Englishwomen will easily accustom themselves to the 'rationals' [Mrs Amelia Jenks Bloomer's 'alternative bifurcated ensembles', an early form of trouser suit] which some strong-minded souls think the ideal garment for cycling.

(*Jackson's Oxford Journal*)

OCTOBER 21ST

1998: On this morning, a young squirrel caused havoc in Christ Church Cathedral during morning service. He came into the building and started bouncing up and down the nave before disappearing behind the high altar. Members of the congregation watched fascinated as vergers started to search for him under pews in what was described in the *Oxford Mail* as 'scenes strangely reminiscent of Basil the Rat's escape in TV's Fawlty Towers'. The first person to notice the squirrel at about 7.20 that morning was cleaner Glyn Lyon, who tried unsuccessfully to lure him into a garden nearby. When the cathedral officials joined in, he panicked and made a beeline for the altar. The Revd Justin Lewis-Anthony, Precentor of the cathedral, said that it was lucky that there were no more services until 6 p.m that evening. He did appreciate that anyone seeing two vergers and the Precentor running up and down and looking under pews must have wondered what on earth was happening. The problem was eventually solved using a bag of fruit and nuts produced by verger Matthew Power. A fruit-and-nut trail tempted the squirrel into the sacristy for the rest of the service and then to the cathedral door. (*Oxford Mail*)

OCTOBER 22ND

1900: Male Oxford University students were given a chance to play their part in the academic future of the country on this day. The fertility unit at Oxford's John Radcliffe Hospital launched a campaign to persuade these gifted young men to deposit sperm, and placed advertisements in the *Oxford Student* newspaper at the start of the academic year. Donors were offered £12.50 per session as opposed to something like $250, which would be paid to donors in the United States. Dr Bill Ledger, the programme's director, explained that donations should be made before the men's sperm count decreased with age and added that the amount paid would be more attractive to students than to working people. However, he believed the motivation was not money but because the work was considered valuable and they wished to contribute, as they would to appeals for blood or bone marrow. Sperm collected was frozen for six months and potential donors were subject to stringent health checks. Dr Ledger stressed that the unit was recruiting from a broad background, not just students, who formed less than half the participants. Many people, he believed, would prefer donations from those of a similar background. (*Oxford Mail*)

OCTOBER 23RD

2000: Filming started on *Harry Potter and the Philosopher's Stone* – the first multi-million-pound screen version of a J.K. Rowling Harry Potter novel – at Christ Church and in the Bodleian Library. The film company Warner Brothers and the University entered into a contract brokered by Dr Robert Gasser, Bursar of Brasenose College. He stressed that filming would not be allowed to disrupt normal student life. Apart from Christ Church and the Bodleian itself, the University's Divinity School was transformed into the Hogwarts hospital wing, and Duke Humfrey's Library, part of the Bodleian, was used as the Hogwarts Library. Other scenes were shot locally at Didcot Railway Centre, where the famous young wizard Harry Potter is shown being waved off to school on board the Hogwarts Express. The female lead in the Harry Potter series, Hermione Granger, was played by Oxford schoolgirl Emma Watson. Another Oxford connection was actress Dame Maggie Smith, who lived in Cowley and performed with the Oxford Playhouse School of Theatre in the 1950s. She plays the part of Minerva McGonagall, second in command at Hogwarts. Oxford was also used for *Harry Potter and the Chamber of Secrets* (released 2002) and *Harry Potter and the Goblet of Fire*, 2005. (Various sources)

OCTOBER 24TH

2000: One of the best-known city-centre buskers was threatened with prosecution by council officials for selling his CDs in the street on this day. He had received a warning letter from the city's Street Trading Enforcement Officer, his third warning about selling his CDs without a street trading licence, which could have cost him £3,000, although they did not object to his busking. The previous year, flute player Frei Zinger of South Oxford had signed a profitable recording contract worth £11,500 when a talent scout heard him play in Cornmarket Street and ordered 5,000 CDs then and there; the money went towards the production of a new album. However, he had not been out on the city streets recently because of the council's ban. Mr Zinger said the situation was ridiculous as bands were allowed to come from outside the city to play and sell their CD there with no licence, and that he was singled out because he was a well-known face about town. He added that the only place he had met this restriction was in his hometown but he had been actively encouraged in Reading, Croydon and Portsmouth. A council spokesman said he should buy a licence like everybody else. (*Oxford Mail*)

OCTOBER 25TH

2006: On this Kazakhstan Republic Day in 2006, the country's, ambassador Erlan Idrissov, spoke to the Oxford Union ahead of the release of the Sacha Baron Cohen film *Borat: Cultural Learnings of America for Make Benefit Glorious Nation of Kazakhstan*. The spoof film had drawn criticism because it showed the former Soviet republic as being backward and ignorant and this was what the ambassador aimed to disprove. *Borat* shows the reporter, played by Sacha Baron Cohen, take in Americans when he pretends to be a naïve journalist who makes very offensive remarks while hiding behind the role of an innocent foreigner. At the same time, he tricks his victims into exposing their own prejudices. Kazakhstan is portrayed as a country where women are second-class citizens and this angered the authorities. The visit included a talk about the film and a question-and-answer session. Idrissov had already criticised Cohen for taking advantage of the lack of public knowledge concerning Kazakhstan and told *The Guardian*: 'Britain prides itself on its sense of fair play. By all means laugh at *Borat* if you will, but I suspect that once you know something of the true Kazakhstan his antics will leave a nasty aftertaste. Indeed, you may not laugh at all.' (*Oxford Mail*)

OCTOBER 26TH

1920: More than forty of the first women to graduate from the University of Oxford took part in a ceremony in the Sheldonian Theatre on this day. It is not possible to state precisely the name of the first woman graduate. Before this date female students were not permitted to become members of the University, although from the late 1870s they were able to attend lectures, take examinations and even gain honours – but not have degrees conferred on them as their male equivalents did. A new University statute which came into force in October 1920 changed the situation, as it allowed women to be admitted to full membership. In addition, those who had already reached the required standards could both matriculate and be awarded, in retrospect, the degrees to which they were now entitled. Among them was Annie Rogers, the first woman to gain honours in a university examination intended to be the equivalent of that taken by men for a degree. In 1877 she had gained first-class honours in Latin and Greek in the Second Examination for honours in the recently instituted 'Examination of Women'. In 1879 she followed this achievement with first-class honours in Ancient History. (Various sources)

OCTOBER 27TH

1998: On this day it was claimed that, apart from 'bits and pieces', Oxford University History graduates didn't know their English history. Modern History don, Dr John Maddicott, put this down to the syllabus, 'which failed to give students a working knowledge of how their country had evolved'. He called it 'a sort of self-service restaurant, where the menu is exclusively à la carte and the tables are almost all separate'. He pointed out that one could get a History degree without understanding major topics such as Magna Carta, the Black Death, the Glorious Revolution of 1688, the Industrial Revolution, or the 1832 Reform Act. Dr Maddicott blamed a 'decline in academic confidence, an easy acceptance of what is fashionable and an overriding reluctance to try to decide what the subject of history at Oxford ought to be about'. He went on to say that thirty years previously the core of the syllabus was a study of the subject from the end of Roman Britain to the middle of the last century, which enabled students 'to observe the slow process of evolution and change' and ' met the need of English citizens to know the history of England in some detail'. (*Oxford Mail*)

OCTOBER 28TH

1998: Anthony McPartlin, half of the duo Ant and Dec and described as a 'children's TV star', was taken away by police after a punch-up outside a nightclub in Oxford on this day. The twenty-one-year-old Geordie was interrogated at St Aldates police station concerning a fight outside the Park End Club, which had broken out after a punter allegedly insulted Ant as he was leaving the premises. It was claimed that one of his friends punched the man in the face, so starting the clash in which a barman was hurt as he tried to stop it. The television presenter was driven away in a police car, along with two of his friends, but all three were later released without any charges being brought. The man who had been injured stated that 'someone shouted something' which Ant's friend thought came from his group and so he hit him in the mouth. He fell, and someone started kicking him. A spokesman from the club said they had looked at the CCTV footage of the incident, which gave no clues as to what had sparked off the incident. He also said that Ant was a regular there and that he was never any problem. (*Oxford Mail*)

OCTOBER 29TH

1964: On this day, a baby girl called Yasmin Parvaneh was born in the city, the daughter of an Iranian father and an English mother. In her teens she was discovered by a local modelling agency while she was working as a sales assistant, and competed in beauty contests in the area before taking up modelling full-time. At first she took part in a few fashion shows and did a large amount of hand modelling. She moved to London in 1983 and was given a trial by the Models 1 agency. So successful did she become during the 1980s that, by 1989, the girl from Oxford was one of the highest-paid models in the world, working for such big names as Calvin Klein, Christian Dior and Karl Lagerfeld, and appeared in the first American and British issues of *Elle* magazine. However, she became better known as Yasmin Le Bon after her marriage to the lead singer of Duran Duran, Simon Le Bon, whom she married on 27 December 1985. A few weeks after the birth of their first daughter Amber in August 1989, Yasmin returned to modelling; daughters Saffron and Tallulah followed. (Various sources)

OCTOBER 30TH

1998: On this day, after a lifetime in show business, veteran compère, dancer and comic Bruce Forsyth received an unexpected accolade. No less than three of his catchphrases were selected for inclusion in the newly published *Oxford Dictionary of 20th Century Quotations*. One of them, 'I'm in charge', was taken from his compèring the hit television variety show *Sunday Night at the London Palladium* (1957–61) and the other two, 'Didn't he do well?' and 'Nice to see you, to see you nice', were from the long-running Saturday evening show, *Bruce Forsyth and the Generation Game* (1971–77 and 1990–94); from 1973–9, he was married to Anthea Redfern, the hostess on the show. In order to compile the latest edition of the dictionary, fourteen University researchers spent five years on the computer trawling through magazines, and TV and radio scripts. The editor, Elizabeth Knowles, said: 'By their very familiarity, catchphrases become a part of the public consciousness. With Bruce Forsyth, the quotations are very much associated with his personality.' Brucie did indeed do well to be listed along with Sir Winston Churchill, Bertrand Russell and T.S. Eliot, who were among the most quoted icons of the twentieth century. (*Oxford Mail*)

OCTOBER 31ST

2003: From this day homeless people in Oxford were given the chance to train as part of a scheme aimed at getting them back to work. Named 'The Aspire Bike Doctor' and managed by the Oxford Cycle Workshop, which mended and sold abandoned bikes, it was in partnership with Aspire, a company in Osney Mead that employed homeless people. The idea was that cyclists would be able to drop in at various points round Oxford on specific days to have their bikes fixed while they waited. Principal customers were expected to be shoppers in the city centre, rail travellers and students; the venues would be the University Science Area, the railway station, Oxford Brookes University and the New Road Baptist Church in Bonn Square. All the repair sites were offered rent-free and Oxford University offered to pay for repairs for their staff as part of their cycling initiative. Aspire hoped that at least those trained in bike repair would later find full-time employment. The scheme had a number of backers, including the University of Oxford and Oxford Brookes University, Thames Trains, Barclays Bank, the City Council and several charities, representatives of which were invited to arrive by bike at the launch at the Baptist church. (*Oxford Mail*)

NOVEMBER 1ST

1937: On this day, the funeral of Miss Annie Rogers of St Hugh's College took place. As a schoolgirl, Annie came top in the Oxford Local Examinations, only to have the accompanying scholarships offered to a boy. The service was at St Giles' Church where Miss Rogers had worshipped for many years, followed by interment at Wolvercote Cemetery. She had died after a collision with a lorry, probably as a result of her erratic way of riding a bicycle. The heads of most of the colleges, many university officials, as well as past and present members of St Hugh's, were present at the memorial service held for her later in the week at the University Church. In the appreciation published in the *Oxford Times*, it was stated that to many she 'must have been a familiar sight, with the keen face and rather old-fashioned hat above it – the sturdy thick-set figure, rather bent of late years – yet only a few realised how full of purpose and of labour had been that old lady's career, and how closely it coincided with the "march of women" during the last 80 years'. It concluded: 'her death leaves the gap made by a strong personality.' (*Oxford Times*)

NOVEMBER 2ND

1891: On this day, many members of the Oxford Photographic Society and their friends gathered for a 'lantern evening', during the course of which magic lantern slides were shown to an enthusiastic audience. Modern photographers may find the coverage in *Jackson's Oxford Journal* of historic interest. On this occasion, all the slides had been made by Mr E.A. Ryman-Hall and were remarked on as being 'very fine examples of his method of toning'. All of the negatives were taken on Eastman film, by using a hand camera, and the lantern plates were 'an "Alpha" toned with a modification of a formula given for the Alpha paper'. The views of the Lake District were singled out for admiration, as were snap-shots taken from one of Salter's steamers during a boat trip down the Thames. The majority of the pictures shown to the Photographic Society were voted by its members as 'simply perfect and could not have been excelled if taken by the ordinary method and the most elaborate calculation of exposure &c. The pictures were a miscellaneous lot, but all were extremely good and interesting, showing excellent taste and judgement in selection and careful workmanship'. (*Jackson's Oxford Journal*)

November 3rd

1899: On this evening, the reaction of the reporter from *Jackson's Oxford Journal* to 'The Japs' performance was not entirely complimentary. According to him:

> [The] voice of the gentleman Jap, who is obviously a Frenchman, is painful at close quarters and with one exception, I think the masking is a good idea; one sees as much as one wants to see of them without prying behind the bands of lace and the patch of blackness ... but the thing I really went to see was the performance of little Miss Valli Valli, a clever child who sings and dances quite childishly, with a quaint attractive imitation of grown-up artistes.

Most of the songs in her repertoire were deemed suitable, such as 'a droll song descriptive of amateur attempts at French conversation', however 'It was not pleasant to [see] a child, though happily she was too young to understand what she was singing about, go through a painfully suggestive song which mars one of our otherwise amusing musical comedies. To watch a grown-up girl sing such [a] thing makes one feel sick and ashamed, to hear them from the lips of an innocent child makes one despair of human nature.' (*Jackson's Oxford Journal*)

NOVEMBER 4TH

2003: It was reported on this day in that a relative of a pioneer Polar explorer was disappointed by the lukewarm reception to his suggestion of a Blue Plaque. Stephen Haddelsey was annoyed by the decision of the city's Blue Plaques Board not to honour Frank Bickerton, who accompanied Sir Douglas Mawson in 1911 and was selected by Sir Ernest Shackleton for the doomed Endurance expedition three years later. It was Bickerton who first discovered a meteorite in the Antarctic. He served on the Western Front as an infantry officer in the First World War, volunteered for the Royal Flying Corps, and became first a fighter pilot and then a test pilot. His birthplace, The Elms at Iffley, now the Hawkwell House Hotel, was considering renaming suites of rooms after the family, and the City of Oxford Museum was interested in holding an exhibition, said Mr Haddelsey. The family had already been commemorated by Bickerton Road in Headington, which is named after Frank's father, Liberal councillor Joseph Bickerton. Mr Haddelsey was planning to publish a biography, *Born Adventurer: The Life of Frank Bickerton*, to mark the 50th anniversary of his relative's death the following year. The Plaques Board denied any snub, saying that not enough detailed information had been given them. (*Oxford Mail*)

November 5th

1954: Norman Longmate wrote of this date:

A visitor to Oxford on Guy Fawkes Night might suppose that he had stepped back several centuries into the atmosphere of a medieval witches burning. Broad Street and St Giles are thronged with undergraduates, many of them shouting, some throwing fireworks about in the crowd, while a few of the bolder spirits are busily engaged in smashing windows in the entrance doors of the Playhouse Theatre in Beaumont Street, or assaulting solitary policemen and attempting to steal their helmets. At the junction of the two streets where the Martyrs Memorial stands – favourite target for Oxford climbers – a bonfire is burning and some individuals will be attempting to drag down nearby road signs, or to uproot from their foundations the wooden benches provided by the city, to add them to the flames. In the background a great mass of undergraduates and citizens are standing, looking profoundly bored and possibly singing the well-known Oxford carol Lloyd George Knows my Father [sic] – a sure sign that they are uncertain what to do next.'

Guy Fawkes Night continued to be a flashpoint well into the 1960s. (Norman Longmate, *Oxford Triumphant*)

NOVEMBER 6TH

1947: On this day sports commentator Jim Rosenthal was born in Oxford, where he went to Josca's Preparatory School and then on to Magdalen College School. Since childhood he has supported the home football team, Headington (later Oxford) United and is still remembered for wearing a U's hat while hosting the ITV coverage of the Milk Cup final from Wembley Stadium in 1986. In 2010 he joined the Club's board of directors. Jim extended his attachment to the place of his birth when he went into the newspaper business when, joining the staff of the *Oxford Mail*, and broadcast on local and national radio. Jim's parents were well-known Oxford characters. His mother, the former Maud Levy, attended the Sorbonne, where she read Literary Studies, then the universities of Florence, Freiburg and Heidelberg, and finally the Courtauld Institute in London to study Art History. She met her husband Albi Rosenthal, son of a Munich bookselling dynasty, when she was doing research at the Wallace Collection. He established an antiquarian bookshop in Curzon Street and when this was bombed moved to Oxford. In 1947 Maud and Albi married and, as their family grew, bought Half Acre on Boars Hill, where they stayed for the rest of their lives. (Various sources)

NOVEMBER 7TH

2008: This was the day on which the newly restored and returned ceiling paintings from the Sheldonian Theatre, the ceremonial hall of the University, were in place and ready for the first public viewing at a degree ceremony the following day. The thirty-two panels which make up the ceiling were done in 1668–9 by Robert Streater, serjeant-painter to King Charles II, in his studio in Whitehall, London. The separate panels were brought up to Oxford by barge as far as Abingdon and then taken on by carts. The largest panel measures over 6 x 3.6 metres and the theme of the ceiling is 'Truth descending upon the Arts and Sciences to expel Ignorance from the University'. After investigation into the suspected movement of the wooden cornicing around the perimeter of the auditorium late in 2004, it was decided to take away all of the panels from the Sheldonian for conservation and repair work. This involved the erection of scaffolding which took up the entire auditorium so that the panels could be removed intact and attached to their stretchers rather than be rolled up. The work was done in their Bristol studios by International Fine Art Conservation Studios Ltd. (Various sources)

NOVEMBER 8TH

2002: On this day, the main library of Oxford University, the world-renowned Bodleian Library, celebrated its 400th anniversary. It had been founded by scholar and diplomat Sir Thomas Bodley in order to re-establish the much-depleted university library. Bodley's library opened on 8 November 1602 and was described by Sir Francis Bacon as an 'ark to save learning from the deluge'. To celebrate the anniversary, the University conferred honorary degrees on four internationally respected figures with connections to some of the other most important research libraries in the world. These were James Billington, librarian of the American Congress in Washington, who had been at Oxford as a Rhodes Scholar; Lynne Brindley, chief executive of the British Library; Professor Sir Brian Follett, Chairman of the Arts and Humanities Research Board; and Paul LeClerc, chief executive of the New York Public Library. The degree ceremony came as a fitting end to a year of Bodleian birthday events – concerts, exhibitions, and the inauguration of the Libraries Capital Campaign for Oxford. The Bodleian is one of the five copyright libraries in the British Isles, entitled to a copy of any book published in the country, and the second largest in Britain, after the British Library. (Programme of the event)

NOVEMBER 9TH

1695: Anthony à Wood notes how William III came to Oxford and was received in the Sheldonian Theatre on this day.

Now so it was that the Masters, Bachelaurs and Undergraduats, being confined to their galeryes, and the women to their, there were only some gentlemen and ordinary people and attendants in the Area, who rudely scrambled away all the banquet and sweetmeates, all sorts of souse fish, fruit, etc. – about fifty large dishes besides very many little or small dishes intermix'd – who swept all away and drank all the wine.

The Universite had employed William Sherwin, the inferior beadle, to go to London and provide all rarities that could be; were at great charge; and when all was done, few scholars participated, few gents, and no women.

The Universitie was at great charge in providing a banquet for the king; but the king would not eat anything, but went out and some rabble and townsmen that had got in by the connivance of the stairers (and some when the king went in and out) they seyzed upon the banquet in the face of the whole Universitie, and, in spite of their teeth, all looking on and would not or could not help themselves.

(*Life and Times of Anthony à Wood*)

NOVEMBER 10TH

2001: On this day, an ancient building which has hosted a variety of composers and virtuosi, from Handel to Kennedy, was the venue for the performance of a new classical work by a former Beatle. Sir Paul McCartney brought his fiancée Heather Mills to hear the choir of Magdalen College perform the composition entitled 'Ecce Cor Meum' (Behold my heart) at the Sheldonian Theatre in Broad Street. Earlier in the day he had overseen the final rehearsals in the company of the President of Magdalen, Anthony Smith. The idea of the oratorio had come to Sir Paul after he and his late wife, Linda, heard the choir sing during a visit which the McCartneys made to the college chapel in 1997, so that it was especially written for the Magdalen choir. Conductor Bill Ives said that Sir Paul had been pleased with the debut performance. He had the impression that its composer was excited to finally hear it backed by an orchestra, as it was the first time that he had heard everything together. In addition, it was the first time that Sir Paul had ever been in the Sheldonian. Bill Ives described him as 'thrilled to bits'. (Various sources)

November 11th

1867: The *Daily News* reported that on this night a serious disturbance broke out in Oxford, which was alleged to have been started by certain undergraduate members of the University. They had heard that there was to be a bread riot that night and had made up their minds to prevent it. At about 10.30 a Town and Gown skirmish started in St Aldates and continued until the Proctors and their attendant Bulldogs intervened and sent the brawling students back to their colleges. With Gown safely behind locked gates, the rougher elements of Town took themselves off to Alderman Grubb's bakeries in Queen Street and Cornmarket Street where they started smashing the windows. Fortunately, the Mayor, backed by city and University officials, soon arrived on the scene. They arrested some twenty of the rioters, who were hauled off to the University police station where all except one were given bail. Several college windows were broken and the Mayor himself narrowly escaped injury while attempting to subdue the rioters. One of them threw a stone at him which narrowly missed his head and ended up crashing through a nearby window. The streets were not cleared until nearly 3 a.m. (*Jackson's Oxford Journal*)

NOVEMBER 12TH

2007: This was the day that Oxford learnt that three academics in Germany had produced a five-volume study in which they expressed doubt about the authenticity of some of the Michelangelo cartoons owned by the Ashmolean Museum in Beaumont Street. The reason for their claim is the fact that the hundreds of drawings claimed to be by him – which are to be found all over the world – cannot be genuine because his contemporaries refer to his having burnt the majority of them before his death in 1564. Even worse, this was just the tip of the iceberg, as they were among the 40 per cent of sketches by the Renaissance genius which they believe should be classed as copies, the rest being in the British Museum and the Royal Collection. Keeper of Western Art, Timothy Wilson, responded by saying that the museum staff welcomed 'intelligent and informed debate about all aspects of works of art in its care', and added that there were 'very detailed and authoritative catalogue entries for all the drawings attributed to Michelangelo in the Ashmolean'. He added that they looked forward to reading the new studies by the German scholars in detail in order to make a proper assessment of them. (*Oxford Mail*)

NOVEMBER 13TH

1002: On this feast of St Brice, members of Oxford's peaceful and established Danish community were forced to take refuge in the priory church of St Frideswide, the precursor of today's Christ Church Cathedral, when they came under attack from their Saxon neighbours. When the mob reached the church, their barricaded the innocent Danes inside and set fire to it, burning them all alive. Among those killed that day were Gunnhild, the sister of the King of Denmark, and her family. The blame for this atrocity can be laid squarely at the door of the English king, Ethelred II, the Unready, whose royal charter refers to Danish settlers as 'sprouting like cockles among the wheat', and states that they were killed 'by a most just extermination'. Furthermore, the victims had ruined the doors of St Frideswide's when they frantically tried to escape the flames. The loss of books and damage to the church were evidently felt to be more important than the lives of those who perished. The charter also includes the information that Ethelred felt responsible for the rebuilding of the church, 'with God's aid'. In rapid retribution, Sweyn Forkbeard burnt Oxford to the ground. (Various sources)

NOVEMBER 14TH

2000: On this day it was suggested that the reduction in the number of applications to Magdalen College could be traced to the popular television programme *University Challenge*. There had been a 22 per cent drop in students wanting to come to the college that autumn after the increase which had followed the success of Magdalen teams when they won the contest two years running in 1997 and 1998, and this was put down to the fact that the college did not take part in 2000. The President, Anthony Smith, commented that the college was back in the position it held before its television successes. That year Magdalen had attracted adverse publicity when the then Chancellor Gordon Brown unfairly accused it of elitism when it turned down comprehensive pupil Laura Spence. Fortunately, state school pupils were not put off by what became known as the Laura Spence affair. Out of 400 applications for the 120 places on offer, 48 per cent were from state schools as opposed to 39 per cent from those in the independent sector, the remaining places being taken by students from overseas. Mr Smith added, 'The good thing is that applications to the University overall were up by one and a half per cent.' (*Oxford Mail*)

NOVEMBER 15TH

1876: On this afternoon, Thomas Wyndham, Fellow and tutor in Natural Science at Merton College, shot himself. The first anybody knew about it was when Mr Wyndham's bed-maker came into his room at 5 p.m. and found his body on the floor with a gun beside it. Although a very successful scholar, the deceased had been very much tied up in his studies and was considered by many to have been somewhat eccentric. He had been rather depressed during the previous week, and one of the two letters found by his body was read out at the inquest. Addressed to his medical advisor, the well-known Sir Henry Acland, it said, 'Dear Dr Acland, I must be put into a lunatic asylum. Please put me in.' The second letter, addressed to a lady to whom Wyndham had been engaged, was not produced. The verdict of the inquest was 'that the deceased had destroyed himself while in a state of unsound mind'. According to the report in the *Hampshire Telegraph*, 'The deceased gentleman bore a high character in his College for his devotion to his work and had given a lecture to his pupils within two or three hours of his body being discovered.' (*Jackson's Oxford Journal*)

November 16th

1963: A very special convocation was held in the Sheldonian Theatre to celebrate its restoration, which had been helped by the Historic Buildings Appeal, on this night. The theatre had been closed for four years and University ceremonies were held elsewhere. Another purpose of the ceremony was to confer honorary degrees on several people involved in the work. The Chancellor, the Earl of Stockton, conferred the degrees of Doctor of Letters on the architects Godfrey Allen and Sir John Summerson, Doctor of Music on Benjamin Britten, and Master of Arts on John Thomas, a well-known local photographer whose work had greatly assisted the architects. Godfrey Allen had been involved with St Paul's Cathedral, so, said the Public Orator speaking in Latin, Sir Christopher Wren might be 'rejoicing in the Elysian Fields' at the honour being conferred. Sir John Summerson had worked in the office of Sir Giles Gilbert Scott and become Curator of Sir John Soane's Museum. Britten's *Noye's Fludde* had recently been performed in the University Church and John Thomas had been spotted climbing 'masterfully over roofs and gables, well equipp'd with tripod tall and telephoto lens'. A lecture by Sir John Summerson, entitled The Sheldonian in its Time, concluded the proceedings. (Various sources)

NOVEMBER 17TH

1718: An exhibition notice appeared in *Jackson's Oxford Journal* on this day:

> Dear Sir, Young Mr Palmer brought me a picture set in Gold and made by order of K. Alfred, who, it is said, wore it about his neck. It was found some years ago in Somersetshire and intended by Mr Palmer's father, lately dead, for Oxford, and his son has put it into my hands for the Bodleian Library. Mr Palmer says that notice is taken of it in Dr Hicke's Thesaurus and the Philosophical Transactions [of the Royal Society]. I wish I knew the story but have neither of the books in which it is to be found. The University is much obliged to Mr Reynolds for his present …

The picture referred to is the Alfred Jewel which had been discovered in 1693 at North Petherton in Somerset, only about 8 miles from Athelney. The Jewel, which bears the inscription *Aelfred mec heht gewyrcan*, or 'Alfred had me made', was bequeathed to Oxford University by Colonel Nathaniel Palmer (c. 1661–1718) and can be seen today in the Ashmolean Museum. The Alfred Jewel was the inspiration for the Inspector Morse novel *The Jewel That Was Ours*, which was later screened as *The Wolvercote Tongue*.

(From 'Local Antiquarian Gleanings' in *Jackson's Oxford Journal*)

NOVEMBER 18TH

1820: On this day there were public rejoicings when news of the abandonment of the Bill of Pains and Penalties – which had accused the Queen (Caroline of Brunswick) of adultery – reached the city at about 9 p.m. Despite the fact that it was so late, crowds of people turned out on the streets. They were there in order to demonstrate their approval of the decision and their support of the Queen, who they considered to have been treated abominably by the great and the good, in particular by George IV whose own personal life was not above suspicion. The common people showed their joy by repeatedly shouting out her name and making sure that the celebratory bonfire which had been built in Carfax was kept burning all night. The following night, the mob compelled all the citizens to display lights in the windows so that the whole of the city centre was illuminated. When these unruly celebrations threatened to go on for several days, to the disruption of trade and study, both Town and Gown stepped in to introduce measures to return normality as soon as possible, despite the unpopularity of their actions in some quarters. (*Jackson's Oxford Journal*)

NOVEMBER 19TH

1883: On this day, the Vice-Chancellor's Court heard how The Honorable Charles H.S.F. Trefusis of Christ Church and Mr David C. Guthrie of New Inn Hall had assaulted PC Beckwith; Mr Guthrie was further charged with wilfully breaking a pane of glass at the police station.

The constable stated that that evening several undergraduates had crossed the street, and had met him and one said, 'Well, Bobby, have you got any more reports for the Proctors against us?' The previous week he had had to report an offence to the Proctors and the gentlemen were severely dealt with. One of them said, 'Let him have it' and part of a pineapple was thrown at Beckwith, striking him in the face. He seized Guthrie and with the assistance of another constable, was taking him to the station, when Mr Trefusis also struck him in the face. They were both then taken to the station, and while there Guthrie saw a constable looking through a glass door, and he put his hand violently through it, remarking at the same time, 'That is for you.'

The defendants pleaded guilty and were fined £10 each and had to pay costs and damages. (*Jackson's Oxford Journal*)

NOVEMBER 20TH

2006: On this day, journalist Richard Heller, a graduate of Balliol College, came up with the novel idea of holding a 'name and shame' ceremony in direct contrast to the annual Encaenia, when famous people are given honorary degrees. He asked the Chancellor of the University, Chris Patten, himself a Balliol man, to give the suggestion some thought and give Oxonians the opportunity to make what he termed a moral statement about candidates who are considered particularly dishonourable. Each June, at Encaenia, the University confers about six honorary degrees to those it feels are outstanding in their particular fields of expertise and have made a positive contribution to it. Mr Heller told the *Oxford Mail* that there were so many people in the world who deserved to be shown up as being dishonourable. Although the President of the United States had sprung into Mr Heller's mind as making the ideal first candidate for nomination, on reflexion he felt that his shaming by the people of America was probably sufficient disgrace. The nearest thing that Oxford has to Mr Heller's suggestion is the right to veto a candidate's nomination for an honorary doctorate at Encaenia, but this is rarely publicised. (*Oxford Mail*)

NOVEMBER 21ST

1995: This was the day on which the Prince of Wales visited researchers and students at Oxford University's Department of Zoology in South Parks Road, as well as taking part in the celebrations for the 440th anniversaries of both Trinity College and St John's College. Prince Charles' visit to the Department of Zoology was in recognition of the research into biomimetrics (using structures or behaviour from nature to solve human problems) led by Dr Andrew Parker, Senior Research Associate at the Department and E.P. Abraham, Research Fellow at Green College. Dr Parker demonstrated his research into the role of colour in nature, and illustrated how these colours can be replicated artificially and ultimately applied commercially, with the assistance of researchers from the Departments of Physics and Engineering. The Prince also met representatives of the Food Animal Initiative, a long-term project aimed at improving animal welfare, food safety and environmental sustainability in farming. After he had spent some time talking to students and staff at the Department of Zoology, the Prince of Wales went on to visit first Trinity College and then St John's College, both of which were founded in 1555. (*Oxford Mail*)

NOVEMBER 22ND

2000: On this day, some rugby-loving pets turned out in the cold to support their team when the Dark Blues were playing Major Stanley's XV. Fortunately the owners of Jamie and Charlie had been considerate enough to make sure that they were well wrapped up against the chill of the side-line. Jamie, a cocker spaniel belonging to Gordon Ponting of Kidlington, was wearing a smart matching tartan coat and bonnet, and cross-breed Charlie was cradled by a member of his family throughout the game. Despite being in a wheelchair, Gordon, a great rugby fan, went to all the big matches at Twickenham – but for these Jamie had to stay at home. Charlie, on the other hand, who belongs to the family of Simon Danielli, was all set to go up to Twickenham to cheer on Simon making his second appearance as a winger in the Varsity Match against Cambridge. Charlie, who lives with the Daniellis in Dog Lane in a village just outside Gloucester, has his own club badge. He seemed to be a good luck mascot at the Stanley game as Simon scored a hat-trick of tries which gave the Dark Blues a narrow victory. (*Oxford Mail*)

NOVEMBER 23RD

1875: On this day, the Roman Catholic church in the Woodstock Road, built by the Jesuits, was dedicated to St Aloysius with much pomp and ceremony at a service in which Cardinal Manning officiated. Of particular note was a valuable painting of St Aloysius and the Holy Family, hanging above the altar, which was presented by the Revd Hartwell Grissell, Chamberlain to the Pope. Every part of the new church was crowded and there was an impressive showing of local Catholic dignitaries, including members of the aristocracy and clerics; many of the 'clerical gentlemen' mentioned in the newspaper account were 'seceders from the Church of England, and were either at Oxford or Cambridge'. Cardinal Newman himself had been expected to attend but was unable to do so. The sermon was given by Cardinal Manning, arrayed in full cardinal's scarlet, a cope with rich gold embroidery, stole and alb of deep point lace and a jewelled mitre. Covering the ceremony, the reporter from *The Times* commented on Manning that 'Less than thirty years ago the same man was one of the most familiar preachers in the same city, but in a very different character' – as Select Preacher to the University. (*Jackson's Oxford Journal*)

NOVEMBER 24TH

1880: On this evening a recital was held in the Clarendon Assembly Room for the benefit of the Oxford Crèche. The main performers were child stars the Misses Webling, Josephine, Rosalind and Peggy. The programme included songs, a piano recital and excerpts from Shakespeare, Shelley, Tennyson, Macaulay, Matthew Arnold and Edward Lear. The variety of these 'afforded good opportunity for the display of various forms of elocutionary ability'. The acknowledged pet of the party was certainly the youngest of the sisters, Miss Peggy, who had a talent for comedy. This was given full scope by Barham's 'little vulgar boy' which earned two encores. Also much appreciated was what the *Journal*'s reporter refers to as 'Lewis Carroll's exquisite piece of nonsense, "The Shipwright and the Carpenter"'. However, some renderings were less successful and required 'a fuller development of voice and ideas than are likely to be found in children unless they are unusually unnatural'. The review concludes rather ambiguously, 'As regards the policy of allowing children, except under very special circumstances, to thus minister to the entertainment of the public we have our own opinion, but if anything could reconcile us, it would be the performances of the Misses Webling.' (*Jackson's Oxford Journal*)

NOVEMBER 25TH

2002: On this day, it was reported that Oxford builder Ian Beesley had become so exasperated at being kept awake at nights by the noise made by vehicles driving over a road hump outside his home in Ferry Hinksey Road that he had dug it up with a mechanical digger. It had been installed outside the Beesleys' home as part of a £90,000 scheme to slow down traffic going in and out of the Osney Mead industrial estate. On either side of the hump were pedestrian crossing lights for children to get to West Oxford Primary School in safety. After being featured in the local paper and making twenty-six phone calls to the council about the thumps from lorries and the screeching of air brakes with no success, he reached breaking point. It took Ian, the owner of a construction company, a little over an hour to get rid of the 'sleeping policeman', armed with a JCB and pneumatic drill, and helped by two friends who wanted to remain anonymous. He told the *Oxford Mail* that he was prepared to go to prison for what he'd done and didn't regret it in any way; in fact, if it was replaced he would certainly dig it up again. (*Oxford Mail*)

November 26th

1870: This death notice appeared in *Jackson's Oxford Journal* on this day:

'Excessive Mortality in One House' was reported when 'a goods porter named William Everest, formerly in the employ of the Great Western Railway Company, died at his house [in] Osney after suffering for nearly twelve months with incipient consumption. On the same day one of his children died of scarlet fever; on Tuesday another child died from the same cause; and on Wednesday the remaining three were buried in one grave in Osney Cemetery. The funeral was attended by Mr Inspector Johns and a body of the deceased's fellow-workmen. Everest had been a member of the Great Western Railway Provident Society, which allowed him during illness half pay and his widow will receive 6*s* a week from the Widows and Orphans' Fund of the same valuable Instuition.

(*Jackson's Oxford Journal*)

———◆———

1870: On this day the Volunteer Fire Brigade met at the engine house, Clarendon Hotel Yard, and then marched to the Corn Exchange to practise the ladder drill, raising and lowering the long ladders to and from the gallery, splicing ladders, securing ladder clips to hose, suspending the hose from the ladders and demonstrating the proper way to carry ladders. After the drill, each member was given a printed copy of their duties at fires, and they fixed the date for the next drill.
(*Jackson's Oxford Journal*)

NOVEMBER 27TH

2008: This was the day that hundreds of undergraduates, lecturers and visiting academics and staff turned up at Magdalen College in order to welcome the Queen and the Duke of Edinburgh. They all gathered in St John's Quad to see the royal couple, who were there to commemorate the college's 550th anniversary. However, this was just the finale to a series of anniversary celebrations. The Queen and Prince Philip were driven into the quad a few minutes before 1 p.m. that afternoon and were greeted by the President of Magdalen College, Professor David Clary and his wife Heather. With them were the Vice-President, Dr Ralph Walker and the Home Bursar, Mark Blandford-Baker, and she was presented with a book about the college's treasures. The names of students and staff had been entered into a ballot to establish who would have lunch with the Queen and Prince Philip; there were 900 applicants for 120 places. The Home Bursar said that it was a great honour for the monarch to visit Magdalen on its birthday. Her last visit had been in 1948 when she was still Princess Elizabeth and had visited a number of other colleges and received an honorary Doctorate of Civil Law. (*Oxford Mail*)

NOVEMBER 28TH

1832: This was the day that the last case of cholera that year was reported in Oxford. The deadly epidemic reached the County Gaol on 24 June. The total number of cases which are most frequently quoted, and therefore presumably accepted as official, is 174, although some sources say 171, others as high as 184. The last case in England during that outbreak was on 31 December 1832. (*Oxford Triumphant*)

———— •◆• ————

1951: On this day, the results of a survey conducted by *Isis* were published. The student magazine had sent out a questionnaire about working habits and plans for the future to 400 undergraduates. The information gained from the 200 students who replied showed that three quarters of them had no idea what they were going to do when they went down to find jobs. Only those who were reading 'vocational' subjects such as Jurisprudence and the medical students, not surprisingly, had some sort of plan worked out for their future lives. Otherwise, the idea of specialisation in their university courses in order to use what they had studied in any future career hardly seemed to exist. Two thirds of the subjects stated that they did not imagine that their degrees would be of any direct use to them in life after Oxford. (Various sources)

NOVEMBER 29TH

2001: Workmen, office staff and managers at the Oxford and Chiltern branch of developers Berkeley Homes, based in North Oxford and Abingdon, followed the famous and very successful example of the Women's Institute by producing a pin-up calendar for 2002, with each month starring a different member of staff, including the building manager to the commercial manager, in order to raise money for the Helen & Douglas House hospice for terminally ill youngsters. Their aim was to make £8,000 from selling the calendars at £10 a copy. The proceeds were to go towards buying a mobile unit equipped with fibre optics, multi-coloured lights, toys and mirrors aimed at stimulating the senses of those youngsters staying at the hospice who were unable to leave their beds. A spokesman for Berkeley Homes said that the women in the sales team had come up with the *Calendar Girls*-style idea as a fun way to help the charity. At first some of the staff at Berkley Homes, in particular the male ones, were somewhat bashful about taking part in the project, but they soon entered into the spirit of it; indeed, some were even competing to be photographed without their shirts on. (*Oxford Mail*)

NOVEMBER 30TH

1855: On this evening, as usual, 'a meeting of the Scotch members of the University' met for dinner in Mr M'Laren's Fencing Rooms at the Masonic Hall in Alfred Street. In the chair was Sir James Fergusson, Bart MP, formerly a member of University College, and lately serving in the Crimea, who had come down from Ayrshire especially for the dinner. Forty-six gentlemen sat down to eat in a room 'tastefully decorated with evergreens and the flags of the British, French, Turkish and Sardinian nations; and on scrolls round the walls were to be seen as usual, inscribed the names of the most celebrated Scottish worthies, poets, chieftains, generals and philosophers'. One toast was to Prince Albert as 'Laird of Balmoral'. The Duke of Sutherland and the Marquis of Stafford were gracious enough to send along their personal pipers to play at the event and 'during the evening the company were enlivened by the strains of the national music of Scotland, Adams's band playing at intervals'. After the dinner finished, reels, highland flings and other Scottish dances went on until midnight, when, in accordance with University regulations, most of the company had to be back in their colleges. (*Jackson's Oxford Journal*)

DECEMBER 1ST

1877: On this day, patrons were sought for an Institution which was not so well known or liberally supported as others as its work was 'carried on in a very quiet and unostentatious manner'. The Oxford Refuge for Fallen Women had been founded some three years before by two of the city's clergymen as a 'Preparatory Home in connection with the long-established Penitentiary in Holywell'. It was thought that if such a place of safety was not available for them, 'their evil associates [were] certain to regain a hold on them'. However, a reformed life required a good deal of time and patience; rehabilitation and training therefore took at least two years as it had been proved that it took that long to make the adjustment from 'an existence of utter lawlessness and excitement' to 'the religious calm and strict discipline of a regularly organized Home'. It was feared that the change might prove 'too sudden for their wayward and impulsive temperaments'. The refuge doors were open day and night 'as it is generally under cover of darkness that these poor wanderers resort to those who they have reason to hope will assist them'. Inmates were regularly employed in laundry work, which helped with the refuge's expenses. (*Jackson's Oxford Journal*)

DECEMBER 2ND

2003: It was reported on this day that a number of primary schools in Headington had adopted a groundbreaking scheme to reward pupils who behaved well, and to encourage them to take responsibility for their schoolmates. The Sunshine Friends project was first set up at Bayards Hill School in Barton, with fifty Friends in the 5th and 6th Years, and was then extended to others in the area: St Andrew's, Windmill and Wood Farm schools. The idea was that pupils were chosen by interview and then received training in counselling and meditation in order to become a Sunshine Friend. Friends were to be responsible for helping younger pupils at their school, especially any with emotional and/or behavioural problems. Friends were to look after them in the playground and during meals and were able to give out 'rays of sunshine awards' to others, which were to be displayed on charts in the classrooms. These were given for conscientious and helpful acts. Those with the most 'rays of sunshine' at the end of term received a certificate in recognition of their achievement. (*Oxford Mail*)

December 3rd

1679: Anthony à Wood noted on this day how:

One Mr John White (student in Baliol Colledge) was most barbarously butcher'd by a cursed villain, who, understanding that the Student had money, broke open his door and trunk and took away his money and together with it some linen, but in the meantime the Scholar came up and caught him in the fact; then the rogue being betray'd, most cruelly and inhumanely knock'd down the said Scholar with a hatchet which he had in his hand, cut a piece off his chin, beat his nose flat, cut one of his ears in two places, and brake his scull in several places and having most wonderfully abused the body of the deceased, made his escape. The next day the body was found weltering in its gore, whereupon present enquiry was made. 'When had he been seen?' Answer was returned 'Not since the evening of the day before,' at which time the murderer was seen to go towards his chamber. Then diligent search was made for this fellow; he was found and apprehended who had in his custody above 20 pounds of the murdered person's money, with a shirt of his on his back and upon strict examination confessed the whole fact.

(*Life and Times of Anthony à Wood*)

DECEMBER 4TH

1862: This day saw the first Jewish student, Sackville Davis, graduate from Oxford University. Traditionally, Jews, as well as non-Anglican Christians, were excluded from the older English universities by the necessity to subscribe to the 39 Articles, or allegiance to the Church of England. Since 1581 this had been done at matriculation and it was not until the Oxford University Reform Act of 1854 that students no longer had to take any oath or declaration. Davis matriculated in 1859 as a member of Worcester College, which was afterwards seen as broadminded. Later research, however, revealed that his ethnicity had not been questioned nor had he given any indication of it. After one term Davis requested to opt out of any divinity paper on the grounds of his religion. Realising that they had admitted an infidel, the horrified college decided he should either leave or migrate to another college. After unsuccessful approaches to Pembroke and Christ Church, Davis kept his name on the books at Worcester on condition that he kept away from chapel, hall or lectures in college. He did not sit the exams for honours but settled for a pass degree and so became an Oxford graduate. (Various sources)

DECEMBER 5TH

1827: A suspicious death which took place on this day is recorded in the Register of the Vice-Principal of Brasenose College. It was connected with the sinister Hellfire Club which flourished between 1828 and 1834. Such clubs were not uncommon at the period and were imitations of the one which met in the caves at West Wycombe, Buckinghamshire. The Brasenose Hellfire Club met twice a week and was not exclusive to that college. The venue was a set of rooms on the left of the foot of Staircase VI, which looks out over Brasenose Lane. Before the official start of the club, a woman named Ann Crutchley had died in Brasenose Lane as a result of having accepted a glass of brandy passed out of a college window. The donor, H.J. Radcliffe, was rusticated until the following academic year. The club's activities were brought to an abrupt end by the death of its President, which was accompanied by delirium tremens in 1834. These two deaths helped give rise to the story of the Devil arriving at Brasenose, seizing a blasphemous student in his claws, and flying away with his prey over the rooftops of the Bodleian Library. (Various sources)

DECEMBER 6TH

2006: It was reported on this day that Australian singer and former *Neighbours* star Jason Donovan nominated the soon-to-be-opened Oxford Children's Hospital as the charity which would receive the hundreds of thousands of pounds which he earned for his appearance in the reality show *I'm a Celebrity Get Me Out of Here*. After spending more than twenty days in the Australian jungle, with only the most basic supplies, Jason left feeling 'relieved and exhilarated'. He said that he'd really missed his family. Because he was fortunate enough to have two healthy children, he was determined to stay the course and help the sick children who would be treated by the new Children's Hospital. He described himself as 'thrilled to have completed this amazing adventure' and said that he was looking forward to coming to Oxford the following week for a Christmas Concert. The 106-bed hospital, which opened in January the following year, was built on the John Radcliffe site in Headington and was expected to treat more than 65,000 children each year from a wide area of the country. Jason's connection with Oxfordshire is that he and his wife Angela have a home in the countryside near Wantage. (*Oxford Mail*)

DECEMBER 7TH

1777: On this day, residents of the city and members of the University alike were invited to earn themselves some money to buy Christmas presents by replying to the following advertisement:

WANTED immediately, Two Front TEETH in the upper Jaw, for transplanting to another Person; they must be of a middle Size and beautiful white without any Blemish in the Enamel Whoever will dispose of such Teeth, and have them drawn by Mr Moor, dentists, at the Time he shall appoint for it, shall receive of him One Guinea, and Mr Moor will supply the Vacancy with artificial ones, made with the Enamel so as not to be distinguishable from human Teeth, and shall answer the Person the same Purpose as natural ones.

Mr Moor recommends his Dentifrice for the Teeth and Gums; the Efficacy of the above is sufficiently known in the University and most capital Places in England; it is therefore needless to describe its particular Virtues. Sold by Mr Moor in Holywell and Mr Jackson in the High-street, Oxford; Mr Fairfax in Worcester; Mr Rollason & Co in Birmingham and Mr Burdon in Winchester.

(Jackson's Oxford Journal)

DECEMBER 8TH

1894: On this day *Jackson's Oxford Journal* contained the following advertisement:

> LADIES should know of the most wonderful medicine ever discovered for all irregularities and obstructions, however obstinate or long-standing.
>
> Thousands have been relieved by this miraculous remedy and thereby saved trouble, illness and expense. Perfectly harmless and astonishingly effective as testified to by hundreds of married and single females, PILLS ALONE ARE USELESS and only bring disappointment. Stamped addressed envelope for price list. The only effective remedy on earth. Try and judge for yourselves.

(Jackson's Oxford Journal)

December 9th

1980: On this day, the 450th anniversary of Gill & Co. Ltd (Ironmongers) was celebrated. It is very unusual for a business to be able to trace its history directly from the reign of Henry VIII but this was just what Gills could do. It is possible that its start may have been even earlier, if an ironmonger who appeared in the 1380 poll tax was connected with it. It is certain that the company descends from the Smythe family, until it went to a Mr Bush in 1785. Later it became Bush and Pitcher, until around 1840 when Mr (later Alderman) Gill became involved. He ran it for the next thirty-nine years and it took the title of Gill & Co. in 1922. It's uncertain where the original premises were, but in the early twentieth century they were in High Street, before finally settling in Wheatsheaf Yard. Although drastically downsized, it still carried some 4,500 lines and was known as a place where you could get anything as there were various depots of stock around the city. In 2010, despite having survived the reigns of twenty monarchs, it closed – a victim of the recession and competition from chain stores. (Various sources)

DECEMBER 10TH

1931: On this day Henry Daniel Seymour was executed at Oxford Prison for murder. The body of a fifty-four-year-old widow, Mrs Anne Louisa Kempson, had been found in her ransacked Oxford home in August 1931. She had been battered to death and a sharp instrument had been pushed through her throat. During house-to-house enquiries police learnt of a vacuum-cleaner salesman named Seymour, who, claiming that his money had been stolen, had borrowed some from a housewife living nearby. He then said he had missed a bus and stayed overnight at her house, where a parcel containing a hammer and chisel were later found. A local ironmonger remembered selling these tools and he gave police a description of the purchaser, a man who had previously sold a vacuum cleaner to Mrs Kempson. In Aylesbury, the manager of a hotel had retained a suitcase in lieu of payment and found a well-scrubbed hammer inside with the brand labels removed. Police identified the owner as Seymour and traced him to Brighton where he was arrested and, on 15 August, was charged with murder. Seymour's trial opened at Oxford that October. Several lies were exposed in the course of his defence and on the 24th he was found guilty. (*Oxford Times*)

DECEMBER 11TH

2007: On this day, nearly 800 people formed a queue – which at its longest reached round the Divinity School and into the Proscholium – to get a view of the manuscripts which formed the Bodleian Library's one-day exhibition titled 'Magna Carta at Oxford'. Three of these 'engrossments' (official documents from the Chancery bearing the monarch's seal) date from 1217 and the last from 1225 are four of only seventeen survivors which were made prior to 1300. During the lunch hour, Professor Richard Sharpe, Fellow of Wadham College and Professor of Diplomatic, gave a gallery talk on Magna Carta in the Divinity School. He also explained why so many examples have survived. With each issue, a manuscript was written, sealed and sent from the Chancery to each county. Agreed by King John at Runnymede in 1215, the document was revised and re-issued over the next eighty years by his successors. Three of the four Magna Carta examples were bequeathed to the Library at the close of the seventeenh century by the antiquarian Anthony à Wood. Magna Carta is seen by many historians as the most significant early influence on modern constitutional law, influencing the American Constitution and Bill of Rights. (*Oxford Mail*)

DECEMBER 12TH

1928: On this day, in the run-up to Christmas, a new daily evening newspaper was launched in Oxford and has been a favourite ever since. This was the *Oxford Mail*, a daily sister paper to the *Oxford Times*, a weekly broadsheet which had been in print since 1862. One of its claims to fame was that in 1922 T.E. Lawrence 'of Arabia' had commissioned *Oxford Times* to typeset and print an advance private edition of *Seven Pillars of Wisdom*, which became known as the '1922 Edition' or the 'Oxford Text' of the work. The *Mail* was the idea of two former Liberal MPs, Frank Gray and Sir Charles Starmer, the head of the Westminster Press. The *Oxford Times* fought back by attempting to bring out a rival daily paper but the two soon merged to eventually become Oxford and County Newspapers. A furniture warehouse in New Inn Hall Street was converted into the papers' headquarters and renamed Newspaper House. The new company used a fleet of Austin Seven vans to make its deliveries and by 1934 it graduated to a fleet of new Morris Cowley vans. It moved to new large premises in Osney Mead in February 1972. (Various sources)

DECEMBER 13TH

2004: On this day, with Christmas fast approaching, children were left disappointed because letters from Santa Claus were delivered at their homes in envelopes which had been opened and had had gold-wrapped chocolate coins removed. The Royal Mail denied the possibility that the children's Christmas post had been targeted by thieves and said that the problem was due to the fact that sorting machines were not equipped to deal with envelopes which had lumps in them. The Royal Mail put the blame on the *Oxford Mail*, which had been helping Santa to send the letters, for sending them off with the coins inside them. However, this was the first time since it went into partnership with Santa that the paper had received any complaints concerning the envelopes arriving opened or with chocolate missing. Then, with only a fortnight to Christmas, the promotion team received eight complaints from parents and grandparents about envelopes with one end cut open and in each case, although the letter and card arrived safely, all but three of the chocolates had gone. More than 1,200 letters, costing £2.99 each, had been sent out to date, each stamped with a message reading: 'From Santa, North Pole, Christmas 2004.' (*Oxford Mail*)

DECEMBER 14TH

1650: On this day the hanging of Anne Green, a serving maid, took place. She was condemned for the murder of her bastard child, fathered by the grandson of Sir Thomas Reade of Duns Tew, in whose service she was at the time. As soon as the hanging had taken place at Oxford Castle, well-wishers hung on her legs and hit her on the breast and stomach to ensure a quick death by her neck being broken. After half an hour the girl was cut down and her corpse taken off to be anatomised by some young medical students, as was the fate of murderers at that time. However, on reaching the dissection room, while the rope was still tight around her neck, it was discovered that she was still breathing. As an 'act of charity', one man stood upon her breast and a soldier struck her with the butt of his musket. Despite all this she continued to breathe whilst preparations were being made to dissect her, so of course they changed their plans and resuscitated her. Not surprisingly, this caused something of a sensation and the story of her recovery was printed, with verses added by the young poets of the University. (*Life and Times of Anthony à Wood*)

DECEMBER 15TH

1827: The following extract from *Jackson's Oxford Journal* was published on this day:

We have this week the painful duty of recording an atrocious murder committed on the body of an unfortunate woman of the town named Ann Priest (but known by the name of Ann Crotchley), twenty-four years of age who was discovered about quarter past twelve on Thursday night in Blue Boar Lane in a state of intoxication and totally insensible. She was removed into a passage adjoining and in little more than an hour afterwards the watch found her in the same place, bleeding most profusely and apparently in a dying state. She was conveyed to her lodging in St Thomas's parish where she died early on Saturday morning. Previous to her death, she told her landlady that she had been ill used by some man whom she did not know. Two surgeons who examined her person stated on the inquest that her death was occasioned by a wound inflicted with a sharp instrument on her body. The nature of the case will not admit to stating the particulars but our readers will learn from the evidence of the witnesses examined that the crime was of the most inhuman and diabolical description.

(*Jackson's Oxford Journal*)

DECEMBER 16TH

2004: This was the day when history was made at the British Universities Championship when Kaleen Love represented Oxford at boxing in the first women's Varsity Match. Kaleen fought the Light Blues welterweight Katherine Tubb in the first match of the tournament, although she was defeated in the third round. She fought well, particularly as she had only taken it up three months beforehand and her opponent had been boxing for over a year. Eight Dark Blues, seven men and Kaleen, travelled to Dundee for the tournament and returned home with one gold medal and two silver ones. Lightweight James Whitman outclassed all competitors in the run-up to the semi-final, in which he fought fellow Oxonian Fred Brown. This all-Dark Blue contest turned out to be one of the best fights of the competition, with Whitman taking the honours in the semi and then storming through to take the title in the final. Silver medals went to David Amiekumo in the middleweight category and Azar Salomon in the light heavyweight final. Team co-captain Peter Ho said that the Oxford team had put on a good show at the championships and he was feeling confident for the match against Cambridge in March. (*Oxford Mail*)

DECEMBER 17TH

2004: It was announced on this day that the final cost of the Institute of Mathematics, the first new building destined to go up on the site of the Radcliffe Infirmary, was estimated at £40 million. The University, which took over the site when the Infirmary closed in 2007, was said to be deciding on an architect who would draw up a master-plan for the whole of the 10½-acre site not far from the city centre. The University intended to hold an international competition, in cooperation with the Royal Institute of British Architects, to obtain the best designs. It was stressed that it was essential for the RI site to become 'part of the must-see list in Oxford' as well as acting as the principal focus for University plans for extending teaching and research facilities over the next twenty years. As a guide to architects regarding its vision for the site, the University stated that it was to become the main campus, with administrative offices, academic departments and research facilities, possibly incorporating underground buildings and with room for expansion for years to come. It was felt that this futuristic development would, without doubt, mark the beginning of a new phase for the centuries-old University. (*Oxford Mail*)

DECEMBER 18TH

2000: In a cul-de-sac off the Botley Road in West Oxford, the residents were showing that the Dunkirk spirit was alive and well on this day. Bullstake Close was one of the worst-affected parts of the city when the nearby Thames burst its banks and spread beyond the flood plain. Some of the residents were evacuated to drier parts of Oxford but others chose to stay in their homes and help each other out, with the water lapping up to their doorsteps. Sandbags were placed at the most vulnerable places and duckboards put down so that people could get around. George Stratford, who made pottery animals in his spare time, used some of his excess clay to make seals to put round two of his neighbours' doors in the flats below him. He said that he was not personally worried about being flooded as he lived upstairs. Another resident, seventy-eight-year-old Cecilie Harris, spoke about her determination not to leave her bungalow unless her electricity packed up. She was sure that the water would recede before it reached her doors, despite the fact that her garage and conservatory were already underwater. Everyone agreed about pulling together and helping each other out. (*Oxford Mail*)

DECEMBER 19TH

2000: On this evening, thousands of pounds worth of damage was done during an attack on Fat Phil's Angling Centre in the Abingdon Road. Vandals used bricks to smash the window and damage stock. The Saturday before, shop owner Phil Cross had spent hours dressed up as Father Christmas, fishing in the floodwater which lined the Abingdon Road and keeping motorists and bus passengers amused as they were stuck in the flooded, traffic-jammed road. Before the attack, Mr Cross had already decorated his shop ready for Christmas, complete with a lit-up and red-nosed Rudolph. The ultimate insult was a brick which hit the reindeer squarely on the nose and gave him an electric shock. Mr Cross, who was disappointed that his attempts to cheer up passers-by at a difficult time had misfired, was convinced that his fishing act had drawn the wrong sort of attention to his business as his was the only shop to be targeted. Security alarms went off at about 6 p.m. and police began to search through video footage from security cameras to see if they could catch the culprits. Fortunately nobody was injured in the attack but security at the Angling Centre was increased. (*Oxford Mail*)

DECEMBER 20TH

2004: In was reported on this day that a former US serviceman who had been stationed at both RAF Brize Norton and RAF Croughton, donated a star-spangled banner to the Churchill Hospital in Oxford to say thank you to the staff there who had saved his life, and in honour of his father. Jim Webb, who lived at Grove, near Wantage, presented the flag to the hospital after noticing that the existing one, which commemorated the hospital's strong Anglo-American links (as it was once leased to the United States Army) was tattered and torn. He described its condition as 'absolutely horrendous' and, as he had a flag, he thought he would give it to the hospital. The Stars and Stripes which he presented was the ceremonial flag which had been used at the funeral of his father, Frederick, who had been a Master Sergeant in the American Air Force until 1971. It was handed over on the anniversary of his death as a lasting gift before the family moved back to the United States. Mr Webb said that in 1997 he had had a serious viral infection which at one point put his life in danger, but the staff at the Churchill Hospital literally saved his life. He spent a month in hospital followed by five months recovering at home. (*Oxford Mail*)

DECEMBER 21ST

1880: The servants of Jesus College were invited to bring their wives and families to the college on this day. Along with the choir of St Michael at the North Gate, they were entertained 'by the kindness of Mrs Wharton', the wife of the college's Classics Fellow. The hall was specially dressed for the occasion and must have made a great impression on the guests, and after tea 'Mr Henry Taunt of Broad-street was engaged and very much delighted the company for about two hours by his trip round Europe &c'. Then came supper and 'full justice having been done to all the good things, the Hall was cleared for dancing and was enjoyed with much spirit till about twelve o'clock when three cheers were given for Mrs Wharton and the company dispersed, all having thoroughly enjoyed themselves'. (*Jackson's Oxford Journal*)

DECEMBER 22ND

1900: The following is an extract from *Jackson's Oxford Journal* published on this day:

So there are two ways of playing the game of Christmas. We can treat the whole concern as an insufferable bore or rush into ecstasies of delight over the return of the festive season. The former growls at the carol singers, grumbles at the Christmas bells, grudges Christmas presents and resents the offer of plum-pudding as an insult. The latter lives on mince pies for some weeks in anticipation of the event, arranges the snapdragon, is on the top round of the ladder decorating the Christmas tree, probably joins the waits or the mummers on the lawn, is stage manager for the Christmas play, carves the turkey and gives the handsomest Christmas presents. The typical Christmas and the typical 'Christmaser', if we may coin such a word, have been for all times enshrined in the pages of DICKENS and WASHINGTON IRVING. We feel that both are terribly out of fashion today, and the rush from the country to the town, especially to London, is to a great extent responsible for the change. One associates the idea of Christmas with the country house.

(Jackson's Oxford Journal)

DECEMBER 23RD

1893: On this day, the following ingenuous and somewhat desperate appeal appeared in *Jackson's Oxford Journal*:

GRANDPONT SCHOOL

The walls of the above urgently needed School are now rapidly rising. To get the work done I have been obliged to make myself solely responsible for the £808 still needed. I entreat your readers to help a veteran Rector in his seventy-fourth year who has laboured for thirty-four years in this poor Oxford parish. Prompt help will be most brotherly. Pray cross your cheque or postal order kind reader thus –
'Messrs. Parsons and Co., Old Bank, Oxford, for Grandpont School Fund' and send it to me before you forget your generous intention. Do not let me die in debt!

A.M.W.CHRISTOPHER, St Aldate's Rectory, Oxford

It is good to relate that Canon Christopher did not die in debt. In fact, he was to live until 1913, although he resigned from the school in 1905. During his time there, he made St Aldate's influential in the city and University for its evangelical ministry; the church was remodelled and enlarged twice, a parish room built, the rectory made inhabitable and a large daughter church, St Matthew's, built in 1890–1 with schools added in 1893. (*Jackson's Oxford Journal*)

DECEMBER 24TH

1821: From Mary Latimer's Diary of this day:

I got up at half past seven, and Edward read the prayers. After breakfast I learnt my German lesson. Mr Mechelin came and did not leave until after an hour and a half. My father had lunch at home and spent the evening with my mother in her bedroom. The ladies J. & J. Bricknell had tea with us. We had music, and then Miss Roberts and I played whist with them. We had supper. Because it was Christmas Eve, all choristers of the church came to sing hymns. A robin came into the room through the window, and I kept him until morning and then let him go. The Misses Bricknell left at a quarter to midnight, and then at midnight the bells started to ring for an hour. A mistake happened yesterday. We went to All Souls Chapel to attend an ordination ceremony. The Bishop of Oxford (Dr Legge) and his chaplain, Mr Levett, first read the liturgy but, in the end, they omitted the liturgy itself. Then Mr Dolby, Exeter College, preached a long and excellent sermon. Afterwards they began to ordain the young man. We stayed there for a long time, but not until the very end of the ceremony.

(Mary Latimer's Diary, Oxfordshire CRO)

DECEMBER 25TH

1891: This Christmas Day in the Oxford Workhouse:

> … was marked by a certain amount of gloom as, in consequence of an epidemic of influenza in its most severe form in the house, there were the unparalled number of ten deaths in a week and the hospital wards were filled with critical cases so much so that the services of two Acland nurses were required in addition to the usual staff. This sad state of things probably accounted for the small number of visitors [4] to assist at the Christmas dinner.

However, the dinner was up to its usual standard, and included roast beef and mutton, baked potatoes and other vegetables, followed by as much plum pudding as anyone could eat and it was all washed down with a pint of beer per person. After the meal, the Master heard one inmate say, 'I have had a jolly good dinner' which made all the work and planning worthwhile. Three cheers were given for the visitors to the workhouse who had worked so hard to organise and finance the meal, and to the Master and Matron, Mr and Mrs Stedham. 'The proceedings then terminated and pipes, tobacco, snuff and other "goodies" were distributed.' (*Jackson's Oxford Journal*)

DECEMBER 26TH

1878: This Boxing Day was a complete anti-climax after all the jollity and excitement of the previous few days when many people had come to Oxford to spend the festive season with family and friends. Earlier in the week, they would have been able to go along to the Queen's College, when the hall was open to the public and the ancient Ceremony of the Boar's Head took place. Accompanied by its own carol, the head was brought in wearing a crown and flags bearing the college arms. That year the boar, which weighed 25 stone and had been reared on one of the college farms, had a head which weighed well over 5 stone. In contrast to this spectacle, Boxing Day was observed as a bank holiday:

> ... with an almost complete suspension of business, but there was comparatively nothing in the way of amusement going on, if we except the Theatre, which had opened for a short season; a 'long quadrille' held in the large room at Mr Conacher's, Great Clarendon-street in connection with the North Oxford Amateur Dramatic Society, and which was well attended; and the annual ball at the South Oxford Working Men's Club, which took place in the Town Hall.

(*Jackson's Oxford Journal*)

DECEMBER 27TH

1826: On this day, William Fletcher, three times Mayor of the city, philanthropist and antiquarian, died in his house at No. 46 Broad Street which he had leased from the City Council in 1787. *Jackson's Oxford Journal* of 6 January 1827 contains a lengthy account of the funeral, which explains how a vault had been prepared in Yarnton Church:

> ... in readiness to receive the leaden coffin and its lifeless contents, a massive stone coffin with its original sculptured lid which were dug up at Godstow [Nunnery] many years since and presented to the Alderman by the Earl of Abingdon. The funeral service was read with great emphasis by the Rev. Vaughan Thomas.,Vicar of Yarnton, and the body was lowered into its dark and silent abode ... The site will hereafter be indicated to the enquiring visitant by the figure of the Alderman in his official robes and a plain unassuming inscription, cut into a brass plate, simply shewing that he died on the 27 December 1826, eighty-seven years of age, and upon another piece of brass this quaint and characteristic addition:

> Yarnton, my childhood's home!
> Do thou receive
> This parting gift –
> My dust to thee I leave.

(*Jackson's Oxford Journal*)

DECEMBER 28TH

1861: On this day, *Jackson's Oxford Journal* contained an account of how, following the sudden and unexpected death of Prince Albert, the City of Oxford Rifle Corps had held a church service as a tribute to him. The Prince Consort had died of typhoid at the age of forty-two, on 14 December, and had been buried on the 23rd. Members of the Corps assembled in Broad Street, each man wearing a black crépe band on his left arm. Under the command of Captain Parson, they marched behind their silent band to Carfax Church. The building was packed to capacity and the hanging of black cloth on the pulpit and reading desk must have made a deep impression. The Mayor (Alderman Ward) and Aldermen Sadler and Spiers attended in their corporate roles, although they were all three members of the Rifle Corps. After the singing of 'I know that my Redeemer liveth', the service began. The Revd J.S. Sidebotham, Chaplain of New College, spoke of Albert's many virtues, the entire nation's shock and distress, and the necessity of being constantly prepared for death. After the 'Dead March' from *Saul*, the congregation left the church. The Corps reassembled in Queen Street ,where they were dismissed. (*Jackson's Oxford Journal*)

DECEMBER 29TH

2000: This was the day when it was noticed that the life-size wooden cut-out of Abanazar, the villain in *Aladdin*, had gone missing from outside the foyer of the Oxford Playhouse. For some reason his co-stars, Widow Twankey and Aladdin himself ,were still there. The three figures were made by the theatre as part of a promotion for that year's pantomime, and stood outside the main entrance of the Playhouse, in Beaumont Street. The theft of Abanazar was thought to have been a drunk's idea of a joke. All three had been outside all day but when the Playhouse staff closed up after an evening performance they noticed that Abanazar was no longer there. A member of staff said that he could imagine the thief waking up with a hangover to see Abanazar staring at him from the other side of the bedroom. The consensus was that he had been kidnapped by party-goers on their way home or that he had got fed up with standing about in the cold day after day and had made his way to a pub. The Playhouse was offering a family ticket to see the pantomime as a reward for his return. (*Oxford Mail*)

DECEMBER 30TH

2010: On this day, two of the country's leading authors, both from Oxford, went on record as saying that Oxfordshire County Council's plans to put a stop to funding for twenty libraries was 'shameful', and stated that their loss would deprive local communities. Award-winning writers Philip Pullman and Colin Dexter both launched attacks on proposals by the council to save £2 million over a period of four years by cutting back on its library service. Unless volunteers could be found to man the libraries which were under threat, they were in danger of closing the following year under the Conservative-run council's budget plans. Mr Pullman described the cuts as a 'political decision' which other councils had managed to avoid. He said that closing twenty out of forty-three libraries was 'an absolutely shameful number', and 'not inevitable'. Earlier that week, Mr Pullman had been among the writers who forced the government to scrap plans to axe funding for Bookstart, which gives free books to young children. According to Colin Dexter, a saving of £2 million seemed like peanuts in the council's budget but one which would cause great damage that could not be easily repaired and would 'markedly degrade the experience of life for many people in Oxfordshire'. (*Oxford Mail*)

DECEMBER 31ST

1892: On this day penny dinners for the poor of the city started to be given out at Oxford Town Hall. 'The committee of ladies having this laudable object in hand commenced supplying penny dinners from the kitchen of the Town Hall, and soup was provided for around 400 applicants.' On the following Tuesday, the number increased to well over 600, as it did on the Thursday, by which time word must have spread. However, 'the quantity of vegetables hitherto charitably given had been rather small and consequently it was found necessary to buy more largely than usual. Help both in money and in this respect will be thankfully received, and Miss Tawney of No. 63 St Giles-street is the treasurer of the fund.' (*Jackson's Oxford Journal*)

———◆———

1999: On this Millennium eve a daringly successful raid was carried out at the world-famous Ashmolean Museum. The thieves used scaffolding on an adjoining building to get onto the museum roof. They then managed to break in through a skylight and make off with a painting by Cézanne, 'Auvers-Sur-Oise'. Because other valuable works were not taken, it was supposed that the painting was stolen to order. (Various sources)